Immediate
Seating

Immediate Seating

A Look at Movie Audiences

BRUCE A. AUSTIN

Rochester Institute of Technology

WADSWORTH PUBLISHING COMPANY
Belmont, California
A Division of Wadsworth, Inc.

Communications Editor: Kristine M. Clerkin
Production Editor: Leland Moss
Editorial Assistant: Melissa Harris
Designer: Donna Davis
Print Buyer: Barbara Britton
Copy Editor: Anne Montague
Compositor: Graphic Typesetting Service
Cover: Donna Davis
Signing Representative: Dawn Beke

Chapter opening photo credits: Chapters 1, 4, 5 and 8
Phototech; Chapters 2 and 3, IMP/GEH Still Collection

Printed in the United States of America   49

1 2 3 4 5 6 7 8 9 10—93 92 91 90 89

Library of Congress Cataloging-in-Publication Data

Austin, Bruce A., 1952–
   Immediate seating: a look at movie audiences / Bruce A. Austin.
      p.   cm.
   Bibliography: p.
   Includes index.
   ISBN 0-534-09366-3
 . 1. Motion picture audiences.   I. Title.
PN1995.9.A8A97   1988
302.2'243—dc19   88-5899
                                                            CIP

Contents

CHAPTER FIVE

Contexts of Moviegoing
and Movie Attendance 80

CHAPTER SIX

Movies and Attitudes 93

Preface

"I have a theory: It is not to bore the audience." [1]
—William Wyler

uestions about the kinds of movies that have been made and how movie images might be interpreted have been posed for nearly a century. A cursory examination of virtually any library reveals so many books about the form and content of movies that years of religious devotion would be needed to read them all. But though film is clearly more than just the projected image, the study of film has, by and large, been limited to it; that is, the thinking and writing about movies have been fixed on the history, criticism, and appreciation of the surface phenomenon of movies while disregarding the important issues of who is watching the screen, why they go to the movies, what they like and dislike.

People watch movies. People respond to films—they have cognitive, affective, and behavioral reactions to the images projected before them. People have reasons for going and not going to the movies. Even if our scrutiny of the library shelves were meticulous, our chances of uncovering texts on movie audiences would be slim indeed.

What is movie audience research and why study it? Audience research is about what people think and feel about movies. Audience research is a means for testing and verifying or refuting the scholarship on the meanings of film images. Audience research does not negate the value of aesthetic questions but provides a wider group of people to study. Film is a mass medium, so understanding the "popular" response serves an important purpose. The message and its meaning are not synonymous; the meaning of a film is created by those who view it. What the meaning is and how it is created, therefore, fall within the purview of audience research.

Audience studies focus on movie consumers and therefore are of interest to the business side of the movie industry. Audience research, for instance, could be designed to determine viewers' responses to specific institutional strategies, policies, and practices. Audience research might also be used to help formulate, implement, and evaluate policy. Policy decisions and policy-making that are directed at and have implications for mass communication audiences must be developed and evaluated in terms of their behavioral implications. Chapter 7 provides an analysis of the movie industry's self-regulatory policy by using audience research.

Research on moviegoers directs our attention toward such questions as how audiences respond to what is on the screen and why they respond in the ways they do. It also examines the decision and motivation processes people use before they set foot in the movie theater, before they decide which movie they will go to, and before they even choose moviegoing as an activity to engage in. Once we develop some ideas or theories about why people go to movies, we can begin other kinds of audience research.

Perhaps the most important reason for studying movie audiences is that movies are not just art or commodities or a business; movies are a medium for communication. This means that films have social consequences. For good or ill, movies have the capacity to move people. If for no other reason, the social implications of movies mean that it is important to study audiences. This book seeks to bring to the study of film audiences the scholarly apparatus, rigor, and attention that heretofore have been applied only to the study of film content. The terms *film, movie, cinema, motion pictures,* and the like are used interchangeably in this book to refer to *commercial, theatrically exhibited, full-length* motion pictures that are at least ostensibly designed and viewed for the purpose of *entertainment.*

The following chapters examine the history, development, and present state of research on the audiences for motion pictures. The book discusses how the film industry and the scholarly community study film audiences. The results of such research are reported along with a synthesis and interpretation of this literature. Because this book is an introduction to research on film audiences, some issues will not be examined at all or in detail. The effects of media violence and sexually explicit materials have been addressed by numerous other texts; attention to these issues is not included in this book. A final purpose of the book is to provide ideas and incentives for future research on film audiences. Where, for instance, the quantity of data on particular issues is sparse, its quality is cited to indicate the potential for fruitful avenues of further research.

Chapter 1 examines methods for and types of industry research on movie audiences. Chapter 2 places motion pictures and their audiences in the context of leisure activities. Motivational dimensions of moviegoing are discussed in

Chapter 3; Chapter 4 covers the research on the reasons people attend a specific film as well as the film industry's marketing and advertising efforts to attract attendance at particular films. Chapter 5 explores various forms of the moviegoing experience and reports in some detail on the audiences for three particular forms. Chapter 6 discusses attitudinal concerns in relation to movie audiences. In Chapter 7 the movie rating system (G, PG, PG-13, R, X) is evaluated, using audience research. The final chapter offers historical background on the impact of communications technologies on movie audiences and reviews literature on the contemporary "communications revolution" and its effect on theatrical film audiences.

I am indebted to several people for their assistance and advice as I wrote this book. Stan McKenzie read nearly every line and dash I composed. He helped me to understand why what I had written needed polishing, clarification, rewriting, or serious therapy (though I began to wonder what he meant about the last item). He was generous with his time, spending many hours reading my prose when he probably wished he could have been building his house. Ruth Hermann expertly and professionally typed the manuscript. While no doubt grateful to the invention of word processing, she remained patient, cheerful, and supportive despite my many revisions. At the University of Illinois, Anita Specht typed early drafts for at least two chapters, made delicious coffee, and probably did not regret at all my returning to Rochester. I am also indebted to several professionals at Wadsworth. Dawn Beke urged me to stop talking about and actually write the book's proposal. Kris Clerkin found reason to believe that I really would write the book. Leland Moss guided the production process and Donna Davis carefully attended to its "look." Anne Montague somehow managed to maintain her wonderful sense of humor and interest in the book's subject while at the same time improving its readability. Both the book and I benefited from the wonderful resources of the University of Illinois's library as well as the reference staff at RIT's library.

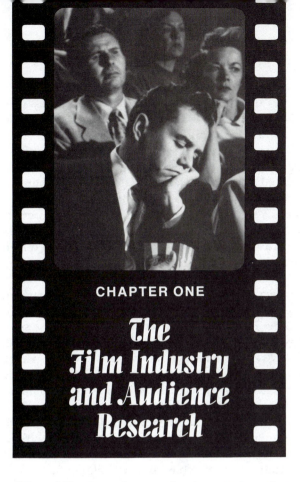

CHAPTER ONE

The
Film Industry
and Audience
Research

"The public always knows what it wants just after it has seen it."[1]
　　　　　　　　　　　　—Samuel A. (Roxy) Rothafel

An analysis of movie audiences should start with a look at the film industry because without the movie manufacturers movie audiences simply would not exist. Also, because much of the remainder of this book analyzes film audience research from a social, or non-industry, perspective, the business aspects of moviemaking must not be ignored, and an important component of that business is selling movies to audiences. Summarized here are the methods used by the film industry to research its audiences and the kinds of studies that it conducts.

To research means to look again, that is, to *re*-search: "What the research attitude presumes is that the first look—and every later look—may be prone to error, so that one must look again and again, differently and thoroughly, each time."[2] Research methods are the procedures and operations followed in the looking and looking again; they address the issue of *how* one can discover the information needed to answer particular questions. In an often repeated story, the infamous Harry Cohn, tyrannical president of Columbia Pictures, claimed he had a "foolproof" method for predicting the success of a movie: "If my fanny squirms, it's bad. If my fanny doesn't squirm, it's good. It's as simple as that." Cohn believed he could judge the audiences' interest in a picture using the "tush test"; that is, detecting restlessness was his "research method."[3] As will be seen, unlike the social sciences, the industry uses only a few research methods. Furthermore, the admonishment to look repeatedly at the same phenomenon, using multiple methods, has generally been ignored.

The film industry uses audience research to answer one question: How can people be attracted to see a particular film? Even though any one distributor usually has several movies in release simultaneously, movies are "sold" to the public on a one-at-a-time basis. Underlying this sales posture is the notion that every movie is different and thus must be individually promoted and marketed. This "uniqueness assumption" implies that results gathered from the study of any single film and its audience cannot be generalized to the next feature that unspools; every picture has to be researched and sold independently. At the same time, however, another article of faith in the industry is the "big engine theory": A mega-hit for one studio acts like a powerful locomotive that pulls a long train of other movies in concurrent release. Further, a successful picture is frequently used as a model for promoting subsequent releases.

Movie industry researchers have little desire to develop sophisticated theories explaining audiences' behaviors or motivations. Explanation and understanding, two essential functions of theory, are clearly less important than the hope of learning how to maximize attendance at a specific film. What follows is a description of the organization of the major studios' marketing departments, a brief history of movie marketing, an analysis of the special problems relevant to movie marketing researchers, and an examination of the methods for conducting audience research used by the film industry.

MARKETING ORGANIZATION AND STRATEGY

Completion of production doesn't mean the end of expenses. According to Aljean Harmetz, "The average cost of making a major studio movie [in 1987] was about $16 million, with an additional $8 [million] to $10 million spent on marketing."[4] The marketing research department works closely with the sales, advertising, and publicity departments. Sales is responsible for booking a film into the theaters, determining when it will open, developing its release pattern, and establishing the financial terms with exhibitors. The advertising department determines the creative "look" of paid advertisements, trailers, and posters, as well as the specific media buys (concerning which media paid advertising will be placed in—TV, radio, newspapers, and so on—and the strategies used in distributing advertising money). The publicity department attempts to generate attention for a movie in ways that do not involve direct expenses—for example, guest spots by the stars on TV talk shows. This department, or sometimes a separate division called promotion, is also responsible for developing product tie-ins, such as *Star Wars* drinking glasses sold at Burger King. Together these departments attempt to help to create and mold a clear, consistent, and attractive image of a film.

Perhaps the most important task for marketing is to ensure that a movie opens to the "right" audience: either a huge one at hundreds of screens or a smaller but influential one in an exclusive run. The film's release pattern strategy is shaped by marketing research. A wide release pattern is advantageous for films for which poor word of mouth is anticipated. The goal is to fill theaters in every city and shopping mall before people can tell their friends how little they enjoyed the movie. John Friedkin, vice president for advertising and promotion at 20th Century-Fox, once stated, "All that guarantees [exhibitor guarantees of a certain amount of money to be paid] and promotions can buy is a couple of weeks' business and after that it has to be word of mouth. If the picture is bad, you might as well shoot everybody coming out of the theater—they will quickly enough kill any film."[5]

Friedkin was too generous in saying "a couple of weeks' business" could be generated by promotion. Most industry personnel agree that the time span is much shorter and that especially negative word of mouth travels much faster. Typically a promotional and advertising blitz buys only the first weekend's audiences. Clark Ramsay, who handled the release of *Jaws*, claimed that "you can't hype your way to success in this business. The movie has to be good. What we did was create an opportunity for *Jaws* to take off. The advertising and promotion might have been responsible for the first three-day run, but it was word of mouth that carried it to the top."[6]

Conversely, opening a film on a limited-run basis attempts to capitalize on word of mouth by building interest, creating excitement, and offering an allure of exclusivity. Opening *The Deer Hunter* in just one or two theaters in such major markets as Philadelphia, coupled with a heavy advertising campaign, resulted in noticeably long lines and the hoped-for positive word of mouth. (The resulting financial success of the film helped assuage an exhibitor concern: Because of the film's three-hour running time, only one show an evening could be offered rather than the usual two, thereby diminishing potential box office.)

Film marketing research efforts must be coordinated with sales, advertising, and publicity. But even very close coordination does not guarantee success. One of the most spectacular examples of this was *The Great Gatsby* (1974). The intense promotion and publicity effort included numerous product tie-ins: DuPont's white finish Teflon cookware; Ballantine's Scotch; Glemby International beauty salons, which featured Gatsby hair styling; and Robert Bruce Sportswear, which offered a Gatsby clothing line. Ironically, the opulent movie floundered at the theaters, but the products tied to the film were quite successful.[7]

HISTORY

Analysis of a commodity's consumers by the manufacturers makes simple business sense. The economic motivation to study film audiences should have provoked keen interest within the industry. But the powers in Hollywood during its heyday were antagonistic toward and disdainful of audience research.

As Leo Handel, founder of the Motion Picture Research Bureau, recounts, "In 1942 there was only a handful of persons who did not reject film research outright. Most condemned it without trial."[8] Today Hollywood does conduct audience research, but the *feeling* about such research may not be too different from Handel's assessment more than 40 years ago. Even those who conduct audience research demonstrate a preference for the personal, intuitive touch over the scientific approach.[9]

A form of audience research was being conducted as early as the 1920s. Carl Laemmle, the founder of what would become Universal Pictures, began his film career doing "field studies" of the audience for Hale's Tours:

> For two days the little man from Oshkosh [Laemmle] stood down in State Street [in Chicago], moving just enough to keep from being conspicuous, while he counted the attendance that went in to see Hale's Tours pictures. When he got through he had an accurate notion of what kind of people went to see the pictures, what hours of the day they found the time to do it in, and how many of them there were per hour and per day.[10]

Similarly, the film exchange system

> established a route of communication from audience through exhibitor to distributor and producer, enabling the nickelodeon patrons to make their wishes known to the makers of pictures. If spectators enjoyed a film and applauded it, the nickelodeon owner scurried around and tried to get more like it, and if they grumbled as they left the show he passed on the complaints to the exchange, and the exchange told the manufacturer.[11]

These initial forays into the field of audience research, however, were little more than shots in the dark. None offer anything in the way of generalizability of the "data" to wider audiences. One industry insider summarized audience analysis within the film colony this way in 1954:

> We have usually worked in the past on the thesis that if we stand in the dark and throw a rock and hear a crash, we've hit the greenhouse. This is not an altogether dependable method. It means that if you don't hear a crash, you may no longer be in the motion picture business.[12]

The early popularity of films is a frequently mentioned reason for the industry's lack of research. During the long Golden Age when people went to the movies in droves, the industry assumed a complacent, "who cares why they go" posture. The weakness of this reasoning, as history would show, was its shortsightedness: It assumed an ever-increasing, or at least stable, movie audience. The industry ignored, or refused to acknowledge, the possibility of competitive media and alternative leisure pursuits. Nor is it simply hindsight that reveals the flimsiness of this rationale; as early as the mid-1920s, when radio was introduced, the industry could have anticipated that the size of its audience and growth of its profitability would, at some point, reach a ceiling or at least would not continue to expand so dramatically.

Perhaps the most frequently heard reason for Hollywood's resistance to audience research was that movies are an artistic endeavor. Powdermaker's anthropological study also reported the pervasive disdain for applying merchandising methods to what was essentially a creative process. But Hollywood's claim to artistry is quickly dismissed by Handel: "We would gladly accept this statement if the same people did not tell us, after turning out a series of utterly commercial cliché pictures without batting a solitary eyelash, that movie making is just a business like any other."[13]

Some have suggested that industry executives distrusted and therefore avoided researchers. As Handel explained: "Some moviemakers misinterpret the function of audience research. They see in it not an instrument for their use, but a substitute for executive acumen."[14] Although industry executives' fear of usurpation by researchers was not unfounded, the astute executive might readily benefit by the results of audience research, thereby enhancing the status of his or her acumen.

Handel reported in 1953 that

> the industry still clings to some archaic methods of measuring audience reaction, such as uncontrolled sneak previews, preview cards, too much reliance on fan mail, and naturally, the mystic "feel" of the market, which seems to reach its heights of potency in the air-conditioned private dining rooms of Bel Air and Miami Beach.[15]

Certainly by 1930 the methods of social science had been developed to such an extent as to make such methods of audience research obsolete.

Industry personnel in large part did not perceive the benefits of audience research. Or perhaps it may be more accurate to state that the industry created an environment in which the benefits of audience research were not permitted to be revealed. Some reasons for the inattention to audience research—the appeal to art, for instance—are plainly myths, self-aggrandizements, or self-delusions. Others are the result of unjustified laziness and heedless observation of a changing market environment. In sum, remarkably few solid explanations exist for Hollywood's reluctance to research its audiences.

Two significant factors explain the development and growth of movie marketing research. Most important was the introduction of television in the 1950s. TV destroyed established movie attendance patterns. With fewer and fewer people going to the movies less and less frequently, Hollywood sought ways to hold onto its audience. Marketing research, with its aura of "science," was thought to be one way of achieving this goal.

Another reason for the increased emphasis on research methods other than seat-of-the-pants: The movie industry saw marketing techniques as a means for improving its image in the eyes of Wall Street and the banking industry.[16] Hollywood had been stigmatized as a fly-by-night industry built on glamour, with few concrete, tangible assets. Movies were considered a disposable commodity and one that defied accurate prediction of success or failure, never mind profit margins. By implementing marketing research and marketing techniques, Hollywood took on the appearance of other, less ephemeral, industries.

In the decade following the end of World War II, the demise of a guaranteed audience, the loss of the major producers' theater chains, and menacing developments in politics (red-baiting, McCarthyism, the Hollywood Ten) and labor (unionization, strikes) increased the risk factor for lending institutions. Turning to the long-established business tradition of research as a substitute for intuition made economic sense.

PROBLEMS

There are particular difficulties in marketing movies and conducting movie marketing research as compared with other commodities. Samuel Marx, in his book *Mayer and Thalberg*, describes the film consumption process this way:

> Theatres are the stores where customers buy entertainment, but unlike most merchandising outlets, the [buyers don't] take [their] purchase away. [They pay] for it and [look] at it, then [leave] with only the memory of it. When the last customer has paid and looked and left, the material that was bought still belongs to the [person] who sold it.[17]

Likewise, Chris Musun, in *The Marketing of Motion Pictures*, states that "the financial results of a 'unique' film coupled with 'unique' selling and distribution techniques hardly lends itself to prediction."[18] Whether or not movies are truly a unique product is debatable. Nonetheless, movies possess attributes distinct from those of other products and services that consumers might purchase; thus the researching and marketing of movies must be conducted in a special way.

Movies are essentially a luxury (or discretionary) product; they fulfill none of the basic human needs necessary for continued existence. Movies neither maintain people's health nor do they enhance their appearance. Further, movie attendance is neither a status symbol nor is it publicly displayable like a car or clothing. Movies are an indulgence to which people treat themselves. Therefore, consumers must be persuaded to purchase movies for perhaps less than "rational" reasons. Discovering and exploiting the arguments and reasons to persuade consumers is the challenge faced by marketing research.

The actual consumer purchasing behavior in regards to movies can be characterized as an "impulse buy." The decision to attend a movie is typically made shortly before attending; a *Los Angeles Times* study found that 45 percent of its sample usually made their decision to go to a movie on the same day they actually went. The decision to go to a movie, however, is unlike picking up a candy bar or magazine while standing in the grocery store checkout line and is also unlike the decision process involved in purchasing an appliance. Showtimes prohibit purely spontaneous behavior, like candy bar purchasing; at the same time, intensive consumer research, as for buying an appliance, rarely plays a major role. The *Times* study also found that two-thirds of the respondents reported that they went to the movies "in streaks" rather than "on a fairly regular basis" and that convenience played a significant role in their attendance: 67 percent traveled five miles or less to get to the theater the last time they went to the movies.[19] This does not mean that movie attendance is unthinking or inadequately considered. For movie marketers, though, predicting the behavior of consumers involves a wider range of more amorphous variables than is the case for other products. Movie marketing research seeks to reveal which variables are most important and how to best exploit them for a particular film.

Unlike many package goods, movies do not offer the consumer trialability. Smaller, less costly versions of movies are unavailable, manufacturers' discount coupons for the product are not produced, and product returns based on consumer dissatisfaction or failure of the product to perform as expected are impossible. Moviegoers, therefore, cannot sample the product with minimal risk. (Neither theatrical trailers nor other forms of advertising provide a fully analogous form of product sampling.)

All of these attributes, of course, are a result of the fact that the consumer does not purchase a generic product. Although we may talk about going to *the* movies, in the end we go to *a* movie, and the film consumer enters into the "purchase agreement" with little knowledge of the commodity itself. The form is familiar, but the specific content is not, because (unlike other consumer products) there are few repeat purchases. Most people attend a movie only once. (*2001, Star Wars,* and *The Rocky Horror Picture Show* are the exceptions, not the rule.) Marketing and selling a movie is an all-or-nothing proposition, both for the marketer and the consumer. Thus from both the manufacturers' and the consumers' perspectives, the inducement to purchase must be especially compelling, for there is only a limited time to sell the product by the manufacturer and little recourse available to the consumer once the product has been purchased.

The fact that moviemakers have only a brief time to offer their product to consumers presents a special marketing concern. Each individual movie has an extremely short theatrical shelf life. On the average, a movie is theatrically available for some four to six weeks. The marketing process must consider the *costs* of manufacturing the movie (including the actual cost of production, interest expenses, advertising, and duplicating of prints) as well as its *competition* (including other movies already in or being prepared for release by the same studio, other studios' movies, and the many alternative leisure activities consumers might choose). Film marketing needs to achieve a high penetration in and a large share of a market characterized by limited growth potential. Olen Earnest, who conducted marketing research for 20th Century-Fox and Universal, describes the film market as one "characterized by quick entry and quick exit, and the majority of box office gross must be made early—for there may well be no later." The average box office drop-off after one week of release is 15 to 20 percent, even for a popular film, and attendance declines even more rapidly thereafter.[20]

Moreover, the industry favors only three release periods for its pictures: summer, the Christmas holiday season, and the Easter holiday. Marketing must attract and hold the attention of potential moviegoers and persuade them that a particular movie, out of all the others available, is *the* movie to attend. The specific marketing strategy must consider the number of movies opening in a given week, the total number of annual movie releases, and the relatively small annual attendance of moviegoers.

The potential audience for most movies is limited to the relatively narrow age group of 12- to 34-year-olds. Thus, unlike car manufacturers, who can create different models of the same product for different market segments, moviemakers create a product for a much more specialized, less diverse (which is not to say homogeneous) market.

Movie marketing research and its methods face two further difficulties. First, again unlike other consumer products, movies can't be test-marketed the way other products might be. Second, movie marketing research is difficult to conduct with any accuracy prior to actual creation of the product.

Unlike consumer package goods, the movie product has no established brand leaders, no brand loyalty among consumers, and, indeed, no actual brands. When introducing a new hand soap, for instance, the marketing researcher knows that: (1) there is a clearly definable market for hand soaps; (2) the development (growth, decline, stability) of the market can be traced; and (3) the share of market held by various existing hand soaps can be ascertained. When testing the new hand soap on consumers, the marketer can ask consumers to compare the new product against existing brands and assess the new product's perceived benefits as related to consumers' previous and present experience. Such "knowables" are not present for movies.

Prerelease research can only tap emotional, attitudinal, preference, and cognitive dimensions of the consumer; it does not and cannot discover the most important dimension, the behavioral aspects—actual movie attendance. At best, the behavioral component, which is clearly the criterion by which success is measured, can only be inferred. Prior to actual release of a film, the only tangibles available to researcher and respondent are proposed advertising campaign materials such as newspaper illustrations and other visuals. Moreover, the competition is unknown; both researcher and the public have little or no idea of what the alternatives will be, a point of special significance when attempting to conduct research on a movie that may not be exhibited for another six months.

The "uniqueness assumption" about movies postulates that each film is a product unlike other products within the same class. Although facial tissue is pretty much the same whether its brand is Kleenex or Scott, the same cannot be said for motion pictures. Movie marketers try to position a film in the marketplace in such a way that it is perceived by audiences as a new experience that nevertheless retains some positive familiarity with their previous experiences.

The way that movies are purchased will have an impact on behavior. Few people go to the movies alone. The most common attendance unit is the couple. As a result, one person's responses to market research questions may indicate very little about how he or she will actually behave once presented with the true opportunity to make a movie selection decision. The presence of another person in the attendance decision and the specific film choice process can result in geometrically larger numbers of variables. In some cases the involvement is direct; in other instances one individual will weigh the appropriateness for a date or the preferences of the other when choosing a movie.[21]

As a result of these limitations, the movie industry has resorted to a rather selective set of approaches to selling its products.

METHODS FOR AND TYPES OF RESEARCH

The major film companies' research is oriented to the marketing of one picture rather than to developing or uncovering generalized principles and concepts. Analysis of particular subgroups of the target audience is also forgone; though the age bracket of the most frequent moviegoers is well known, finer discriminations within that age bracket are rarely given serious consideration.

Preproduction Research

A 1983 *Variety* article about research by the film industry reported that preproduction research was rare. Marvin Antonowsky, who has headed the research departments at Columbia and Universal, was quoted as saying that "conceptual research is a waste of time." Another industry marketing person flatly stated that "research should not be used to determine [whether] a movie should or should not be made." The resistance to preproduction research is largely related to the amorphous nature of the product. One veteran movie researcher said, "Anything that is innovative is hard for market research to clue in on." Another noted, "In a movie, you're selling an image for an image. It's not something you can take home and wear." A third asked, "How can you research an idea or a story line? How do you describe *One Flew Over the Cuckoo's Nest* or *On Golden Pond*? It all depends on execution." And a fourth asserted, "Anyone who bases his decision to go ahead with a picture only on research is a fool."[22]

Concept tests. Despite such comments, preproduction research does occur, sometimes with ironic results. Typically, it employs concept tests using a questionnaire composed of 50- to 100-word synopses of several film stories. Respondents, who are frequently solicited at shopping malls, are asked to imagine that they have decided to go to the movies and to indicate on a scale how likely they would be to attend each movie described. Columbia turned down the option to produce Steven Spielberg's *E.T.*, for instance, based on their research, which found that the film would be of interest only to children.

Concept tests were first performed by the Audience Research Institute (later called Audience Research, Inc.), founded by George Gallup in 1937, two years after he established the Gallup Poll. ARI invested considerable energy in refining its methods for conducting concept tests. Initially attention was focused on the length and number of the synopses presented to respondents. After testing synopses ranging from just one or two sentences to 3,000–5,000 words, ARI settled on a length of about 60 words and six to eight story ideas to be tested during one personal interview. Paul K. Perry, former president of the Gallup Organization, recalled that despite the methodological refinements, "people were unable to identify the reasons for their liking or disliking a story." Thus ARI researchers found it difficult to discern accurately the story elements that appealed to the respondents.[23]

Concept tests, however, continue to be conducted, although perhaps as low-priority projects. Among "exploitation" filmmakers, the results of concept tests are apparently given crucial significance. In 1983 the *Los Angeles Times* published writer Lee Grant's detailed "diary" of the development and research conducted on *Private School*. Compared to mainstream Hollywood productions, *Private School* was produced on a bargain-basement budget using second-echelon actors (Sylvia Kristel, Phoebe Cates, Matthew Modine). The budget for marketing research, however, was expansive. To determine how to treat the story, three concepts were tested: a raunchy sex approach, a sexy comedy, and an innocent romantic comedy. The sexy-comedy version of the concept test read as follows:

> There are wild times at an exclusive Dallas girls' school when a busty, beautiful gang of ready-for-anything seniors take sex education into their own hands. The sex-starved fraternity nuts from a nearby men's college are happy to help, but the girls' own spinster headmistress does all she can to stop the all-night action. And a ruggedly handsome new teacher causes still more crazy commotion when two of his students compete to seduce him.

Results indicated that this sexy-comedy treatment tested best among the 13- to 30-year-olds in the five-city telephone survey sample. Females found the raunchy treatment offensive and unappealing, and most of the sample viewed the romantic version too saccharine. Armed with a full script and supporting research, producer R. Ben Efraim cut a distribution deal with Universal; *Private School* went on to earn almost $45 million.[24]

As in the past, present methods for performing concept tests possess several limitations. First, as ARI found, the number of concepts must be restricted, because developing lengthy questionnaires is expensive, data interpretation is complicated, and people are less willing to answer a lengthy questionnaire than a brief one. Moreover, people typically do not choose to attend one movie by selecting from ten or more movies. Psychologist George Miller's social science dictum concerning "the magic number seven, plus or minus two"[25] reminds us that above a certain point, the greater the choice, the less reliable the judgments.

The order in which the concepts are presented may also pose a problem. Concepts appearing toward the end of the questionnaire may receive less attention than those at the beginning; the first and last concepts may receive disproportionate attention because of their prominent position. Creating different versions of the questionnaire in which the concepts appear in different orders can compensate for this bias.

A final problem of methodology is the halo and contrast effect: the impact that one concept may have on another. Even though respondents are asked to evaluate each concept separately from all others, the other concepts can have a contaminating effect. Consider, for instance, how you would respond to a "want to see" question asked about the following films, presented in the following order: *Empire of the Sun, September, Nuts,* and *Three Men and a Baby.* Your appraisal of *September* may be colored by the way in which you responded to *Empire of the Sun.* Alternately, would your want-to-see rating of a film be affected by being surrounded by two obscure movies as compared to two sequels (for example, *Rambo III* and *Jaws 3D*)? To minimize this kind of contamination, no more than five concepts are tested, and two anchor concepts are included at the beginning of the questionnaire. A positive anchor is a film that most people will presumably respond favorably toward, followed by a negative anchor (one that presumably most people will respond unfavorably toward). Responses to these two anchors then define the end points of the rating scale so that the data can be interpreted more accurately.

Concept testing apparently carries little actual weight in most production decision making. One independent movie marketing research firm reports that from their experience, the initiation of and the results of concept tests "are most often used to reinforce preconceived ideas or to convince *someone else* when there is an internal dispute, rather than to gather real information on which a decision will be based."[26]

Casting tests. Another type of preproduction research is the casting test. Paramount is said to have based budget decisions on statistical analyses of stars' "marquee values" as early as 1929; the methods and data sources for these values are unknown.[27] In the 1940s ARI developed some casting tests to determine which actors and actresses would best enhance the market value of a particular movie. A related research project, called the Continuing Audit of Marquee Values, was developed by ARI to ascertain the relative drawing power of screen personalities. It was developed as a result of other ARI research indicating that a star's marquee value accounted for some 16 percent of the variance in movie rentals.

ARI used several methods to conduct its casting and Marquee Values tests. In general, a national quota sample of 500 to 1,000 people was drawn to represent demographic characteristics of the movie audience as sorted by frequency of moviegoing. ARI employed interviewers in 76 communities to conduct the tests for the Audit of Marquee Values. One Audit approach presented respondents with a list of as many as 150 names and asked them which names they would make an effort to see if the person named were appearing in a movie. Because the respondents had no concrete referent—only the star's name listed on a theater marquee—the results were of questionable value. Another ARI method tested cast combinations: stars were presented to respondents in various pairings (for example, Katharine Hepburn with Ronald Colman or with Walter Pidgeon) to determine how drawing power might be maximized. Additionally, studios tested casting and casting combinations as related to titles of films, film concepts (stories), and both titles and concepts.[28]

In the 1970s, Universal became known as the leader in use of the "casting computer." Though rumors and anecdotes about computerized casting abound, the industry is mum. When film scholar Thomas Simonet interviewed industry researchers on this subject, he found uniform denial that casting research was being performed.[29] A frequent response was that such research would be superfluous, that casting is usually "a foregone conclusion." The demise of Hollywood's "star system" of the 1930s and '40s, with its means for contracting a stable of studio stars, along with the rise of agent-constructed "packages" no doubt have reduced the incidence of this kind of research. Further, the practical value of these performer appeal and familiarity studies may be slight, given the weak predictive power of the results. Such top-grossing movies as *Star Wars, Rocky*, and *Alien* had no big-name stars; research on the audience appeal of Harrison Ford, Sylvester Stallone, or Sigourney Weaver at the time the projects were in development would have revealed little of value to the studios, directors, or producers.

Emotional-response tests. Both concept and casting tests involve in-person interviews with respondents. A more recent type of preproduction research used more impersonal methods. In the late 1960s through mid-1970s, the Emotional Response Index System drew considerable attention. Introduced by Peter and Lee Zoellner in 1968, ERIS attempted to predict the success of a movie based on an analysis of its script or treatment as measured against the emotional responses of a 7,000-person sample gathered years before the script was written.

People's emotional reactions to a variety of issues and themes were measured physiologically by means of galvanic skin response (GSR). GSR purports to indicate general emotional arousal and anxiety by measuring the electrical conductivity of a person's skin, which changes with level of perspiration. GSR responses were collected over several years and stored in a computer. Movie scripts were analyzed for qualities of affluence, affection, status, and security. These four dimensions of the scripts were then rated and charted in comparison to the GSR responses collected earlier. Beyond the concern for the predictive accuracy of this method was the problem of the validity of the GSR instrumentation; some researchers question whether GSR actually measures what it claims to measure. No mention of this technique has appeared in the literature since 1978.[30]

Perhaps the most successful preproduction research to date was conducted by Sunn Classic Pictures in tandem with a special method of film distribution. During the 1970s Sunn spent about $85,000 per film on preproduction research, asking people in person and by telephone about the kinds of themes and issues that would attract them to the movie theater. Once the topic, or theme, for the proposed movie had been decided, Sunn once again surveyed people to determine the exact treatment. Sunn identified as its market working-class families who rarely went to the movies more than twice a year. Sunn was interested in attracting this "fringe" audience because they represented as much as three-quarters of the U.S. population. Additionally, Sunn produced only G-rated "family films" such as *The Life and Times of Grizzly Adams*, which would attract a larger attendance unit than the typical couple, thereby increasing box-office return. The films were distributed by a method known as "four-walling," in which Sunn rented fully staffed theaters from exhibitors for a specified period of time and kept virtually all admissions revenues. Further, Sunn used heavy television advertising campaigns to emphasize the limited engagements of its films.[31]

Despite Sunn's success, preproduction research has generally not been favored by the industry. The central problem with such research is that the existing methods do not permit accurate and interpretable answers to production decision questions. More reliable research can be accomplished at the prerelease stage. Components of the product such as the title and advertising strategies are things that can be more clearly presented to people for their evaluation.

Research During Production

Once the process of filmmaking has been set in motion, market researchers begin to design research projects to answer such questions as: What kinds of people will react favorably and unfavorably to this film? Where might advertising dollars best be spent? What kind of advertising (its design, layout, and "look") will be most effective? What will the word of mouth on this film be?

Three kinds of studies are called for during the filming, preparation for release, and distribution of the picture. *Promotional research* seeks to determine which aspects of a film most appeal to moviegoers so that those aspects can be stressed in the advertising and promotion of the film. Audiences might react to the story, the characters, the starring talent, the scenery, the title, or any number of things. *Advertising research* attempts to uncover the best advertising strategies for three significant media: print, television, and in-theater trailers. *Awareness studies* occur during production and postproduction of a film as well as at release to determine the extent to which people have heard about the movie. In general, today the methods for obtaining this information include telephone interviews and in-person interviews, most frequently at shopping malls. The samples range in size from 500 to 1,000, heavily skewed to the 12 to 49 age group. A few key cities are selected for the research, with a balance struck between more and less cosmopolitan locales (Boston and San Francisco along with Des Moines and Kansas City, for example).

Title tests. Once in production, research on the picture's title begins.[32] In 1947 George Gallup was quoted as saying that a good title can add $300,000 to a picture's gross earnings. Today most industry researchers agree that the title can make a difference in the final analysis, but by itself the title will not make or break a film. Twentieth Century-Fox began testing the *Star Wars* title more than one year before its release to discover moviegoers' perceptions about the film based solely on the title. Results indicated that by itself the title generated little interest in seeing the film, because it suggested a violent science-fiction film.

A 1987 Tri-Star release first called *Skip Tracer* had its title changed to *Squeeze Play*. A comedy starring Michael Keaton and Rae Dawn Chong, its original title failed to convey the film's humor and, moreover, was thought to be too obscure. Originally, the film's marketing had to explain what a "Skip Tracer" meant (someone whose business it is to track down delinquent bill payers). Despite the title change, however, the film performed poorly.

Audience interest in film titles, as with other kinds of movie research, is typically measured by a want-to-see question. Respondents are asked to indicate the extent of their interest in seeing a movie on a five-point response scale ranging from "very interested, would definitely like to see" to "not at all interested, would definitely not want to see." Leo Handel pointed out that the phrasing of the want-to-see question can influence the responses. Compare, for instance, how you would respond to questions phrased in the following ways: "Do you want to go to see," "Are you interested in seeing," "Would you buy a ticket for," "Would you yourself buy a ticket for." The more specific, personalized, and action-oriented the phrasing, the greater the likelihood of accurate response.

In general, there are three criteria for a good title. By itself, the title should be enticing, communicate the essential theme of the movie, and be easy to remember. These criteria are not necessarily mutually exclusive, nor are they necessarily hard and fast rules applicable to all films. Nonetheless, they offer a basis for the design, execution, and evaluation of research. A title that by itself communicated little and indeed was obscure to most people was *The China Syndrome*, yet the movie was commercially successful. That the 1979 accident at the Three Mile Island nuclear plant occurred virtually at the same time the picture was released, and hence the phrase became well-known, could not have been anticipated by Columbia; the attendant publicity from TMI did not hurt the film. On the other hand, sequels, prequels, and remakes that use titles similar to those of the original are not necessarily guaranteed an audience; for instance, neither *The Sting II* nor *Butch and Sundance: The Early Days* performed well at the box office.

Title tests are constructed to measure the relative appeal of various titles and to learn what audiences think a film is about. Relative appeal is measured by having the sample respond to the want-to-see question when confronted with five to seven titles. Respondents are typically requested to imagine that they have made a decision to go to the movies but have only the titles before them as their information and choice selection. This is obviously a highly artificial situation, yet industry marketing researchers believe that they can gain a sense of the sample's preference for one title over the others. Frequently this procedure is followed by a second questionnaire page in which the studio's three most preferred titles (based either on intuition or previous testing) are presented, along with a 20- to 30-word description of the film. Respondents are then asked to rank each title in terms of their want-to-see. The memorability of the titles presented in a title test is determined by asking the respondents to name all the titles presented in the test once they have completed and returned the questionnaire.

What a title communicates to audiences on its own is usually discovered by interviews conducted independent of related title test studies. Respondents are presented with one title and then asked to explain what they think the movie is about. Or the respondents are presented with the title and a series of adjectives and are asked to mark those adjectives that best match their feeling about the title. More elaborate title tests involve a kind of multiple-choice test in which one title is presented along with several 20- to 30-word plot descriptions. Respondents are then asked to match the title with the one description they think best reflects what the title conveys.

Generally, title testing offers marketing personnel a sense of the attractiveness of a particular title and information on how the film might best be positioned. Title tests can also provide information about the kinds of publicity and promotional campaigns that would be most effective. For instance, *10*, which starred Dudley Moore and Bo Derek, was a relatively meaningless title to many people. However, an advertising campaign emphasizing the meaning of the title gave the film prominence. Similarly, for *E.T.*, the biggest-grossing movie ever, title testing alone would not have predicted its tremendous success; inspired promotion, clever advertising, sneak previewing the movie a week and a half before opening it, and booking the film into 1,100 theaters all helped to generate positive word of mouth.

For *Gandhi*, Richard Attenborough's three-hour epic, Columbia's early research clearly indicated that few among the key moviegoing audience under 35 years old had heard of Mahatma Gandhi, and virtually no one under 20 had any inclination to see a movie about a man who had been dead for more than a quarter-century. Still, the title, obscure though it may have been to the biggest and most frequent moviegoing group, was kept. Columbia launched a massive educational and promotional campaign, delayed the film's opening until December, and tied the release to a series of premieres benefiting UNICEF in several key cities. Thus the results of title tests are but one dimension of the overall marketing campaign and by themselves are of limited value.

Ad research.   Along with title research, advertising and promotion research are also conducted during the production of the film.[33] Despite the fact that a finished product is unavailable to show to moviegoers, studios attempt to learn which aspects of a film are most appealing so that they can exploit them. Typically the basic framework of the movie is presented to respondents, including such elements as the plot synopsis, a brief description and the names of the characters, and any special effects (visual, aural, or story-related). In the early stages of this research, studios do not necessarily attempt to discover which advertising strategies earn the highest or most favorable response; rather, the research tries to learn the basis for audience interest in order to ensure that the advertising campaign's *intent* matches the audience's *understanding*. For

An Officer and a Gentleman, Paramount tested at least ten campaigns before choosing the one that emphasized the romantic aspects of the movie over those emphasizing themes of militarism or masculine rites of passage, which were found to be less appealing. Mismatching of advertising and audience expectations can result in poor or, even worse, little word of mouth. This might have been the case for two Clint Eastwood vehicles, *Honkytonk Man* and *Bronco Billy,* in which Eastwood was cast against type. (On the other hand, *Every Which Way But Loose* and *Every Which Way You Can* both proved successful at the box office.)

Advertising must effectively and accurately convey a movie's subject as well as offer enticement to attend. Misleading advertising may result in a short-term benefit of drawing people to the film but ultimately, once word of mouth takes hold, the result is diminished attendance. An example of a "problem film" for advertising was *Prizzi's Honor.* The film was essentially a black comedy concerning the relationship between two professional hired guns (Jack Nicholson and Kathleen Turner). Conceivably, the movie might have been advertised as a gangster film or a romance, though these elements were secondary to the main thrust of the film. To position the film as a black comedy involved special risks; in particular, if the audiences did not "get" the humor, their expectations upon entering the theater would not be met, resulting in negative word of mouth. The advertising copy, illustrations, TV spots, and trailers all focused on the creative mix of humor and drama in order to convey accurately the essence of the film while at the same time distinguishing it from the strictly gangster-oriented themes of two other recent releases, *The Cotton Club* and *Once Upon a Time in America.*

A problem inherent in such research is that written descriptions of a film do not allow respondents to conceptualize the movie accurately and realistically. As a result, when asked questions that rely on this method, respondents often use previous experiences with aspects such as the film's genre to make their judgments. Thus *Star Wars* initially tested poorly based on its science-fiction theme and perceived juvenile appeal. According to Olen Earnest, who directed the marketing research, the research did reveal one concept that seemed capable of broadening the appeal to a larger, adult audience: The adventures of Luke Skywalker were a space-age equivalent of Homer's *Odyssey.* Twentieth Century-Fox created several advertising strategies to emphasize this analogy, including the line "An odyssey to the edge of your imagination and beyond, far beyond."

In the preliminary stages of advertising tests, focus-group interviews are frequently conducted, rather than sample surveys.[34] This research method involves a trained facilitator leading two to ten people in a group discussion about, for instance, their expectations concerning a movie advertised in a particular way. Usually the focus sessions are videotaped, thereby preserving the data and allowing for analysis at some later time.

Focus-group interviewing is relatively inexpensive, permits a broader range of responses than a structured questionnaire, and has the potential for chaining-out among group members (one person picking up on another's comments and extending the dialog). Perhaps of greatest utility to the researcher is the qualitative nature of the data generated by focus groups, which allows for the discovery of unexpected findings, thereby inspiring additional research questions. The focus-group method is an especially apt one for a film that may not have a clear "image" or seems difficult to promote

Columbia used focus groups in order to decide whether to distribute *Emmanuelle* in 1974. *Emmanuelle* was an especially problematic film for several reasons: it was French and was sufficiently sexually explicit to earn an X rating. American distributors are wary of foreign films because they have traditionally performed poorly, with the exception of early silent movies in which language, of course, was irrelevant. And the X rating might imply that the picture lacked socially approved values. Furthermore, the movie featured no name-recognizable stars. Focus-group results, however, indicated that the film was not associated with typical X-rated, hard-core porno movies and that it could be sold as a "quality film." The advertising campaign featured the line "X was never like this," which emphasized both the rating and the uniqueness of the film and also managed to suggest the appeal to socially sanctioned sensuality over hard-core sexuality. The focus-group results also indicated that women enjoyed the movie, which led Columbia to use a female announcer for the *Emmanuelle* radio ads. The research for this film was conducted with a completed film in hand; the method's value for testing advertising and promotional materials for films still in production, however, is clear.

Research on media buys. Research while a film is in production also analyzes the best, most cost-effective media buys to be made. By the 1970s it was not uncommon to spend at least as much as and often even more than the cost of producing the film to advertise it. Placement of advertising, in addition to what the advertising "says," is essential to maximize effectiveness and control costs. Before the introduction of television, newspapers, movie magazines, and national magazines all accounted for a large proportion of advertising expenses. Movie advertising on television now exceeds $100 million annually. And cable TV is increasingly being used to promote movies. Spot purchases as well as music videos derived from the film and programmed on MTV have been credited for the success of such films as *Flashdance* and *Footloose*.

To determine the most effective media for advertising a film, researchers frequently rely on sample surveys. In the past, data on a film's potential audience were cross-tabulated with the "reach" of various media. Movie advertisers interested in reaching, for instance, college-educated, middle-income, married women with children sought a similar demographic profile for their media buys. By the early 1970s, a trend toward psychographic, or "people," research emerged. Using such acronyms as VALS (values and lifestyles program) and catchy titles such as PRIZM and FASTRAC, these research programs gather data on media use, lifestyles, and buying behavior. The audience is then segmented into a number of more or less discrete groups and, based on what media they use, advertising is purchased.

Even without the sophisticated analyses of such psychographic research, the film industry naturally wishes to ensure maximum reach and exposure of its advertising. For example, print advertising for movies frequently includes college newspapers as an inexpensive means for reaching the audiences for films such as *Stripes* or *National Lampoon's Vacation*.

Trailer tests.   Trailer tests analyze the effectiveness of "previews of coming attractions" for a film, a particularly important marketing tool. Because trailers speak directly to moviegoing audiences, they are the best medium to reach a receptive population. Trailers not only make audiences aware of the upcoming release of a film, they also permit analysis of audience reactions to get a sense of what kinds of individuals will be inclined to see the movie.

Essentially, two approaches are taken to test trailers: in-theater interviews and focus-group analysis. In the former, audience members are interviewed after they've watched the trailer and the feature film. Interview items include recall of the title, the want-to-see question, and problems in the promotional strategy for a film. Focus groups permit lengthier, more in-depth, qualitative analyses of fewer people's reactions to a trailer.

Promotion research.   Promotion research results can be used as one means for determining the extent of marketing campaigns for a film. Preliminary research, conducted while shooting of a film is still in progress, may suggest how aggressively a movie needs to be promoted. More refined analysis of this same factor may occur once production is completed and the movie is sneak previewed.

Awareness studies.   The last kind of research performed while a movie is in production and which continues through release is awareness studies or penetration (to what extent and among which groups, do people know about a film?). According to Gallup's Paul Perry, penetration accounts for about one-third of the variance in film rentals. The goal of this research is to determine a movie's opening potential strength and the impact of the advertising campaign on moviegoers. Awareness studies are generally begun no later than about one month before release. The method for this kind of study is usually a nationwide tracking study, conducted weekly, using telephone interviews in the top 30 or so movie markets. Respondents are asked to report the titles of new movies they have heard about or have seen advertised. This provides an index of the respondents' spontaneous, unaided awareness of movies. Respondents are then read a list of all other current movies not mentioned by them and asked which titles they have heard of, thereby providing an index of aided awareness. According to Olen Earnest, a minimum awareness level of 60 percent prior to release of a film is necessary (but by itself not sufficient) for a successful opening. (Earnest reports that *Star Wars* opened with a 64 percent awareness level, eventually exceeding 85 percent.)

Postproduction Research

Once a picture has been completed, several kinds of research are conducted.

Sneak previews.   The sneak preview is the best-known strategy for pretesting a movie. The concept of sneak previewing a movie is nearly as old as the industry itself.[35] According to writer Jill Kearney, the first sneak occurred in 1911, when Thomas H. Ince invited a rather biased group of industry insiders to view his latest Western, *Custer's Fight.*

Two kinds of sneak previews, or "advance screenings," as they are more commonly and accurately named now, are used: production previews and marketing previews. Rarely today are movies genuinely "sneaked" in the sense that audiences do not know what movie they will be shown. Still, at least on occasion, films are brought to audiences for help in constructing the movie's final look. These are known as *production previews.* The legendary Irving Thalberg, production chief at MGM (and the model for F. Scott Fitzgerald's *The Last Tycoon*), institutionalized and, as Aljean Harmetz termed it, "shaped the ritual" of the production preview. Taking his cue from theatrical producers who tried out their plays in Philadelphia and Hartford before bringing them to Broadway, Thalberg viewed sneaks as a kind of field test, a means to adjust the timing of scenes (so that audience laughter, for example, did not step on subsequent lines) or discover where the exposition was too verbose or scant. In Thalberg's era, sneaks were economical, because the sets could be left standing on the studio lot and the cast was under studio contract; reshooting or adding scenes was not a problem.

With near-military secrecy, Thalberg would arrange for screening privileges in outlying suburbs, such as Glendale and Long Beach. The film was delivered by guards in unmarked cans; only a very few of the studio brass had even a glimmer of an idea about when a sneak would occur. For these early sneaks, unlike those of today, there was no advertising of the event and no public prescreening information disclosed; only the theater marquee announced "Major Studio Sneak Preview Tonight." Thalberg observed the audience during the screening and might distribute preview cards soliticing audience opinion about the movie.

More recently, producer Jon Davidson previewed *Top Secret* (1984) while it was still in the rough-cut stage. The movie was targeted at a college-age film-buff audience, so theaters in three university towns were selected: New Haven, Connecticut; Hanover, New Hampshire; and Madison, Wisconsin. The "recruited" audiences were not told the title or type of film they were being invited to see, and the movie was presented without credits and with only an improvised music score. They were told that their opinions about the film would be solicited.[36] Columbia likewise sneaked several versions of Sidney Pollack's *Tootsie* before the final release of the film. Numerous examples of changes in film endings as a result of audience tests can be cited. In the Sylvester Stallone vehicle *First Blood* (which introduced the character of Rambo), audiences were asked to choose between the ending we are all familiar with and another alternative: Rambo dies. The unchosen ending, of course, would have precluded a sequel. Audiences who saw the test marketing of *Risky Business* (starring Tom Cruise) were offered a choice in which the Cruise character does not go on to Princeton University. They—and subsequently the studio—rejected this downbeat finale. Finally, in *After Hours*, the alternative ending had leading actor Griffin Dunne trapped in a plaster cast without hope of getting out.

Frequently studios will solicit individuals for production previews rather than relying on individuals who self-select in response to a newspaper ad, not so much to control the sample scientifically as to avoid exposing an unfinished project to critics.

Another fear among studio executives is that critics will attend an advance screening, especially a production screening, and hurt the film's opening potential. In 1977 Columbia sneaked Steven Spielberg's *Close Encounters of the Third Kind* in Dallas. The film's shooting had been shrouded in secrecy, its budget had become greatly bloated, and Columbia's executives were nervous. Two weeks after the sneak, *New York* magazine published a severely critical review of the film and Columbia's stock fell three points. But *Close Encounters* went on to be a monumental success. On the other side of the coin, for instance, is Michael Cimino's *Heaven's Gate* (1980); its special screening for critics was met with such devasting reviews that it was sent back to the editing room; that did not help, and the picture became the best-known financial fiasco in recent memory, ultimately leading to the sale of United Artists by its parent, Transamerica.

Numerous methods, from the sublime to the ridiculous, have been used to gather data from audiences at production previews. Questionnaires and focus-group interviews are mainstays. Applause and laugh meters were frequently employed in the late 1940s, and concealed microphones picked up patrons' comments as they left the theater. A 1946 *Hollywood Reporter* article discussed the development of a tiny electronic recording instrument that would be placed under a specified number of seats to unobtrusively monitor the patrons' heartbeat and breathing rate.[37]

Various mechanical feedback devices have enjoyed continuing popularity since the 1940s.[38] Perhaps best known among past devices is the Lazarsfeld-Stanton Program Analyzer, originally designed to measure listeners' responses to radio programs. Other brands included the Hopkins Electric Televoting Machine (used by ARI), the Cirlin Reactograph (itself an outgrowth of the Lazarsfeld device), and the Meier Audience Response Recorder (more often used for theatrical plays). They all had respondents hold a mechanical device that permitted them to record their reactions to a film as it was being screened by either twisting a knob or pushing buttons to indicate the extent of their interest or enjoyment. The results of the audiences' twisting or pressing were recorded on a continuous roll of paper from which shot-by-shot analyses of audience reactions could be plotted.

The Schwerin System, which attempted to approximate the method of the mechanical devices, used questionnaires and large numbers that were flashed on a separate screen from the movie; this "number cueing" directed the sample to indicate their reaction at the time cued on the survey form. For all systems, focus-group interviews were conducted following the picture. During the 1940s and '50s, these methods were widely used by, among others, Columbia, Disney, RKO, and The March of Time.

But these mechanical devices have a set of distinct limitations: People may forget to activate or deactivate the device. They may respond unfavorably to characters such as villains, who are created to provoke an unfavorable response. The most severe limitation is that these devices are extremely intrusive and, if the respondents are conscientious about their task, very distracting, which of course then skews the response.

Infrared photography was used to observe audience reactions in the 1950s. Although this approach was clearly superior to mechanical devices insofar as it was unobstrusive and the "respondents" were unaware that their behavior was being observed, teasing the meaning out of the "data" was clearly problematic.[39]

Simple observation is also employed, particularly in theaters that are not specially designed for research testing. For instance, counting the number of trips viewers take to the restroom during a horror movie may be an indicator of anxiety; coughing may suggest nervousness; whispering and increased concession stand purchases may indicate restlessness or boredom. A crucial problem in using these methods is that of establishing a normative value for the behavior being measured.

Today companies such as ASI Market Research, which owns the Preview House in Hollywood, and the National Research Group continue the tradition of production previews.[40] The usual array of questionnaires, focus groups, mall interviews, and telephone interviews, in addition to "wired theaters," are deployed in order to better understand audience response to a film nearing completion. *Marketing previews* attempt through questionnaires and follow-up telephone and focus-group interviews to discern who the audience for a film will be and what the word of mouth will be. Surveys distributed to the audience gather data on their overall evaluation of the film, how strongly they would or would not recommend it to a friend, how they would describe it to others, their frequency of moviegoing, their demographics, and other movies seen by them. If, for instance, the data reveal that the preview audience had a high, positive want-to-see before viewing the film but a negative response to the film, the best distribution strategy might be to open the film wide before word of mouth kills it. Data on other movies seen can be cross-tabulated with respondents' evaluations of the preview film and their anticipated recommendations to determine the kind of audience to which a film might be targeted and positioned. In short, marketing previews offer a final opportunity to refine advertising and distribution strategies.

Marketing previews are also used as a promotional device to generate word of mouth and create excitement for a film. *Raiders of the Lost Ark* and *E.T.* both employed such promotional sneaks with great success. Rather than surveying the audience to collect data, the goal is to stimulate positive, early response by inviting opinion leaders who are likely to influence the moviegoing of others. Another approach is to provide local radio stations with free tickets to give away over the air. This serves at least two purposes: free publicity and audience targeting to generate word of mouth, by selecting a radio station whose format and listeners match the audience appeal of the film.

Yet another purpose for sneaks is to gain a distributor for independently produced movies. For instance, *The Stunt Man*, produced by Melvin Simon Productions, an independent, was screened for and turned down by every major studio in 1979; it was assessed as utterly uncommercial, largely because it was perceived as confusing, the very antithesis of the "high-concept" film (one that is promotable using a key phrase of ten or fewer words). To gain a major studio distributor, Simon sneaked the film in several markets and finally opened the movie to general exhibition, first in Seattle and later at Hollywood's front door, in Los Angeles. The combined effect of positive sneak results, coupled with the fact that *The Stunt Man* managed to exceed the amount of business done by all its Los Angeles competition, convinced 20th Century-Fox to distribute it.[41]

Marketing previews have recently fallen from favor in Hollywood. In the spring of 1985 no fewer than six youth-oriented films were being readied for release by the major distributors. Among them were *The Breakfast Club, Turk 182*, and *Vision Quest*. All of these films were heavily sneaked. Only one of the six (*Breakfast Club*) was able to break from the pack and generate significant revenues. After interviewing several studio marketing people, Richard Gold wrote in *Variety* that heavily advertising and sneaking a movie in major markets may actually hurt its box office chances by overhyping it.

Two methods of postproduction research were briefly attempted and then never heard of again.

Word-of-mouth control.   From 1976 and continuing through at least early 1979, Columbia Pictures engaged the University of Pennsylvania's Wharton School of Applied Research in a project designed to discover how to manage (or at least provide some kind of control over) word of mouth. Although precise details of the research were never publicly revealed, press reports indicate that the project was less nefarious and manipulative than the headlines suggested; the intent was more along the lines of finding ways to promote positive word of mouth rather than hushing the negative.[42] Anecdotal reports suggest that negative word of mouth travels faster, farther, and with greater impact than the positive. Examples include Procter & Gamble's "man in the moon" logo, which was rumored to be somehow tied to Satanism, the allegation that McDonald's hamburgers were made from animals other than cows, and the 1940s rumor that a leper worked at an L&M cigarette plant.[43] Although the few reports printed on the Columbia-Wharton collaboration are not extensive, it might be accurate to infer that the goal of the research concerned two key issues: the means to squelch misinformation, and the means to promote positive word of mouth without the appearance of hype.

Direct-mail marketing.   The second method given a brief tryout and then abandoned involved direct-mail marketing, an increasingly popular and effective strategy used by numerous consumer product and service manufacturers. Direct mail accounted for $11.6 billion in 1983 advertising expenses (of a total $75 billion) in the United States; some 40 million pieces of direct-mail materials are delivered daily, with the average U.S. household receiving about 1.6 pieces a day. Direct mail offers message senders the ability to tailor their reach to specific audiences by using such criteria as postal zip codes or recipient occupation categories.[44]

In 1982, Paramount initiated the first direct-mail marketing campaign for a movie with the rerelease of *Reds*. Research on the rerelease potential for a film was not a new idea; using direct mail as the research method was, however, innovative. There are two audiences for rereleases: those who would like to see the movie a second time and those who didn't see it when first released but might want to see the reissue. Leo Handel, whose Motion Picture Research Bureau conducted revival studies as far back as the 1940s, found that 97 percent of survey respondents were willing to see reissues of pictures they had not seen. When the respondents' interest in a specific picture's reissue was tested, the favorable percentage dropped, "but in any case they indicate a marked general interest in revivals."[45]

To research the market for the rerelease of *Reds*, Paramount contracted a San Francisco marketing firm, who used zip codes to determine potential audience members in three cities. In September 1982 some 100,000 letters soliciting cooperation for completing an enclosed survey were mailed. The four-page survey booklet included a brief description of the movie, basic demographic items, and, because *Reds* concerned the life of American journalist and Communist John Reed, who witnessed and wrote about the Russian revolution, two questions that probed the respondents' political party affiliation and usual political stance (liberal, moderate, conservative). Additional items sought information on the respondents' awareness of various attributes of the film's story and publicity about the movie, as well as their evaluation of the film, recommendation of the film to others, whether they would see it again, and specific aspects of the film they found most appealing. The cover letter indicated when and where the film would be exhibited in the respondents' area. The strategy behind the campaign was that, based on responses, opinion leaders could be identified and provided with incentives such as ticket discounts in the hope of generating additional patronage from word of mouth. There has been no public comment on either the results generated using this approach or the specific results for *Reds*.[46]

SUMMARY

For years the film industry was content to rely on idiosyncratic methods for learning about its consumers. Leo Handel's pioneering efforts in the late 1940s and '50s to adopt more systematic approaches to the study of film audiences remained largely a one-man effort. Not until the 1970s did Hollywood turn its attention to such research in earnest. Today a studio's marketing research department works closely with the sales, advertising, and publicity departments, and research on the audiences for movies occurs at three points: pre-production, during production, and postproduction. Although confronted with research problems not shared by market researchers in the consumer package goods industry, film audience researchers have tended to employ only a limited repertoire of research methods; among the most common are questionnaires and interviews. Finally, the philosophy that guides Hollywood market research—selling *a* film—has overlooked construction or adoption of any theoretical apparatus by which such research might be guided.

CHAPTER TWO

Movies and Leisure

L eisure has always been with us; the study of leisure, however, is a more recent endeavor.[1] Moviegoing is but one
leisure alternative. A failing of the movie industry's audience research is that
it is conceived and conducted in isolation from other forms of commercial
recreation. Industry research compares awareness of and want-to-see for one
movie against only other movies, as if the only competition for a movie were
other movies. This chapter sketches the growth of commercial leisure since
the beginning of the 20th century, along with how people have spent their
leisure time. The place of movies and moviegoing is examined within a framework of related commercial and spectator leisure activities.

LEISURE: FUNCTIONS AND MOTIVES

Scholars have found it difficult to agree on a definition of leisure. We cannot,
for instance, simply think of leisure as analogous to "free time." For, as soci-

ologist Stanley Parker points out, few would define the "free time" of the unemployed as leisure, certainly not the unemployed themselves.[2] For the present purposes, a simple definition is offered: Leisure pertains to activities that are nonobligatory, consciously and personally selected, and essential to people's physiological and psychological well-being. Leisure is consciously motivated; it is not the result of neural activity, nor coercion, nor instinct. If asked, people can articulate their motivations for pursuing leisure in general as well as particular leisure activities.

Leisure serves many purposes. Two broad categories have been noted. First, leisure acts as a means for balancing, correcting, or compensating for the tensions, strains, and obligations of workaday life. Second, leisure is seen as the means to provide such essentials as self-fulfillment, growth, satisfaction, and self-expression. It is "the central integrating force in life, from which life's wholeness is derived by the individual."[3]

Because leisure is voluntary, we become interested in learning why and how people pursue it. Three functions of leisure that may also be viewed as motives have been identified: relaxation, diversion, and broadening the individual's knowledge.[4] A 1983 study found four generalized motivations for leisure:

1. Intellectual—to expand interests, seek stimulation, be creative, satisfy curiosity.

2. Social—to find companionship, build friendships, gain respect and a feeling of belonging, meet new people.

3. Competency/mastery—to have one's achievement and ability recognized, improve skills, and challenge capabilities.

4. Stimulus avoidance—to avoid social contacts, seek rest, and gain relief from stress.[5]

We can examine the relative importance of these four motives by consulting another 1983 study, in which 1,000 respondents rated the importance of 14 reasons for engaging in leisure activities.[6] Table 2.1 presents the results, sorted into the four leisure motives.

Social reasons for leisure were clearly the most important; 64 percent agreed they were "very important." Stimulus avoidance (the relaxation motivation— the one most nearly the opposite of the social) follows at a close second with 59 percent. Somewhat under half (44 percent) of the sample agreed that intellectual motivations for leisure were very important, and 36 percent reported agreement with the competency motivation.

For particular leisure activities, the number and relative weighting of the motives is subject to considerable fluctuation. Age and the process of aging, for instance, influence the kinds of leisure desired and engaged in, as well as the motivations for such leisure activities.[7] Age and related cognitive development "qualify" people for various leisure activities. Obviously one cannot engage in reading until one knows how to read. Travel is necessarily curtailed until one can afford it.

Table 2.1

Motivations for Leisure

Leisure Motivations	Percent Responding[1]			
	Very Important	Somewhat Important	Not Too Important	Not at All Important
Social				
Spend time with your family	79	18	2	--
Companionship	68	23	5	3
Help other people	46	43	9	1
Intellectual				
The chance to learn new things	60	30	6	3
Think and reflect	57	34	6	2
Keep informed about local, national, or world events	52	35	9	4
Creativity	36	40	16	7
Excitement	33	40	19	8
Cultural enrichment	26	41	20	12
Competency/Mastery				
Exercise	47	34	12	7
Challenge	34	37	20	8
Competition	28	30	26	14
Stimulus Avoidance				
Relaxation	67	28	4	1
Forget about work or worries about daily life	51	31	13	4

SOURCE: United Media Enterprises, 1983, p. 21. Reprinted by permission of Newspaper Enterprise Association, Inc.

[1]Percent of "don't know/no answer" omitted.

These data are the result of two questions posed to respondents: "How important is it to you that you find the following in your leisure activities? (challenge, creativity, relaxation, the chance to learn new things, competition, companionship, excitement, exercise, cultural enrichment)." "How important is it that you do the following in your leisure time? (spend time with family, help others, think and reflect, keep informed, forget about work)." See United Media Enterprises, 1983, p. 152.

COMMERCIAL LEISURE THROUGH 1935

Leisure can be sorted into three types: individual, participatory, and commercial spectator amusements, such as movies, sports, and theater, for which the individual must pay money in order to participate.[8] Here we focus only on those commercial spectator leisure pursuits in which many people can partic-ipate simultaneously and which occur outside the home.

The most significant factor accounting for the development and growth of commercial spectator recreation is industrialization, which resulted in urban-ization and an increase in people's free time and disposable income.

Industrialization

The process of industrialization has been continuous. When we speak of the "Industrial Revolution," we must recall that four such revolutions have taken place so far.[9]

Commercial recreation has been dependent on industrialization for its exis-tence. Indeed, leisure itself "is a direct product of work, for the spare time and the resources to enjoy it that have been made available by the development of industrialism have created leisure as we know it in modern society."[10] This is not to suggest that commercial recreation did not exist before the turn of the century, for the history of commercial entertainment is a long one. Magic acts, puppet shows, acrobatics, and the like had been offered for a fee in taverns and on village greens for centuries. Large outdoor amusements and fairs, fea-turing itinerant entertainers, occurred with regularity on national and local holidays.

The innovation, as the United States emerged as an urban-industrial society at the turn of the century, was the *organization* of commercial entertainment. The barnstorming of wandering minstrels and traveling dog-and-pony shows gave way to scheduled performances at permanent entertainment houses. Moreover, these establishments served only an entertainment function, leav-ing to others the business of lodging and drink. Industrial specialization found a complement in the specialization of the leisure industry. Specialization took place even among the performers themselves. Whereas once an actor might perform a large number of roles over the course of a career, by the mid-1800s a star system had evolved, along with a kind of typecasting. Furthermore, as was true for industry, entertainment entrepreneurs sought consolidation and monopolistic control of their field. An early example was the short-lived Zoo-logical Institute, founded in 1835, which sought to centralize control of the import and exhibition of exotic animals. More imposing and effective was the Theatrical Syndicate, established by three firms in 1896 (the same year in which movies debuted), an attempt at monopoly control of theatrical produc-tion and presentation.

Thus along with the machines for industrial manufacturing came the machines for play. The technology of industry was stylistically duplicated by the leisure entrepreneurs, the standardization of industrial production was mirrored by the standardization of recreation, and the mass production of consumer goods included the mass production of movies.

Time. Industrialization increased productivity while requiring less human effort and fewer working hours from each worker. The average workweek in

1850 was 70 hours. Six-day workweeks were the norm. By the turn of the century, the average number of work hours had dropped to about 55 a week. The number of hours at work diminished even more rapidly following the turn of the century than before.

The shorter workweek before 1900 can be attributed to the rise of trade unions and laws that restricted work hours among women and children and that regulated working conditions in such industries as mining and railroading. But without the "amazing productivity of the American economy," the continued significant reductions in the workweek would have been unlikely.[11]

Money.   Real gains in personal income occurred at the same time that work hours decreased, accompanied by a significant dislocation of traditional personal and social values. The emphasis on efficiency of production, standardization, and nationalization of product distribution and availability meant that a consuming public had to be cultivated. In order to further fuel the fire of industrial expansion, the public would simply have to buy more than it had previously. In his 1935 book *Labor and Modern Industrial Society,* Norman Ware stated: "Time out for mass consumption becomes as much a necessity as time in for production."[12] Spending replaced thrift as a social value.

The rise of the advertising industry was one manifestation of the attack on traditional social values. Crude local attempts at advertising were replaced by the "science" of advertising research conducted by large national businesses. Industrial workers were now presented with slick, sophisticated ad campaigns advising, instructing, and persuading them where they might spend their newfound wealth.[13]

The Recreation Revolution

Between 1900 and 1930, the U.S. population grew by 47 million, nearly two-thirds as much as it had grown in the 125 years prior to 1900.[14] Most of the growth occurred in only a few states, and within those states the greatest proportion of growth was in the urban centers. Industrialization and the increased efficiency of farming accounted for "the most dramatic single movement" between 1870 and 1930: the migration from farm to city. In 1870, more than half of all employed people, excluding children, worked in agriculture, lumber, and fishing; by 1930 only 21 percent of the working population was involved in such work. As would be expected, a simultaneous rise was seen in the percentage of the labor force involved in urban occupations of trade, manufacturing, and professions.[15]

As the United States shifted from a rural-agrarian to an urban-industrial society, enthusiasm for recreation grew rapidly.[16] In particular, commercial amusements flourished at an astonishing rate and became the preponderant use of leisure time. Before 1900, theater was the first organized, commercial amusement to provide mass entertainment. Formerly the province of the wealthy and social elite, theater broadened its audience through lower admission prices and larger auditoriums. Still, theater remained too expensive for much of the working class; vaudeville proved to be the means to meet the interests and pocketbooks of this group. The late 1800s were the era of minstrel shows, boxing, and circuses. From the turn of the century through the mid-1930s were the movie industry's formative years. During these three and a half decades, movies were developed, diffused, and exploited; the economic structure of the industry evolved and solidified, as did movies' place as a commercial leisure industry.

But movies were not the only form of amusement that attracted the public during this period. Attendance at college football games doubled from 1,504,000 in 1921 to 3,289,000 in 1930. Attendance at baseball games also increased. The number of playing card decks on which federal tax was paid tripled between 1900 and 1930, and mah-jongg became a craze in the mid-'20s. Rotary, Kiwanis, and Lions clubs all experienced healthy growth during 1917–29, both in the number of clubs and size of membership. The number of pool halls and bowling alleys rose and appeared to peak in 1921. Although commercial dance halls, cabarets, and roadhouses diminished in number and size between 1921 and 1930, the closed, or taxi-dance hall that catered to male patrons was on the rise. Commercial radio broadcasting was initiated and expanded enormously during this period, both in number of receivers manufactured and purchased and in number of broadcasters. A 1934 report noted that "organized religion is more and more having to compete for public attention with vast secular interests and agencies"[17] and that "much recreation is [now] provided by other institutions than the family."[18] The significance of urbanization for commercial amusements was enormous. All commercial recreations at that time required that people leave their homes to engage in them. Urbanization meant the tight concentration of large numbers of people in a relatively small geographic area. In the city, the neighborhood movie theater found itself surrounded by a huge potential audience numbering in the thousands.

Another factor accounting for the growth of commercial recreations was the regularity with which they were offered. Movies, for instance, were available daily, unlike the 19th-century community events such as fairs, which were typically tied to holidays and other special occasions. Moreover, movies played virtually continuously, at a single location, and offered a variety of stories. These features contrasted sharply with the fly-by-night entertainers of earlier years.

The Movie Boom

Table 2.2 suggests how rapidly movies caught on in the United States even in their first decade. In New York City at this same time, only 76 "live" theaters existed, some of which also included movies as part of their fare. Moreover, it was claimed, movies "are the main American amusement of to-day," accounting for "two and a quarter million [admissions] per day—three time the audiences of all the regular theaters in America put together!"[19]

More people went to the movies than participated in any other form of commercial recreation. Movies ran continuously, were inexpensive and easily

Table 2.2

U.S. Movie Theaters and Their Seating Capacity in 1909

City	Population	Estimated Number of Movie Theaters	Total Seating Capacity
New York	4,338,322	450	150,000
Chicago	2,000,000	310	93,000
Philadelphia	1,491,082	160	57,000
St. Louis	824,000	142	50,410
Cleveland	600,000	75	22,500
Baltimore	600,000	83	24,900
San Francisco	400,000	68	32,400
Cincinnati	350,000	75	22,500
New Orleans	325,000	28	5,600

SOURCE: "The Moving Picture and The National Character," *American Review of Reviews*, September 1910, p. 315.

accessible, and, before the introduction of sound, did not require an understanding of spoken English. They were socially democratic as well. Before the introduction of movies, urban amusements were segregated by socioeconomic class and gender; movies encouraged the attendance of all: men, women, and children, the wealthy and the poor alike.

A recreation survey of 777 Milwaukee children in 1912 found that moviegoing was mentioned most often. One factor accounting for this was "the fact that the children in Milwaukee as in other cities cannot get the play which is perfectly wholesome and normal for them to have without being guilty of a misdemeanor." Among commercial amusements, movies were most popular among the children, it seemed, because few alternatives were available to them. Dance halls, pool halls, and bowling alleys ostensibly restricted admission to adults.[20]

In the California Report of the State Recreational Inquiry Committee, published in 1914, movie theaters ranked third in number behind saloons and pool rooms. The report concluded that "more of the people of the state indulge in commercial recreation than all other forms put together." This finding was not unique to California. A 1915 study of Ipswich, Massachusetts, also documents the popularity of movies and their near-monopoly of commercial recreation: In this small town of 6,000 inhabitants, movies were "the chief commercial amusement."[21]

Table 2.3 summarizes the entertainment menus of five cities in the 1910s and '20s. Some towns either had no stage theaters or did not report them as commercial amusements. Moreover, the seating capacity for the movie thea-

Table 2.3

Commercial Amusements in Five Cities

Type of Amusement	Milwaukee 1912	Toledo 1919	Cleveland 1919	Buffalo 1925	Rochester 1929
Movie theaters	50	49	123	59	37
Stage theaters	12	(NA)	(NA)	(NA)	10
Pool and billiard halls	(NA)	(NA)	443	68	309
Bowling alleys	91	(NA)	160*	35	61
Dance halls	(NA)	54	115	70	73

SOURCES: For Milwaukee, Haynes, 1912; for Toledo, Phelan, 1919; for Cleveland, Moley, 1920; for Buffalo, Weir, 1925; for Rochester, Raitt, 1929, p. 361.
*1918 figure.
NA = not available

ters was very large: the number of house seats multiplied by the number of daily shows.

The two "Middletown" (Muncie, Indiana) studies published by sociologists Robert and Helen Lynd in 1929 and 1937 amply demonstrated the impact and attraction of the movies. Although Muncie residents turned out for and enjoyed theater and opera, their opportunity to do so was limited. With the introduction of movies, the desire to see drama could be easily, conveniently, and inexpensively satisfied. By 1923, Muncie had nine movie theaters. Although the Depression diminished the number of theaters by two, as the Lynds discovered in their second visit to Middletown in 1935, attendance was relatively unaffected.[22]

Another observer in the '30s noted:

> The popularity of the motion picture is shown by the fact that it has continued to attract large crowds in spite of the financial depression. It is apparently a necessary luxury, slow to feel cuts in the family budget. The important role it plays in the leisure time of the masses can hardly be exaggerated. Moderate in cost and almost universal in its appeal, it provides an easily acceptable form of recreation especially adapted for a temporary escape from the routine of daily life.[23]

Early entrepreneurs. The extraordinary expansion of the movies can be largely attributed to the economic ease of entry into the business for movie producers and exhibitors. Producers needed little more than a camera, tripod, and film. In the early days of film, artistic talent and aesthetic sensitivity were less important than the technical ability to operate a movie camera. Because movies were easily, rapidly, and inexpensively duplicated, an extensive distribution network for the same product developed. The product manufacturer enjoyed incredible economy of scale. The exhibitor, too, could operate with very low overhead; unlike stage theaters, movie houses didn't need actors, crews, and technicians. Multiple shows, far exceeding the two performances a day typical for the stage theater, were the norm. An entire series of daily customer admissions could be obtained while using the same product again and again.

Moreover, early exhibitors purchased movies outright, rather than renting them from distributors, with whom they share every admission dollar, as they do today. Thus the producer's initial cost was, by and large, the only variable cost to the retailer. In New York, a city where we would expect exhibitor costs to be the highest, nickelodeon operators paid $25 for a license, while stage theaters paid $500. In 1910, operating expenses for a nickelodeon averaged $500 weekly, while for theaters the cost was $2,500 a week.[24]

THE "PROBLEM" OF COMMERCIAL RECREATION

The development and growth of commercial leisure aroused the concern and outright opposition of reformers, moralists, and government agencies. In 1915, Richard Henry Edwards wrote a lengthy treatise on the dangers of *Popular Amusements*; similar sentiments informed Henry Durant's clearly titled 1938 book, *The Problem of Leisure*, in which he indicts cinema, racing, and gambling. In *The Exploitation of Pleasure*, a 1911 study of commercial recreation in New York City, Michael Davis wrote: "The attitude toward recreation in America . . . [was either] that of the Puritan or of laissez-faire." Davis was quick to dispel the Puritan view that "joy is danger," while at the same time noting that "commercial recreations, developing under laissez-faire, have supplied essential popular needs but brought serious public evils." Not the least among these evils was the notion that commercial enterprises resulted in diminished "human opportunities" for noncommercial recreation on playgrounds or at home.[25]

Crusaders advocated that traditional values be protected by law. Others, less extreme in their position, expressed ambivalent feelings, especially about movies. Jane Addams, the Chicago Hull House social worker, was one. Her concern was that movies were capable of "making over the minds" of the urban population, but she also saw the educational and morally uplifting potential for the medium.[26]

Social worker and municipal reformer Frederic C. Howe wrote in 1914:

> As with many other things, America has turned its leisure over to commerce to be exploited for profit. . . . And commercialized leisure is moulding our civilization—not as it should be moulded, but as commerce dictates. . . . leisure must be controlled by the community, if it is to become an agency of civilization rather than the reverse. [The community] cannot rely upon commerce for the proper development of its needs.

Among other ideas, Howe advocated the organization of museums, colleges, public libraries, and schools "into an extra-mural university" for the people "to wrest leisure from commerce" and provide the "means for the redemption of leisure."[27]

The debates, complaints, and concerns about commercial recreation have yet to end; today, for instance, critics cite the pernicious effects of video games and video arcades.

The Dark Side of the Screen

According to their critics, the evils of movies were many, ranging from deleterious psychosocial effects to physical harm. One example of the latter concern is a 1921 article published in the *American Journal of Public Health* about "Eye Strain in Motion Picture Theaters."[28] Five years later an article in the *American Journal of Physiological Optics* addressed "the question as to whether natural colors in motion pictures reduce or intensify the eye strain which is quite commonly experienced by sensitive individuals witnessing a motion picture exhibition"—30 years before the widespread adoption of color in movies.[29] In 1945, a scholar in the University of Chicago's physiology department reported in the journal *Science* that "it appears that attending motion pictures shows, though looked upon as 'relaxation' in the sense of escape from the humdrum reality of existence, *is by no means relaxation in the physiological sense*." He discovered that muscle tension increased while viewing movies, resulting "in a highly significant rise in body temperature of one-half to one degree F."[30] Several months later, however, another scholar asked whether two confounding factors might account for these results: the type of films shown, especially "disappointing" ones, and the "close contact with masses of other people in a confined space."[31]

Critics asserted other hazards. Unlike noncommercial forms of recreation, which might take place in the fresh air of the playground, movies were viewed while seated in poorly ventilated, crowded, and often dirty rooms. Some early nickelodeon operators took to employing matrons who would spray an "antiseptic" mist while the pictures played (Peter Bogdanovich wonderfully recreated such a scene in his 1976 movie *Nickelodeon*).

The harshest criticism of movies, however, focused on their social and psychological effects. An enormous 1929 study of 10,052 children looked at the social impact of films. Anticipating what would later be said about television, it called movies "the story-book of the age" and "the most powerful narrator of tales the world has yet known." The "problem" of movies was identified thus: "The fact that the movie as a rule is adult in theme and yet is depicted in a manner which is intelligible to immature minds has caused it to be questioned as an institution for children."[32] Movies were said to cause crime and delinquency and pervert the moral character of viewers. Movies were accused of cultural imperialism, but also of "insidiously upsetting our ideas of conduct and slowly but surely altering the standards which at present govern our national life."[33] A 1932 article in a sociology journal was titled "The Motion Picture Versus the Church."[34] A 1912 survey of Nebraska public school administrators concluded that movies exerted "a tremendous moral influence" that was "decidedly detrimental" and that movies were "doing more harm than good, especially in the smaller towns." In particular, the school administrators reported that movies had caused "neglect of home study," "diffused attention and dullness," and a "general tendency toward the coarse and low, the rude and disrespectful" among pupils.[35]

Not everyone, of course, damned the movies. John Collier, the head of a major settlement house in New York City, reported in 1908 that his investigation of more than 200 Manhattan nickelodeons revealed not one "immoral or indecent picture, or one indecent feature of any sort." The greatest social and moral concern, he wrote, should be directed at the penny arcade and the cheap vaudeville, neither of which had elevated itself, and the latter, "if anything, has grown worse."[36]

While the angry denouncements of critics were never completely quelled, an uneasy armistice was reached by 1935. Proposals for national censorship of the movies by a federal agency never reached fruition. Instead, various forms of industry self-regulation successfully kept a cap on such extreme "remedies." The establishment in 1934 of the Production Code Administration, headed by Joseph Breen, along with the looming presence of the Catholic Legion of Decency and a host of municipal and state censorship boards helped mollify the critics. The truce lasted until the mid-1950s.[37]

MOVIES AND COMMERCIAL LEISURE SINCE 1935

Between 1935 and 1945, attendance averaged 80 million to 88 million weekly. It peaked during 1946–48 at 90 million weekly. In 1949, attendance was off more than 20 percent (70 million), dropping still further to 60 million in 1950 and 54 million in 1951. (Too, as attendance fell, so did the number of films released.) Thus in the brief space of three years, average weekly attendance was nearly halved. For movies, the period of unquestioned economic prosperity and steady popular participation had ended.

Table 2.4 shows that as income rose steadily, attendance at movies diminished steadily; the percentage of commercial recreation dollars accounted for by movies also shows a clear pattern of erosion.

The introduction of television and the population migration to the rapidly developing suburbs both contributed to the decline. The baby boom following the war meant that new parents were looking after their children rather than going to the movies. Television, of course, provided a convenient substitute: It was movies in the home. However, television cannot be held solely accountable; the decline in movie attendance had begun long before the ascendancy of television. The population shift to the suburbs also meant a shift in spending habits. Increasingly income was divided among the material possessions "necessary" for the suburban lifestyle and leisure activities other than movies.

A 1948 *Fortune* survey provides insight into the declining place of movies in commercial recreation. It noted that although the U.S. economy was healthy,

Table 2.4

Income, Movie Attendance, and Recreation, 1929–84

Year	Disposable Personal Income (billions of dollars) in 1972 Dollars[1]	Average Weekly Movie Attendance (in thousands)[2]	U.S. Movie Admissions as a Percentage of Total U.S. Recreation Expenditures[3]	U.S. Movie Admissions as a Percentage of Total U.S. Spectator Amusement Expenditures[3]
1929	229.5	80,000	16.6	78.9
1933	169.6	60,000	21.9	84.1
1939	229.8	85,000	19.1	80.3
1940	244.0	80,000	19.5	81.3
1945	338.1	85,000	23.6	84.6
1950	362.8	60,000	12.3	77.3
1955	426.8	46,000	9.4	73.6
1960	489.7	40,000	5.2	59.2
1965	616.3	44,000	3.5	51.2
1970	751.6	17,700	2.9	48.0
1975	874.9	19,900	3.8	51.8
1980	1,021.6	19,700	2.6	42.7
1984	1,169.5	N/A	N/A	N/A

[1]*Economic Report of the President* (U.S. Government Printing Office, 1985), p. 261.
[2]U.S. Bureau of the Census, *Historical Statistics, Colonial Times to 1970*; U.S. Bureau of the Census, *Statistical Abstract of the United States.*
[3]U.S. Department of Commerce, *Survey of Current Business.*

the "story-producing industries" of movies, books, and radio were not. In particular, *Fortune* remarked, Hollywood "is pretty much out of step with the balance of the economy." Movies elicited "the loudest Bronx cheer" among the survey respondents: Only 53 percent reported that they felt contemporary movies were as good as they were two or three years before, and 38 percent stated that movies had declined in quality. Yet quality was not the only reason for the lessening affinity towards movies. Among those who had not attended any movies in the three months prior to the survey, 29 percent reported they were too busy and had other things to do; among those who stated they went to the movies less often than before, a full 50 percent stated that other activities accounted for their less frequent attendance.[38]

Postwar Leisure in America: The 1950s

The U.S. population continued to expand. Although the Depression and then the war had curbed population growth, once these two events were in the past a baby boom began in earnest. Between 1933 and 1955, the population increased from 125 million to 165 million. Americans married at a younger age, had children earlier, and lived longer. Women joined the workforce with far greater frequency than ever before, boosting both individual and family incomes. Occupational trends first noted in the '30s continued unabated through the 1950s. The percentage of people employed in semiskilled as well as professional and managerial positions nearly doubled; among skilled employees, a 50 percent gain was reported. The percentage of those employed in agriculture continued to decline, dropping by nearly half between 1929 and 1953. Thus the growth areas, as income reflected, were in the more prestigious and well-paid occupations. All, however, enjoyed fewer hours of work and more vacation time.[39]

In contrast to the 1930s, when metropolitanism was the buzzword, in postwar America the catchphrase became "The Lush New Suburban Market." Although the beginning of this migration may actually be seen in the 1930s, it was checked first by the Depression and then by the war. With the end of the war, and the ready availability of VA- and FHA-insured loans that featured small down payments and low interest rates, the housing boom began with unmatched fervor.

The suburbs were "rich" in every sense of the term. Suburban families earned incomes 70 percent higher than those of the rest of the nation. Although they accounted for less than one-fifth of the total population, suburban families possessed nearly one-third of the spendable income. Moreover, suburbanites' discretionary income was not simply large, it was *growing*. Suburbia was also the major force driving the expanding birthrate and the consumer economy. Cars, *second* cars, and a variety of home goods including appliances, furnishings, and expensive prepared foods were purchased in massive quantities and with extraordinary frequency.

Despite the vigor of the economy in general and suburbia in particular, there was little good news for the motion picture industry. Chief among the problems were the 1948 consent decree, the scarcity of theaters in the suburbs, and the family obligations of new parents.

The *Paramount* decree divorced the major movie producers from their theaters (*United States* v. *Paramount Pictures* et al.). These theaters had long acted as the certain and noncompetitive retailers for the major studios' movies. This vertical integration of the industry ended, however, at the same time as the population migration to the suburbs began. Although it was not perceived at the time, the consent decree had a silver lining: Those theater holdings that the studios had to give up were concentrated in urban centers, the place *from* which the new suburbanites were fleeing. Indeed, the suburban phenomenon accounts for the dramatic rise of the drive-in from 820 theaters in 1948 to 4,062 by 1954.[40]

Fortune labeled the leisure economy " $30 Billion for Fun." On average, 13.5 percent of Americans' after-tax income was spent on leisure in the mid-1950s. But, as Table 2.4 reports, little of that money found its way to the box office. Movie admissions as a percentage of all recreational expenditures between

1945 and 1950 dropped precipitously, from 23.6 to 12.3 percent, and the decline had only just begun. Despite the fact that spending on commercial amusements was increasing, and despite the fact that leisure spending outpaced income (those with the least income spent a greater proportion on recreation than those with greater income), the movies consistently drew smaller and smaller audiences across all demographic strata. It was not until the postwar baby boomers had reached their teens that Hollywood was able to exploit a new market; this did not occur until 1955, at the very earliest.[41]

The 1950s were devastating for the movie industry, even though some events might have suggested otherwise. In 1952, the Supreme Court ruled that movies did enjoy First Amendment protection, thereby overturning a 1915 decision that had characterized movies as "a business pure and simple." The decision dispelled the censorious cloud that had hung over the industry for nearly 40 years.

Ironically, the 1952 decision had the effect of lessening moviemakers' inclination to produce family films precisely when a boom in families was under way. Thus an era of censorial stability ended, along with movies suitable for viewing by all. TV replaced movies as the medium for inoffensive family fare. Among the young, rock records and radio proved immensely popular media, as did the caravan-of-stars concerts sponsored by such celebrated disc jockeys as Dick Clark and Alan Freed. The movies, meantime, turned to controversial topics that had previously been avoided or disguised. Two Otto Preminger films typify this trend: *The Moon Is Blue* (1953), in which premarital sex was an issue, and *The Man with the Golden Arm* (1955), about drug addiction.

The 1950s proved to be the onset of an era of homebound leisure that has yet to end. Gardening, hobbies, do-it-yourself projects, and the like preoccupied suburban dwellers.[42] Out-of-home commercial leisure continued to flourish, but movies were not the beneficiaries; families played miniature golf instead. In economic terms, the opportunity costs of moviegoing simply became too high to warrant continuance of the previous movie habit. Rather than going to *the* movies, people began going to *a* movie, if they went at all. Although tastes may not have changed, the way people made their decisions about moviegoing certainly did.

Commercial Recreation After 1960

The average number of weekly work hours continues to decline. Generally, the pattern has been about one hour less work a week every ten years. In recent years, however, the decline has been more rapid.[43] Disposable income continues to increase, as reported in Table 2.4. America has experienced unprecedented economic growth and prosperity in the last half of this century. A replay of the disastrous Depression of the 1930s has been averted; recessions have been relatively mild and brief in duration. The movie industry, however, remains plagued by competition from the number of commercial leisure options that also seemingly increase daily (not the least of which is the videocassette). And the home-centeredness of Americans' leisure pursuits that began in the suburban era of the 1950s has, if anything, intensified. Witness, for instance, the introduction of two terms: "couch potato" and "cocooning."

With the exception of movies, commercial recreation in the 1960s flourished; perhaps contrary to nostalgic memories, the mainstream, middle-class amusements proved quite durable even in the psychedelic, countercultural Age of Aquarius. For example, the number of bowlers increased from 6.3 million in 1961 to 7.6 million in 1970. Attendance at horse races skyrocketed from 49.5 million to 69.7 million during the same period. The number of golfers nearly doubled (from 5 million to 9.7 million), and expenditures on other commercial participant amusements increased from $1.3 billion to $1.8 billion between 1961 and 1970.[44]

A 1977 Gallup poll gathered information on Americans' preferred leisure activities. A portion of the results are presented in Table 2.5. The respondents were asked "What is your favorite way of spending an evening?" Thus leisure activities that might occur during daylight hours, especially on weekends, were omitted. Further confounding interpretation for our purposes is the fact that movies and theater were grouped. Nonetheless, it is clear from the table that moviegoing does not hold a prominent position. What makes this finding especially remarkable is that preferences rather than actual behaviors were recorded. Self-reporting of preferences can produce inflated responses, so the movie data are clearly low. Another striking finding from this survey is the dominance of home-centered leisure preferences.

Results of a national Gallup survey of 1,500 households in 1983, shown in Table 2.6, also attest to the popularity of at-home pursuits. The fact that movies appear to rank so high in this table obscures the more relevant fact that moviegoing is infrequently engaged in. Today the movie industry classifies people as "frequent" moviegoers if they attend once a month, a remarkable change from the 1940s, when people would attend once a *week*.

One qualification to these data should be noted. As reported in Table 2.5, the Gallup survey of preferred ways of spending an evening revealed that movies were more attractive to persons under 30 years, to those with higher incomes, and among the college educated. As a group, under-30-year-olds possessed a total disposable income of $450 billion in 1985 and are considered the dominant buying aggregate. A continuing market research survey called the Youth Barometer, conducted by Crossley Youth/Student Surveys, reported that high school and college students attend movies 16 times a year on average.[45] But this age group is often not included in the respondent pool of national surveys and polls. Thus the data in Tables 2.5 and 2.6 may underestimate the place of movies in this group's leisure.

In a 1983 study by United Media Enterprises, 32 hours a week (nearly 5 hours a day) were reported as leisure time, most of it spent at home: Eight of ten leisure activities most frequently engaged in were primarily or exclusively homebound, among them TV viewing, reading, and gardening. The two remaining activities, exercising and talking with friends, might be engaged in outside or inside the home. The difference in home versus outside leisure was most pronounced between teens, singles, and childless couples, on the one

Table 2.5

1977 Gallup Survey of People's Favorite Way to Spend an Evening

	Watching TV	Reading	Home with Family	Dining Out	With Friends (general)	Movies Theater	Games, Cards, etc.	At a Bar Drinking
Total	30%	15%	11%	8%	6%	6%	4%	3%
Education								
College	18	21	11	12	7	10	2	3
High school	33	13	13	7	5	5	4	4
Grade school	43	10	7	3	5	2	4	<1
Age								
Under 30	20	9	11	9	9	11	2	6
30 and older	33	17	12	12	4	4	4	1
Income								
$10,000 and over	27	19	12	9	5	7	4	4
Under $10,000	37	12	9	5	6	4	3	1

SOURCE: *The Gallup Opinion Index*, September 1977, report #146, pp. 14–15.
NOTE: Only selected responses presented; totals may add to more than 100 percent because of multiple responses; data for education, age, and income have been recomputed from original source.

hand, who skewed toward the latter, versus the elderly and parents of grown children, who favored the homebound pursuits.[46]

Several factors account for what seems to be the increased trend toward home-focused leisure. Most significant are that television's saturation in America and the public's strong affinity for it make for more at-home leisure hours. A 1976 Gallup poll found that a majority of those surveyed either preferred to see movies at home on TV or felt there was little difference in watching movies on TV as opposed to on a theater screen.[47] The diffusion and rapid public adoption of TV-related media and entertainment forms, especially since 1975, have strengthened this attachment. Subscriptions to cable and premium cable have risen dramatically, and purchases of videocassette recorders (VCRs) have followed likewise, blurring the formerly distinct lines separating television from cinema. Indeed, among younger people the movie and television experience may be virtually indistinguishable. As a simple example, consider people's behavior in movie theaters. Talking, and not merely whispering, and

Table 2.6

Household Participation in Leisure-Time Activities, 1983

Type of Activity	Number (Millions)	Percent of All Households
Watching television	68	81
Listening to music	54	64
Pleasure trips in cars	37	44
Going to the movies	36	42
Vegetable gardening	35	42
Watching professional sports (TV)	33	39
Vacation trips in U.S.	29	34
Sewing/needlepoint	27	32
Fishing	26	31
Workshop/home repair	25	29
Bicycling	19	22
Bowling	17	20
Camping	17	20
Photography	17	20
Jogging	16	19
Hunting	14	16
Hiking	12	14
Golf	10	12
Tennis	10	12
Power boating	8	10
Horseback riding	8	9
Swimming in own pool	7	8
Racquetball	6	7

U.S. Bureau of the Census, *Statistical Abstract of the United States: 1984* (Washington, D.C., 1983), p. 238.

trips to the concession stand during the movie are not unusual. Theater operators have taken to running brief messages reminding patrons that such activities are disturbing to others.

Sales of home video games also soared between 1977 and 1982. The growth of these games is of particular significance given young people's demonstrated interest in the technology. Home video games, as well as personal computers

Figure 2.1
_____

Leisure Activities in Two-Dimensional Space Along Two Axes

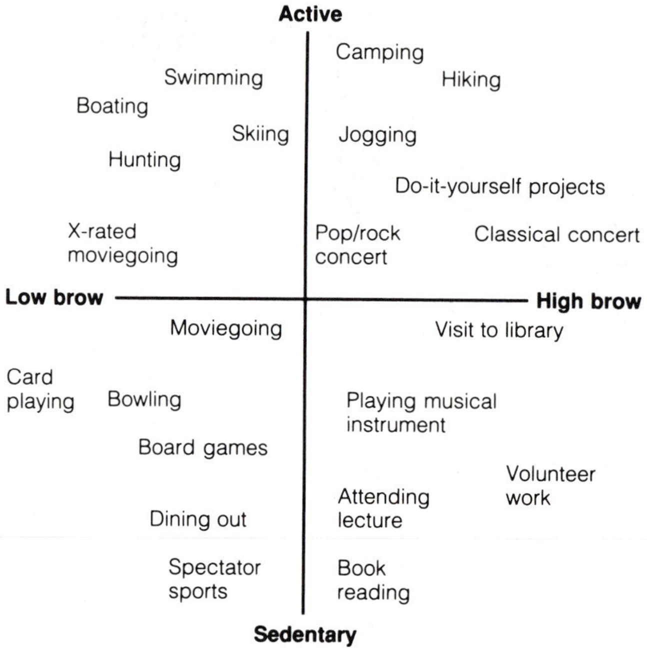

_____

Active

Camping

Swimming   Hiking

Boating

Skiing   Jogging

Hunting

Do-it-yourself projects

X-rated   Pop/rock   Classical concert
moviegoing   concert

Low brow ————————————————————— **High brow**

Moviegoing   Visit to library

Card
playing   Bowling   Playing musical
                                   instrument

Board games

Volunteer
work

Attending
lecture

Dining out

Spectator   Book
sports   reading

Sedentary

_____

Adapted from Morris B. Holbrook and Donald R. Lehmann, "Allocating Discretionary Time: Complementarity Among Activities," *Journal of Consumer Research* 7 (March 1981): 404. Reprinted by permission.

and other video accessories, may result in fewer trips to the cinema and a reversal of the out-of-home leisure orientation among under-18-year-olds, who are among the most frequent moviegoers.

A national sample of 3,288 married Americans were surveyed in 1981 about their participation rates for 50 leisure activities. A "map" of the respondents' leisure activities, presented in an abbreviated and modified form in Figure 2.1, contains two axes, or dimensions, which might be labeled "activity" and "intellectual involvement." As may be seen, moviegoing leans toward the lowbrow end of the intellectual dimension and is midway between the active and sedentary extremes of the activity dimension.

One way to employ this map of leisure activities is to consider the leisure functions and motives discussed earlier. Recall that two generalized leisure functions were balance and personal fulfillment. The four broad motivations for leisure were socializing, intellectual gains, competency, and stimulus avoidance. By tying together the concepts of functions, motivations for leisure, and the dimensions identified in Figure 2.1, a more complete and complex image of leisure results. For instance, book reading might be filed under the personal fulfillment function and the intellectual gain and stimulus avoidance motivations. Moviegoing, we would suspect, should skew more toward the balance function and the socializing motive.

SUMMARY

Leisure was broadly defined as those activities an individual selects for reasons other than sustaining life. Leisure has purpose and value, and the motivations for engaging in leisure are numerous. Analysis of the functions and motives for leisure underscores the fact that leisure is actively sought and offers important rewards.

Commercial leisure involves a cost to the participant, occurs outside the home, can accommodate many people, and is conducted for profit. The growth of commercial recreation is attributed to industrialization and the corresponding increase in people's leisure time and disposable income. Motion pictures were among the most popular turn-of-the-century commercial amusements. This popularity brought with it accusations of moral turpitude. Metropolitanism helped spur the growth of and attraction to movies in the early 1900s; suburbanism led to the decline of movies 50 years later. Today leisure is most often best characterized as homebound.

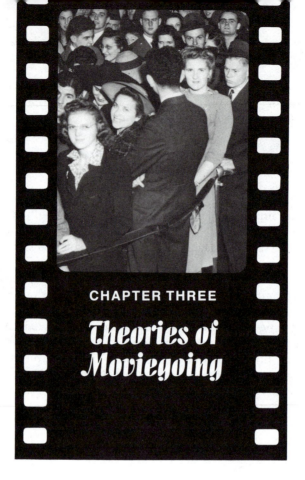

CHAPTER THREE

Theories of Moviegoing

*M*oviegoing was once a communal ritual, often set in an opulent ambience. In 1946, more than one-third of the American public went to the movies more than once a week; by 1983, fewer than one-quarter reported attending a movie once a *month*. Going to the movies meant being in the company of friends and strangers who would sing songs together by following a white ball that bounced across lyrics projected on the screen. It meant being shepherded to one's seat by an usher who was often suited in an elaborate militarylike uniform, while the mighty Wurlitzer organ played in the background. The huge picture palaces were bedizened with gargoyles and other exotic splendors and bordered by balconies and boxed seats. Today most movie theaters are small, boxy, and sterile—except for the popcorn's "buttery flavor" that sticks to your shoes. Today, moviegoing retains comparatively little of the social and experiential specialness it once had.

Despite this transformation of the moviegoing experience, people's basic reasons for choosing movies as entertainment have stayed the same. This chapter examines why people go to the movies.

Research into moviegoing reveals three broad classes of motives: social, psychological, and intellectual, which are also three of the motives of leisure in general. Socially, movies fulfill the need for a moderately priced activity that involves others. And movies may facilitate social contact and discourse in situations far removed from the theater: in daily conversation, for example. You may discuss the relative merits of or your feelings about a particular film, or you may use vignettes from several movies to illustrate a point. In this way movies function as a social lubricant or communication coin of exchange.

How much of your verbal communication is composed of or based on information derived from movies? Have you ever "stolen" a line of movie dialogue? When *The Graduate* was released in 1967, college students especially latched onto the word *plastics.* Delivered in a tone of whispered wisdom, *plastics* was a pithy source of mirth. Ronald Reagan once used Dirty Harry's "Make my day" when he was president.

Or what of nonverbal communication? Perhaps you have seen others mimicking the gestures and actions of movie characters (or actors). Following the release of *The Sting* in 1973, it was not uncommon to see people raise their index fingers to brush their noses lightly and point knowingly at another, just as the two con men played by Robert Redford and Paul Newman did in the film.[1]

Psychological motivations for moviegoing likewise run a wide gamut. Movies offer escape from pressing problems and from boredom. They perform a safety-valve function, relieving anxieties and other distressing psychological states. Understood this way, moviegoing is a means for attaining the psychic equilibrium deemed so valuable by many psychological theorists.

Moviegoing also fulfills intellectual or educational purposes. That most commercial movies are predominantly entertainment-oriented does not mean we should disregard their instructive properties nor the fact that audiences seek those properties. On a simplistic level, entertainment makes the "bitter" pill of education slide down more easily. More significantly, movies provide a way for people to experience and understand things outside of their immediate surroundings. The aesthetic dimensions of film must surely be counted among the intellectual motivations for moviegoing.

MOVIES AS EXPERIENTIAL CONSUMPTION

Little theoretical development on the motivations for moviegoing has been achieved over the years. Kurt Lewin's dictum that "there's nothing so practical as a good theory" reminds us that without a theoretical structure, research and thinking on a topic are slow to advance. Calvin Pryluck wrote, "A good theory helps us to know what we know; it will help organize the evidence, perhaps explain parts of it, and certainly point to other useful evidence worth collecting."[2] It is tempting to transplant theories of buying behavior to the movie context. Consumer research looks at a decision-making *task,* in relation to a *tangible object,* as accomplished by an information-gathering *process.*[3]

Moviegoing, however, demands a more elaborate explanation. The object of the consumer choice is not tangible. Moreover, during the information-gathering process, what research has shown to be the most significant decision-making criteria—a movie's genre and plot—are surmised by the moviegoer rather than known. These qualities of movies complicate the task of consumer research.

Another problem with applying consumer theories to movie audiences is one of labeling. Individually, movies are enigmatic. Though the "product" category is no doubt familiar, each "brand" within the category is not.

But are movies to be considered a product? Or are they a service? Consumer research tends to divide the world into these two classes. Perhaps movies are neither. Products are tangible items or merchandise. Services refer to a type of trade involving the performance of work. A television set is a product; television repair is a service. Only by severely stretching these definitions could movies be classified as either a product or service.

Creating a third category requires answering the question What is the essence of the interaction between movie and viewer? Robert Warshow wrote that "the fundamental *fact* of the movies ... [is] at once aesthetic and sociological but also something more. ... the actual, immediate experience of seeing and responding to the movies."[4] The key term here is *immediate experience.* As film critic Jacob Brackman noted, if we stop to reflect on a film while we view it, we miss the ongoing action. The film is experienced first, and only later do we "rewind" it in our minds to reflect on it.[5]

The intensity or "realness" of this experience is what accounts for our startled response to the "chest-buster" scene in *Alien,* our tear-filled eyes at the end of *E.T.,* our laughter at Donald O'Connor's antics in *Singin' in the Rain,* or our applause when the final credits roll for some movies, despite "adult discount": our knowledge that "it is, after all, *only* a movie." (Indeed, the intensity of the Mia Farrow character's moviegoing experience forms the focus of *The Purple Rose of Cairo.*)[6]

Of those four responses, applause is most intriguing. Who or what is being applauded? Logically it cannot be the creators, nor the actors, nor the movie itself, because the applause is known only to those in the audience. Perhaps the audience is applauding itself, as if to say "We certainly had a wonderful time, didn't we?" This too is curious, since we do not *know* the many strangers who surround us in the theater. Writing in 1916, a Harvard psychologist described "the intensity" of movies' hold on viewers as epitomized by "the applause into which the audience, especially of rural communities, break out at a happy turn of the melodramatic pictures [, which] is another symptom of the strange fascination [with movies]." He warned that "the possibilities of psychical infection and destruction cannot be overlooked."[7] A related view is that of German psychologist Hugo Mauerhofer: "The spectator gives himself voluntarily and passively to the action on the screen and to its uncritical interpretation supplied by his unconscious mind."[8]

Recently consumer behavior researchers have also recognized the inadequacy of the product-service dichotomy. A 1982 article, "The Experiential

Aspects of Consumption," acknowledged that not all consumer behavior could be conceptualized from an information-processing perspective. In particular, people's involvement in art and leisure can only be fully understood from an experiential view of consumption. Such a view "regards consumption as a primarily subjective state of consciousness with a variety of symbolic meanings, hedonic responses, and aesthetic criteria."[9]

A question that arises for the film retailer, movie marketer, and audience researcher is How does one sell an experience? What is the experience like, and how do people experience movies? We can get some idea by examining audience motivations for the experience.

MOTIVATION

In everyday conversation, we may speak of feeling especially motivated to win a place in the starting lineup of a team, or on an off day we might say that we lack the motivation to write a term paper. Rarely, however, do we think about motivation's meaning, the process involved in its actualization, or why and how we come to possess motivation.

To understand the motivation process, we must understand the concept of *needs*. Needs are the physiological, psychological, and social requirements for the continued well-being of an individual. They are often internal states, not directly open to observation or investigation. Needs arise from not only the lack of something but also an excess of something, such as tension or anxiety.

Once an individual becomes aware of a particular need, this consciousness may trigger a drive. Drives are the energy that propels an individual to search for and acquire gratification. Motivation is similar to a drive in that it is a compelling "force" that moves an individual to action; however, unlike a drive, motivation is the reason behind the "energy" of action. In a more general sense, motivation can be understood as a component of and a complement to behavior; one concept cannot be fully understood without the other. At the same time, not all motivation results in behavior.

Motivation research attempts to understand the intentions of goal-directed behavior by examining the internal and external influences on behavior, including the causes of and reasons for behavior. It is conceded that "at least some behavior is impulsive and not preceded by rational considerations."[10] An appreciation of motivation provides a way of understanding the particular behavior of movie attendance.

Expectancy-Value Theory of Motivation

Expectancy-value is a cognitive theory of motivation that focuses on goal-directed activity. Both going to *the* movies and going to *a* movie are goal-directed activities, especially today. The weekly pilgrimage to the movie theater is a thing of the past.

In one form or another, expectancy-value theory has existed for hundreds of years. Benjamin Franklin, one of the first to articulate it, called it his "moral algebra" and applied it to decision making. Moral algebra required that decision makers first identify and then subjectively weigh all the relevant attributes for each option. The weights of each option's attributes were summed and the result compared to all other options. The option with the greatest total sum would be the best.[11] While contemporary formulations of expectancy-value have expanded Franklin's moral algebra and the method of computation, the essentials are the same. Expectancy-value theory tries to explain the selection of a specific option from a relatively homogeneous class of events.

Expectancy-value theory views behavior as a function of two central concepts: outcome values and outcome expectancies. Outcome values are the degree of positive or negative feeling you have toward a behavioral option. Outcome expectancies refer to your judgment about the probability that your specific goals can in fact be satisfied by selecting one or another of the options.

Each outcome value and expectancy is assigned a numerical weighting. Expectancy-value theory predicts the selection of one option from among all the others based on the multiplicative product of the outcome values and outcome expectancies: For each option, the multiplication procedure is performed and one is selected by comparing the mathematical results across options. The behavioral option for which the product is greatest is predicted to be the one selected.[12]

How do we arrive at outcome values and expectancies? In essence, both are beliefs. Martin Fishbein and Icek Ajzen describe three kinds of belief.[13] *Descriptive* beliefs are the result of direct, personal observation of an object or event. For instance, prior movie experiences generate, help form, and modify beliefs concerning movies. A second kind of belief is *inferential.* These beliefs pertain to characteristics not yet directly observed or not directly observable. They are often based on some personal "theory" or intuitively appealing logic. If a particular movie is labeled a Western, we infer certain attributes (such as cowboys, Indians, stagecoaches, deserts) without even seeing the film. Finally, *informational* beliefs are generated from sources outside ourselves, such as friends, advertising, or a movie review, that link certain objects and attributes to a movie. The expectancy-value model assumes that only a limited number of beliefs are relevant to a given behavior at any one time.

How does expectancy-value theory help us understand moviegoing? Consider this example: Moviegoing is but one in a cluster of several leisure options; these might include bowling and miniature golf. The outcome values might include the number of people who can participate or the distance of the recreation from one's home. For each outcome value, you assign a weight based on your subjective evaluation of the outcome's importance or desirability. You also generate an outcome expectancy term, which is your best guess about the probability that choosing each leisure activity will result in that specific outcome. Comparison of the mathematical results predicts which leisure alternative is selected.

In summary, expectancy is "the probability of occurrence of a value-laden event"; value is the incentive or attractiveness of an event. The theory predicts that people select that alternative for which the product of the two terms is greatest.[14] Given the theory's robust utility over a wide range of academic disciplines, including attitude theory, consumer behavior, and marketing research, it is no wonder that so many have chosen it for their own purposes.[15]

Mass Media Uses and Gratifications

Whereas the expectancy approach is broad in its scope, the uses-and-gratifications approach focuses specifically on the mass media. The origin of the uses-and-gratifications approach is frequently traced to a 1959 article by Elihu Katz, written in response to Bernard Berelson's claim that communication research was withering away and that the field was in danger of dying. Katz argued that, on the contrary, it was not the *field* of communication that was dying, but rather the *assumption* about media effects that was endangered. People's use of the media had largely been ignored. Katz advocated that mass communication researchers, to paraphrase John F. Kennedy's (later) inaugural address, "ask not what the media do to people, but what people do with media."[16]

Actually, the genesis of uses-and-gratifications research may be found in a dozen or so articles published in the early 1940s. Research focused on such media content as radio soap operas, quiz shows, and music. Although this was a time when movie attendance was never greater, no research from this perspective was done on the medium and its audiences.

The number of uses-and-gratifications studies grew with the introduction of television in the 1950s, and the corresponding segmentation of format, content, and audience by radio and magazines. As audiences were presented with more and more media choices, more and more research attention was directed at why audiences selected the media and content they did and the rewards they derived from them.

The concept of "uses" is similar to that of motivation. Likewise, the "gratifications" concept resembles the expectancy-value concept of perceived probability that an object possesses a certain attribute or that a particular behavior will have or will produce a certain outcome.

The gratifications approach assumes an active audience.[17] Audiences purposefully select and attend to media and content to satisfy various needs. (Gratifications researchers concede that not all media exposure is purposive, and that it sometimes is more casually initiated.) Different people may use the same medium—and even the same message—for entirely different purposes. TV news, for instance, may satisfy information or entertainment motives, depending on the viewer.

Another assumption of the gratifications approach is that audience members are self-aware and can articulate their reasons and interests for selecting media. Broadly stated, the gratifications approach asks why do people use the mass media and what needs do they satisfy? *How* people make choices among (1) different media and (2) the variety of content offered by each medium is a more complex question.

Audiences create expectations about media and media content and about the ability of media and media content to satisfy needs, and they develop strategies to achieve gratifications.[18] Like expectancy theory, the gratifications approach relies on the concepts of outcome values and outcome expectancies. Prior media experience helps determine media use as a means to fulfill needs, since audiences gain familiarity with various media and media content over time.

In sum, there is conceptual similarity between the gratifications approach and expectancy-value theory, as well as empirical evidence. The two streams of thought dovetail insofar as both are cognitively oriented, action driven, process path-goal approaches "in which the direction of behavior is guided by perceptions of the situation and attempts to gratify needs."[19]

Research on Moviegoing Motives

Much speculation on people's motivations for moviegoing has been offered. A 1952 article asserted that movies appealed to audiences "not because they take them into some other world, but because they make their own world more bearable."[20] At about the same time, the cinema was said to serve several psychological functions. Among these were satisfying intellectual, aesthetic, and religious needs.[21]

Research has at least partially confirmed these early proposals. That movies were sought for and indeed provided a creative and self-fulfilling aesthetic experience was independently documented by two studies in 1977.[22] Other motivations for moviegoing reported by these two studies included the desire to relax and be entertained, to meet social goals, to provide new experiences, and to learn. One kind of learning experience was documented in a study conducted for the Commission on Obscenity and Pornography in 1970. Interviews with 100 heterosexual adult male patrons of sexually explicit movies revealed that one motive for their attendance was to acquire information on sexual practices. These movies were also sought as a stimulus for sexual behavior and as a source for fantasy.[23]

Fantasy or *escape* often have negative connotations: that activities so motivated are habitual, nonselective, and unthinking. Rachel Low, a British cinema historian, referred to nearly one-half of the audience in 1948 as "habitual film-goers who exercise remarkably little choice between films."[24] Yet saying that movie audiences were largely indiscriminate regarding specific film choice does not answer the question of why moviegoing occurred. In 1939, Leo Rosten stressed "that movie-going is a *habit* in the United States." Just one paragraph later, however, he also stated that "the public takes the movies more seriously than we sometimes assume."[25]

Changes in moviegoing behavior over time no doubt account for variations in moviegoing motivations. When Low and Rosten were writing in the 1930s and '40s, people went to the movies every week. By the 1950s, attendance had dropped and the habit was broken. Thus, in 1977, research on moviegoing motivations revealed that—compared with other mass media—movies were not engaged in habitually.

This finding has particular relevance to the media gratifications approach. Ritualistic or habitual conceptualizations of media use contradict the active-audience assumption of uses and gratifications. They suggest that it is the medium itself, rather than its specific content, which is used to obtain need gratification. In contrast, conceptualization of media use as instrumental indicates a goal-directed use of media content in order to gratify needs or motives. We suggest here that moviegoing encompasses both ritualistic and instrumental properties. However, we do not use the term *ritual* to imply the monotonous sameness of habitlike behavior.[26] Rather, the term is applied to the experiential aspects *of* the behavior. The ritualistic use of movies, as well as other leisure pursuits, includes the fantasies, emotions, feelings, sensations, and enjoyment of the experience. As such, the particular ritualistic and experiential dimensions of movies helps "move" the individual toward moviegoing as the means to satisfy this need. Specific movie choice and attendance performs the instrumental functions. The 1977 research illustrates the "inconvenience" of movies as a habitual behavior. That is, while it may be relatively easy habitually to watch TV due to its accessibility, enactment of moviegoing is more difficult. This "inconvenience," however, implies the value of movies to people; although the amount of time devoted to movie viewing is far less than televiewing, moviegoing possesses experiential attributes far greater than televiewing.

European research.   Research on the motivations for moviegoing was conducted as early as 1914. Some of the most ambitious of these early, if unsophisticated, motivation studies were done in Europe. One published in 1929 analyzed responses to a questionnaire distributed in 1914 and 1915 to Swiss schoolchildren ages 8 to 15. Among the questions was, "Why do you like going to the cinema?" Table 3.1 displays the responses from two cities' children. The five reasons reported suggest educational, entertainment, and aesthetic motives for moviegoing. The variation in response by gender is fairly consistent between the two towns: girls more than boys found movies to be interesting and amusing, while the reverse was true for the aesthetic and pastime motives. A response bias may be possible in this study because the children were asked why they *like* going to the movies, rather than why they go to the movies. Nonetheless, the study provides the first empirical glimpse at children's reasons for moviegoing.

The data in Table 3.1 were collected during World War I. In 1944, as World War II raged, another European study of motivation was conducted: 336 Vienna adults were surveyed and interviewed about their movie and theater interests.[27] Table 3.2 presents the results.

Movies were superior to theater in satisfying two of the six needs served: enjoyment and relaxation. Stage shows provided greater satisfaction of inspirational, educational, and aesthetic needs. A study of 3,571 Soviet filmgoers in 1966 found seven reasons for movie attendance (see Table 3.3).[28] Like the

Table 3.1

Motivations for Moviegoing in 1914–15

"Why do you like going to the cinema?"	Neuchatel			Lausanne		
	Girls	Boys	Total	Girls	Boys	Total
Because it is instructive	12.2%	12.6%	12.4%	16.6%	14.8%	15.9%
Because it is interesting	26.6	22.6	25.0	47.9	42.5	45.8
Because it is amusing	28.1	15.6	23.4	15.8	8.7	13.1
Because it passes time pleasantly	6.1	11.0	8.0	13.4	23.0	17.1
Because it is beautiful	22.0	37.2	27.8	6.2	11.0	8.1
Because of the scenery	4.9	1.0	3.4	*	*	*

SOURCE: André deMaday, "An Enquiry Respecting the Cinematograph," *International Review of Educational Cinematography,* November 1929, p. 549; December 1929, p. 644. Some totals do not equal 100 due to rounding.

*Data not reported for this response.

Table 3.2

Comparison of Needs Satisfied by Stage Shows and Movies

Need	Theater	Movies
Inspiration	21.8%	13.0%
Education	20.4	10.2
Enjoyment	28.4	37.6
Relaxation	11.8	29.4
Illusive atmosphere	4.4	1.0
Artistic experience	9.0	2.4
Undecided	4.2	6.4
Total	100	100

SOURCE: Rudolf Lassner, "Sex and Age Determinants of Theatre and Movie Interests," *Journal of General Psychology* 31 (October 1944): 265.

Vienna research, this study showed that relaxation was a primary motive for attendance and, like the Swiss study, it reported that the instructional/interest motivation was especially salient.

A 1983 study of Finnish moviegoers found that respondents with fewer years of formal education were less likely to report informational, social, and

Table 3.3

Soviet Filmgoers' Motivations for Movie
Attendance

Reason for Attendance	Percent
Simple relaxation	32
To find out something new	29
To experience a sharp plot	12
Performance of the actors	9
For the sake of the music	5
Nowhere better to spend one's leisure	4
Skill of the shooting of the film	3
No answer	6

SOURCE: Felice D. Gaer, "The Soviet Film Audience:
A Confidential View," *Problems of Communism* 23
(January 1974): 64.

aesthetic motives for moviegoing than those with more years of education.
The reverse was true for the relaxation/escape motive.[29]

U.S. research. Ironically, the first major effort by Hollywood to study its
audience occurred when the movie audience was fast disappearing. In 1957
the Motion Picture Association of America (MPAA) commissioned an extensive
survey of Americans about their moviegoing behavior.[30] The resulting report,
titled *The Public Appraises Movies,* included fewer than a dozen pages on
"Motivational Factors in Movie Attendance." Personal interviews were conducted between June and July 1957 with 5,021 individuals 15 years of age and
older. Respondents were asked to report what they thought other people's
motives for moviegoing were. ("What do you think are the main reasons
people go the movies?") Such projective methods assume that the response
offered actually reveals the individual's own inclinations.[31] A second question
probed the respondents' own reasons for moviegoing: "The last time you went
to the movies, what was your reason for going?" The two sets of responses are
presented side by side in Table 3.4. The respondents were far more likely to
ascribe recreational and entertainment motives to others than to themselves.
Group II contains six reasons pertinent to seeing a specific movie, or some
element of a particular film, rather than moviegoing in general. One exception:
Educational or cultural reasons for moviegoing may be a general as well as a
specific motive. Seeking information can apply to all movies, not just a particular documentary, because even fictional films may teach as well as entertain.
In any event, the data indicate that this motive was attributed to others by the
respondents, but not to themselves.

Table 3.4

Motivations for Moviegoing in 1957

Reason for Attendance	Other People's Reason[1]	Respondent's Own Reason[1]
I. Recreation, entertainment	57%	7%
Habit	2	1
Just because they wanted to go	1	*
II. To see a picture they're interested in; to see a certain show; to see a particular picture; a picture I wanted to see[2]	9	34
To see a certain actor or actress	7	3
Educational or cultural purposes; to learn something	5	*
Had read the book and wanted to see the picture	*	1
The advertising interested me	*	4
It was recommended to me	*	3
III. To get away from everyday routine; to go somewhere	39	16
To pass the time; to have something to do	23	*
Tired of watching television; to watch something different from television	2	*
Relaxation	*	2

The third group of reasons articulate the entertainment and escapist functions of movies. These responses, especially those attributed to others, point to moviegoing as a means to relax, unwind, and gain respite from the daily routine. These results were interpreted as "a major appeal of the movies" insofar as people perceive movies as an "occasion"; the researchers further suggested that "this appears to be one idea on which advertising and promotion can capitalize." The fourth group of motivations are socially oriented; moviegoing answers the need for an activity in which several people can engage simultaneously.

The Newspaper Advertising Bureau often conducts surveys on issues relevant to motion pictures, to encourage the use of newspapers as an advertising medium. In 1978, 604 respondents were asked to rank the importance of a list of five reasons for moviegoing.[32] As Table 3.5 shows, three of the five reasons generated the most agreement: entertainment, social, and escape. Since motivational salience is expected to vary according to how often one engages in an activity, this study is of particular interest: Compared with the most

Table 3.4 (continued)

Reason for Attendance	Other People's Reason[1]	Respondent's Own Reason[1]
IV. Went with someone else; someone took me	*	17
Took the children; children wanted to go	*	8
Celebration; anniversary, birthday	*	1
Good place to go on dates	3	*
Opportunity to be with other people	1	*
To cool off during the summer	3	2
Relatively inexpensive; less expensive than other forms of entertainment	1	*
Special attractions: stage show, premiums, fireworks	*	1
Had free pass	*	1
Other reasons	5	2
Don't know/don't recall	5	8

SOURCE: Opinion Research Corporation, *The Public Appraises Movies: A Survey for Motion Picture Association of America* (1957), National Association of Theatre Owners file, Department of Archives and Manuscripts, Brigham Young University. Reprinted by permission.

[1]Percentages total to more than 100 due to multiple responses.

[2]Responses to the left of the slash mark indicate the respondent's perception of other people's reason; those to the right represent their own reason.

*indicates responses in this category were not offered or presented as a result of the question posed.

frequent moviegoers, those who attend least often rate escape as more important and entertainment as less important. This finding illustrates that although the motivations for attendance may be relatively stable across time, the salience attributed to the motives can vary within a sample.

A 1973 study showed that the greater the anxiety experienced by an individual, the more likely it was that movies would be chosen over such other leisure pursuits as plays, concerts, sports events, or opera and ballet. The study's author suggested that movies were more socially comfortable than the other activities. Extrapolating from this finding, we can propose that relaxation, escape, and social motives for moviegoing may be more salient among the anxious than the less anxious.[33]

Another report compared analytical and nonanalytical film viewers.[34] Analytical viewers were those who valued movies for self-enhancement rather than only entertainment, were selective about their film choices, and exhibited critical viewing behavior. They attended movies often, enjoyed studying them, and appreciated films that might be difficult to figure out. This does not mean that such viewers have a greater ability to understand these films immediately

Table 3.5

Motivations for Moviegoing in 1978

	Frequency of Moviegoing		
Reason for Moviegoing	2 + per Month	Once a Month	6 or Fewer a Year
To laugh and be happy	37%	35%	33%
To do something with someone	25	25	28
To be able to get away from everyday problems	12	18	21
To keep current or up-to-date with movies	15	12	12
To improve myself and to think	11	10	6

SOURCE: Newspaper Advertising Bureau, *Movie Going in the Metropolis*, 1978, pp. 8, 38. Reprinted by permission.

after viewing; rather, they are willing to try and excited by trying to comprehend them. Thus we would expect intellectual, instructional, and educational motives for moviegoing to apply more to analytical than nonanalytical viewers.

Evidence on both motivations for attendance and differences in motivations among sample subgroups is contained in a recent study of nearly 500 college students.[35] The respondents indicated how closely each of 70 reasons matched their own reason for moviegoing. Factor analysis of the responses to the 70 items revealed seven motivations for moviegoing; statistical comparisons among three frequency-of-moviegoing groups were then performed on each motive. The seven motives and the average score for each moviegoing group are reported in Table 3.6. Frequent moviegoers were those who reported movie attendance of three times a month or greater; occasional moviegoers reported attendance of once or twice a month; infrequent moviegoers attended once in two to six months or less.

Two of the seven motives indicate information-seeking dimensions of moviegoing: learning information and learning about self. "To learn information" summarizes statements referring to movies' ability to provide new ideas and facts about how things work, new things to do, and new places to see. "To learn about self" summarizes statements that relate to the individual directly: Moviegoing is motivated by a desire to "understand and know myself better."

A second pair of motivations reported in Table 3.6 offers an interesting contrast: forget and pass time. The statements that the former summarizes indicated the desire to escape from such "mental" issues as daily pressures, responsibilities, and problems. "To pass time," on the other hand, summarizes statements indicating a "physical" reason for moviegoing: Movies kill time,

Table 3.6

Motivations Among Three Moviegoing Groups: Mean Scores

| | Frequency of Moviegoing | | |
Motivations	Infrequent	Occasional	Frequent
To learn information	1.55	1.64	1.86
To forget, get away, and escape	1.60	1.86	1.97
To enjoy a pleasant activity	2.13	2.41	2.56
To pass time	1.57	1.71	1.68
To relieve loneliness	1.11	1.11	1.19
To impress or conform to others	.84	.88	.91
To learn about self	1.05	1.13	1.34

SOURCE: Bruce Austin, "Motivations for Movie Attendance," *Communication Quarterly* 34 (Spring 1986): 121. Higher mean scores indicate greater agreement with the motivation.

give one something to do, and offer an activity when there is nothing else to do. The latter motive implies attendance as a means to filling a void; the former suggests getting away from what one has. These two motives may be viewed as a refinement of the more general relaxation motive reported by earlier studies.

The third motivation listed in Table 3.6, enjoying a pleasant activity, is analogous to the entertainment motive described by other researchers. This motive was derived from responses such as "because it is so much fun," "to be entertained," and "to feel good." Movies are used to relieve loneliness, a distressing psychological state. People go to the movies "when there is no one to talk with," so that they will not be alone, and because it makes them feel less lonely.

The final motivation for moviegoing was labeled "to impress or conform to others." The two statements that this motive summarizes were "to impress people" and "to be like other people." This motive implies that the actual movie is almost incidental to the social integration value of the behavior.

The overall pattern of responses that emerges from Table 3.6 is that frequent moviegoers place greater emphasis on the motivations (or are possibly more aware of why they go) than infrequent moviegoers, and that they not only seek more from movies, but presumably also achieve more gratification.

SUMMARY

The satisfying qualities of the movie experience demand a unique approach to understanding audience motivations. Expectancy-value theory provides a general approach to understanding the direction motivation will take; the gratifications approach applies tenets of expectancy theory to media use. Within this framework, motivation for behavior is viewed as a function of: (1) the perceived probability that an object or behavior will possess a particular attribute or have a particular consequence and (2) the degree of feeling (ranging from positive to negative) toward an attribute or behavioral outcome.

Research on the motivations for moviegoing points to three classes of motivation: social, psychological, and intellectual. More recent research indicates that the salience of these motives systematically varies by frequency of attendance. Both the theories and literature on motivations for moviegoing presented here are only an initial attempt to understand a complex process. In the following chapter we turn our attention to factors that help explain how people choose to go to a specific movie.

CHAPTER FOUR

Which Show to See?

"*Boxoffice A Wimp As Most Pix Go Limp*"—headline,
Variety, February 29, 1984

$\mathcal{T}$ he theoretical structure of moviegoing presented in Chapter 3 indicates that moviegoing as a form of recreation fulfills various needs. This chapter examines the factors that influence your decision to go to one movie rather than any of the other films available. Diffusion-of-innovations theory is described, as well as a model that attempts to explain how attendance decisions are made. Finally, research on the relative importance of the model's elements is presented. The theory, model, and research provide a means for better understanding movie attendance and why for some films the box office is a wimp while for others it is boffo.

DIFFUSION OF INNOVATIONS

Diffusion-of-innovations theory articulates the process by which new ideas, practices, products, and the like are disseminated and adopted in a society or some part of it. Everett M. Rogers offers a rigorous, critical, and exhaustive explanation of the theory in his book *Diffusion of Innovations.* Rogers traces the intellectual roots of diffusion theory to the turn of the century, when a French judge named Gabriel Tarde wrote a book titled *The Laws of Imitation.*[1] Tarde was primarily concerned with why some innovations catch on and others do not.

American sociologists became interested in the phenomenon in the 1920s and '30s. In 1943, two sociologists interviewed Iowa farmers to study when and how they had decided to begin using hybrid seed corn. The sociologists were interested in describing the process, tracing the pattern, and documenting the rate at which farmers adopted the innovation, beginning with its introduction in 1928.[2]

What had been a trickle of diffusion research became a torrent. Diffusion research was conducted by scholars from numerous academic disciplines. Anthropologists, geographers, and rural sociologists were investigating the idea simultaneously with marketing and education researchers.[3] As measured by published research articles, the field grew from 27 publications in 1941 to more than 3,000 some 40 years later. Diffusion research has focused on such tangible products as pharmaceutical drugs, infant formula, and various consumer products, as well as less tangible concerns, such as birth control and family planning or new models for education.

Rogers defines an innovation as "an idea, practice, or object that is perceived as new by an individual or other unit of adoption."[4] Innovations, therefore, are in the eye of the beholder. Furthermore, "newness" is used comprehensively to include a person's new knowledge about the innovation, new response to it, or new decision to adopt it.

What does this mean for the study of movie audiences? Obviously, few would claim today that movies are an innovation. Yet a specific movie can be defined this way. Any movie that enters the marketplace is an innovation. Adoption of the innovation is attendance at the film.

Diffusion refers to the process by which an innovation is distributed.[5] The scope of diffusion analysis includes the innovation itself, how the innovation is communicated, the time involved in its communication and distribution, and the process by which people accept or reject it. As applied to movies, diffusion theory directs our attention to how a particular film is released, the publicity and marketing efforts involved in its distribution, and the process audiences use when deciding whether to attend it.

How Is an Innovation Adopted?

According to Rogers, an individual proceeds through five steps in the overall process of adopting an innovation.[6]

Knowledge is the first step. On this level, people become aware of and begin to learn something about an innovation. For movies, this means that audiences hear or read about a particular film and perhaps some of its attributes, such as its stars. At this step, the individual seeks information concerning what the innovation is "about" rather than evaluative information on how good or bad, helpful or hurtful it might be. Evaluation enters more forcefully at the second step of the process: persuasion.

Persuasion involves the formation of positive and negative judgments about the innovation. Here the individual weighs the advantages and disadvantages of adopting the innovation. The moviegoer might ask, for instance, "Do I really like Pia Zadora?" The results of the persuasive process moves the individual to the third step: decision.

Decision involves accepting or rejecting the innovation; you either decide to go to the Pia Zadora movie or you decide not to go. For many innovations, the decision to reject can itself be rejected later on. If you learn more about the movie and muster additional favorable arguments for adoption, you may reevaluate your decision and go to the movie a week later (if it's still in town!).

The two remaining steps generally occur only when adoption has been chosen. *Implementation* refers to actually putting the innovation to use. For movies, this step might involve the preparations necessary to get to the theater, such as putting gas in the car or setting a date to attend, and then, finally, actually sitting down in the theater. The final step is *confirmation*. Here the individual attempts to reinforce the adoption decision and to avoid or reduce any dissonance that might arise.

What Affects the Rate of Adoption?

According to one researcher, an innovation's perceived attributes or qualities are better predictors of adoption than are an individual's personal qualities.[7] Rogers identified five characteristics of an innovation as central to explaining the rate of its adoption: relative advantage, compatibility, complexity, trialability, and observability.[8] Additional variables have more recently been suggested: width of adoption, marketing actions, and the financial and social risks related to adoption.[9] The innovation itself does not intrinsically possess these characteristics. Rather, people evaluate the innovation as possessing greater or lesser amounts of each characteristic. Taken together, these characteristics help explain the popularity of some films and, indirectly, movie attendance decisions.

Five of these attributes are positively related to the rate of adoption. *Relative advantage* is an individual's comparison of an innovation to what the innovation replaces. Relative advantage is often measured by such factors as social prestige, convenience, satisfaction, and in economic terms.

Compatibility refers to the innovation's perceived consistency with the person's existing values and needs. The extent to which an innovation can be tested and tried out is termed *trialability. Observability* pertains to how easily the innovation's results may be seen by others.

Width of adoption refers to "the number of people within the adoption unit who use the product, or the number of different uses for the product." Facial tissue may have a greater width of adoption within a household than diapers.

For movies, this concept is roughly analogous to the size (width) of the attendance unit: how many people go together to a movie. (The entire audience in any one theater is composed of many such attendance units.) Obviously, the bigger the attendance unit the faster the movie's adoption rate in terms of sheer numbers of people. (By the same token, width also increases the complexity of the attendance decision process.)

Complexity, financial risk, and social risk slow the rate of innovation adoption.[10] Complexity refers to how well an innovation can be understood and used; financial and social risk refer to the perceived cost of innovation adoption. An example of complexity might be a foreign-language film. Dubbed dialogue reduces complexity, while subtitles may increase complexity. Financial risk could refer to the cost of a movie date. A socially risky movie for some is signified by an X rating.

Marketing actions should also affect the rate of adoption. This attribute, created by the innovator, influences adopter perceptions. The way an innovation is positioned, especially relative to competitors within the same class, can hasten adoption. We can speculate that the size and extent of the marketing effort will serve variously to minimize or maximize some of the characteristics noted above. For instance, the marketing approach can play down the risk factors associated with an innovation.

A MODEL FOR MOVIE SELECTION

Today there is little doubt that movie audiences are quite selective. But this was not always so. A 1941 study by Leo Handel found that nearly half (49 percent) the respondents on the last occasion they attended went to see any picture, while just over one-third (36 percent) went to a particular show.[11] The 1957 study summarized in Table 3.4 also noted an increase in audience selectivity over previous years. The trend toward greater selectivity in movie attendance continues to the present.[12]

How does the choosy contemporary audience choose? Figure 4.1 presents a propositional model illustrating the elements involved in film selection. Also included are the first three steps in the innovation adoption process. Think of the model as a camera lens that possesses a zoom function and a series of focus rings. The zoom action accounts for the ways people decide to go to a movie. The focus rings represent clusters of conceptually similar attributes *of* or *about* a film.

Consider first the zoom capacity, which takes in numerous criteria for selecting a film. When the lens is set in the wide-angle position, a maximal number of movie choices is available. The close-up setting diminishes the number of options.

For those individuals who say they first select a movie and then decide when to attend, the zoom moves quickly to the close-up position. The zoom action does not bypass the focus rings in this instance; rather, it is as if various predispositions have preset the focus rings. An example might be the person

Figure 4.1

A Propositional Model of the Movie Selection Process

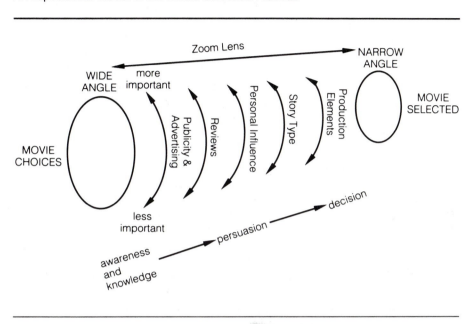

who likes a particular star and tries to attend all movies featuring that star. If you are a Robin Williams fan, your focus rings have been preset. Thus when *Good Morning, Vietnam* was locally available, you found time to see it, giving little consideration to the elements that make up the other focus rings.

Some people select moviegoing as an activity without a clear or fixed disposition to attend any one particular film. In this case, the process begins with the zoom set in the wide-angle position. Compared to the previous example, more focus rings must be manipulated before a film is selected. We can again use *Good Morning, Vietnam* as an example. As noted, you are a Williams fan. This time, however, you are selecting a film to attend as part of a date. Because you feel you must consider the interests of your date, you do not zoom immediately to *Vietnam*. Instead, you may recall what your friends have said about it, along with critics' reviews. This process continues, using many, potentially even all, of the focus rings. The choice of which film to attend on your date is determined by how well the focus rings line up. Once this is accomplished, the entire lens focuses on one movie. The film selected might turn out to be *Vietnam* or might be some other picture.

The process just described also offers an illustration of how the focus rings are manipulated and their interactive effect on one another. To continue the example, we already know you like Williams's acting. As a result, the Production Element focus ring is set in the direction of greater importance (or influence). Suppose, too, you value your friends' opinions about movies. Thus the Personal Influence focus ring is also set in the direction of greater importance. Furthermore, you tend to rely moderately on professional critics' judgments; this focus ring is set midway between important and unimportant. The model predicts that you will choose to attend *Vietnam* only if it is clearly in focus. In other words, your favorable evaluation of Williams along with at least moderately favorable critical reviews and friends' comments must all lock into place. On the other hand, if your friends have pronounced *Vietnam* a bomb, the entire lens shifts out of focus and *Vietnam* blurs as an option. Alternative choices emerge into focus based on various adjustments to the focus rings.

ELEMENTS IN THE DECISION

Figure 4.1 shows five elements (focus rings) affecting movie attendance. The Production Elements focus ring is the most complex in the sheer number of variables it possesses. The Story Type focus ring is the simplest insofar as it possesses the fewest variables; at the same time it is the most amorphous because of how audiences come to learn about and construct an image of story type. Between these two extremes are the focus rings referring to Advertising and Publicity, Reviews, and Personal Influence.

The focus rings in Figure 4.1 are arranged in order of when audiences would become aware of each. Information about a film generally becomes available first through advertising and publicity. Because critics frequently see and report on movies just ahead of a film's release, the Movie Reviews focus ring is second. Word of mouth occurs once a film has gone into release, so the Personal Influence focus ring is third. The Story Type and Production Elements focus rings are (somewhat arbitrarily) fourth and fifth.

Advertising and Publicity

One distinction often made between these two terms is that advertising involves direct costs, publicity indirect costs. Advertising is always in the studio's control; the studio is responsible for its creation and dissemination. Publicity, on the other hand, while often studio-generated and -driven, is not always as directly governable. For example, public protests by gay men during the shooting of *Cruising* (1980) against the film's image of them were widely reported by news media. This certainly functioned as publicity for the film, though the studio may not have found it desirable. This focus ring, then, incorporates both intentional and inadvertent information and persuasion that affect moviegoers' choices. It is perhaps the broadest of the five focus rings, because advertising and publicity may attract public attention to or away from any of the other four focus rings. In many instances, advertising and publicity seek to exploit and capitalize on one element or another of various other focus rings, so that the effectiveness of advertising and publicity in attracting audiences is difficult to judge. An old saying is that half of all money spent on advertising is wasted; the problem is determining which half.

Publicity

Hollywood publicity now embraces virtually all media: Radio and television stations receive electronic press kits featuring film clips and audio bites, music videos derived from films appear on broadcast and cable TV, and TV's "Entertainment Tonight" as well as popular weeklies such as *People* would not exist without stories about movies and movie stars.

Publicity about a motion picture can take diverse forms. The publicity for the 1968 film *Rachel, Rachel* successfully emphasized Paul Newman's directing debut and the fact that he was directing his Oscar-winning wife Joanne Woodward.[13] Promotion for *The Stuff*, a 1986 release, included selling a Tofutti-type ice cream substitute prior to the film's distribution.[14]

Studio-generated publicity frequently begins with the acquisition of the property. Industry trade publications routinely report (based on studio press releases) the purchase of novels, plays, short stories, and feature articles for motion picture production. (Examples of the last category include *Saturday Night Fever, Urban Cowboy,* and *Perfect,* which had their genesis in articles published in, respectively, *New York, Esquire,* and *Rolling Stone.*) Adopting plays for the screen has a long tradition. The industry presumption is that a property with prior public exposure is guaranteed an audience, and they attempt to exploit that audience's interest from the first possible moment.

Another popular method of capitalizing on a "known quantity" is the sequel, prequel, or remake. Sequels follow up the narrative established in the original film. Less common are prequels, in which action occurring prior to the original story is portrayed. *Butch Cassidy and the Sundance Kid* ended with the two protagonists' death. A sequel, therefore, was not plausible for this immensely popular film; the prequel, *Butch and Sundance: The Early Days,* released in 1979, ten years after the original, traced the picaresque heroes' lives before they grew up and became Paul Newman and Robert Redford. Remakes are simply new versions of a story filmed earlier: *Here Comes Mr. Jordan* (1941) was remade as *Heaven Can Wait* (1978), *The Champ* was filmed in 1931, 1953 (under the title *The Clown*), and in 1979. Sequels, prequels, and remakes not only offer publicity opportunities, some studios also believe they enhance bookings by capitalizing on the original film's track record. Moreover, industry marketing and audience research for "Part II" of a popular movie are easier than for an original (and unknown) screenplay.[15]

Between 1964 and 1983 the number of sequels and reissues (rereleases) increased steadily. But, despite the press attention paid to the number of recent sequels and remakes, neither is a new phenomenon. "Sequelitis" was equally prevalent in the 1940s and '50s.[16] Table 4.1 presents the revenues of selected film originals and their sequels. Even using rental revenues unadjusted for inflation, some sequels perform extraordinarily well, sometimes disproving

Table 4.1

Box Office Performance of Selected "Recycled" Films

Film Title	Year of Release	Domestic Rentals
Star Wars	1977	$193,500,000
The Empire Strikes Back	1980	141,600,000
Return of the Jedi	1983	168,002,414
Raiders of the Lost Ark	1981	115,598,000
Indiana Jones and the Temple of Doom	1984	109,000,000
Jaws	1975	129,961,081
Jaws II	1978	52,442,396
Jaws 3-D	1983	26,796,600
Grease	1978	96,300,000
Grease 2	1982	6,500,000
First Blood	1982	22,957,478
Rambo: First Blood Part II	1985	94,000,000
Missing in Action	1984	10,000,000
Missing in Action 2—The Beginning[1]	1985	4,217,312
A Star Is Born	1954	6,100,000
A Star Is Born[2]	1976	37,100,000
The Postman Always Rings Twice	1946	4,000,000
The Postman Always Rings Twice[2]	1981	6,070,000

SOURCE: "All-Time Film Rental Champs," *Variety*, January 8, 1986. Reprinted by permission.
1. Prequel.
2. Remake.

the Hollywood rule of thumb that a sequel will do only half the business of the original.

Product merchandising is an old technique designed to draw attention to a film while offering product manufacturers an opportunity to profit from the film's success. Because the strategy costs movie producers nothing, is certain to generate some publicity, and provides moviemakers with additional revenue (from licensing fees, royalties, or some combination of the two), it is viewed as something that cannot hurt and can only help a film. By the mid-1980s, a reversal of the licensing pattern (from film to product) was seen with products acting as the impetus for films; *The Care Bears Movie* is an example.[17]

An Academy Award nomination generates a great deal of publicity that may boost a film's box office. Certainly the industry itself expends a great deal of money and energy on Oscar. By January every year, innumerable ads fill the trade papers offering this film or that for academy members' "consideration."

Seemingly every other page of *Variety,* the *Hollywood Reporter,* and *Daily Variety* features full-page announcements of special screenings of pictures being touted as "best" in one category or another.

The rule of thumb is that the Best Picture award is worth $5 million to $10 million in exhibitor rentals. This is no doubt true in at least some instances: When the "quality" films *Chariots of Fire* and *Amadeus* won Best Picture, the award seemed to stimulate attendance. A confounding factor, however, is how long an Oscar-winning film has been in release; movies distributed earlier in the year may have exhausted their theatrical legs by the time of the nomination and awards.

But audience research on the importance of Oscar to attendance decisions tends to refute Hollywood's assumptions.[18] The awards' lack of influence on audiences may result from their short-term, seasonal nature.

Advertising

If publicity is the soft sell, paid advertising is the hard sell. A fan magazine article might have an indirect persuasive effect on readers, but a paid ad in the same publication unambiguously telegraphs its intent. From the industry's perspective, advertising and publicity should complement one another, working hand-in-glove to entice moviegoers to a film (hence the term "ad-pubbing").

A rudimentary form of direct mail advertising was used as early as 1910 by Samuel Levin, manager of Chicago's Orpheum Theater. Levin mailed postcards to 8,000 Chicago-area car owners before the opening of *Auto Races at Crown Point* and used the same strategy later to advertise *The Fly Pest,* sending cards to doctors and city health officials.

The early nickelodeon operators recognized that "a theater is its own best advertisement."[19] The Attractograph Company of Chicago, for example, supplied "Moving Picture Signs for Moving Picture Theaters"; Cincinnati's Newman Manufacturing Company sold brass poster frames and easels for theater lobbies. By 1920, handbills, programs, contests, trade publication ads, and slides for screen projection were all established advertising staples.[20]

David Lipton of Universal Pictures noted that advertising for such a highly perishable product as a film is tailored to audiences who seem most likely to be attracted to it: "The major [advertising] effort is concentrated on the point of sale."[21] Point-of-sale advertising includes not only posters and marquees but trailers, or previews.

A hierarchy of influence exists among information sources. A 1984 study indicated that direct prior experience is the most influential source, followed by interpersonal sources and, lastly, the mass media. That is, as diffusion theory also predicts, owning a Mazda (trialability) influences car purchase decisions more than reading *Consumer Reports* or *Car and Driver.* When the highest level source in the hierarchy is not readily available, people turn to the next highest level (and so on down the scale).[22] In looking at attendance decisions, then, we should consider first the forms of advertising that approximate prior experience and then mass media channels.

Trailers.   Trailers most closely approximate the diffusion theory concept of trialability as well as direct prior experience.[23] Anecdotal reports indicating that many people do not perceive trailers as a form of advertising but rather view them as an opportunity to learn about a film heighten the importance of trailers: They are free from the self-serving connotations of other forms of advertising.

They are called "trailers" because in the silent era a title card of a coming attraction followed the presentation of the feature film rather than preceding it. Eventually, trailers were moved to the front of the program. The visual sophistication of trailers evolved from those simple title cards to an elaborate mixture of art and technology; the 90-second trailer for *To Live and Die in L.A.* (1985) contained 247 cuts. Trailers' running times range from 90 seconds to 2½ minutes. Their production is usually subcontracted out to firms specializing in their creation. According to Max Weinberg, a veteran producer of more than one thousand "miniature films," his job is to "make good trailers out of bad movies. . . . If my trailer isn't better than the movie, I'm in trouble."[24]

They seem well worth their cost. Virtually all industry marketers concur on the importance of trailers in selling a film. Trailers address an already interested group in a form compatible with what is being sold (a moving visual). Mid-1950s audiences rated trailers as the most reliable kind of movie advertising (see Table 4.2) and the form of advertising that was most helpful to them in making attendance decisions. A 1984 study confirmed these findings.[25]

Ads in the media.   Of newspapers, magazines, radio, and television, the latter has been rated as the most influential advertising medium in affecting attendance decisions.[26] This is not surprising; of those four media, television is closest in form and content to theatrical trailers. Though it lacks the visual element, radio can create an enticing aural ambience that encourages listeners to visualize scenes. Moreover, exposure to both TV ads and radio spots reinforces the messages presented in each medium. Radio may be the best medium for selling certain kinds of films: Musicals and music-oriented movies are especially suited to promotion via radio, because until recently its high fidelity sound could not be duplicated by TV.

Unlike radio and TV messages, the newspaper message is not transitory; its effectiveness does not depend on the audience's strict attention at the moment of presentation. Newspapers, moreover, provide essential information about showtimes and locations. (In contrast, TV and radio ads may only indicate that a film is playing "at a theater near you.") Several studies attest to the effectiveness of this medium in providing readers with information about movies.[27]

Although expensive, magazine advertising, like radio, provides an effective means of targeting messages to distinct audiences; the readerships for maga-

Table 4.2

Forms of Movie Advertising Judged as Reliable vs. Misleading, 1957

Form of Ad	Reliable	Misleading or Exaggerated	Reliability Index[1]
Previews in theaters	53%	12%	41%
Magazine ads	24	12	12
Newspaper ads	33	22	11
Television ads	20	15	5
Posters in stores	2	7	− 5
Radio ads	6	13	− 7
Signs in front of or outside theaters	13	27	− 14
Large signs or billboards	5	25	− 20
All of them	3	7	—
None of them	9	18	—

SOURCE: Opinion Research Corporation, *The Public Appraises Movies* (1957), p. 23. Reprinted by permission.
1. Obtained by subtracting the percentage saying a particular medium is misleading from the percentage saying it is reliable.

zines such as *McCall's* and *Playboy* are unlikely to overlap. Individualized advertising campaigns can be designed to address these different audiences.[28]

For *Making Love* (1982), about the triangular relationship of a yuppie husband and wife and a yuppie gay man, the placement of the characters in print ads depended on the ad medium's readership: In publications presumed to have a large gay readership, the husband was placed at the apex of the triangle; ads in publications having a high female readership featured the wife.[29]

Together, the industry's hard (advertising) and soft (publicity) sell help to create an image for a film. This image not only conveys information about a film but also functions as persuasion. Consistent with expectancy-value theory and the adoption process, audiences generate expectations about how well a film will satisfy various interests and needs. Because publicity and advertising do not function alone in the selection process in most instances, the other focus rings can diminish or enhance as well as confirm or contradict the information presented in this first focus ring.

Reviews

From their inception, motion pictures attracted press attention; reporters ballyhooed the latest invention of "The Wizard of Menlo Park," Thomas Alva Edison, in 1889. However, it was not until 1914 that serious critical attention was paid to movies. The advent of the newspaper movie critic conferred "a new status of recognition" on cinema. For the first time, theater owners "found a published judgment of the wares they bought, written by someone outside sycophancy of the trade press. . . ." The new race of motion picture reviewers grew rapidly, and in 1925 the list of newspaper film critics totaled four hundred.[30]

The role of critics vis-à-vis movie audiences can be sorted into three overlapping categories: creating awareness about a film, providing information on various aspects of a film, and evaluating and offering advice about attending a film. In the context of diffusion theory, this source of influence can affect both the knowledge and persuasion stages.

Two critical positions can be identified: the elitist critic and the consumer reporter. The elitist function of criticism has been defined as "maintaining the vigor of mores and cultural values in society"; the elitist critic's job is to raise audience standards by being "an exacting judge, constantly positing values *not* yet present in the general public."[31] Consumer-reporter critics evaluate movies according to criteria they believe their audiences hold dear. A 1974 survey of arts critics reported that "more than half the critics said they write their reviews to serve as a consumer guide for readers" and that movie and TV critics "were slightly more inclined toward this practice than others."[32]

The greater the agreement between critics and audiences, assuming that audiences are aware of this consensus, the greater the likelihood that critics can influence attendance decisions. A 1970 study that analyzed evaluations of 5,644 movies by professional critics and members of Consumers Union from 1947 through 1968 found substantial agreement between critics and CU members.[33] A second study, which compared Consumers Union members' and professional critics' evaluations of 636 movies from 1976 to 1981, did not find agreement.[34] As Table 4.3 indicates, these audiences evaluated movies significantly more positively than critics.

The difference in findings between the two studies can perhaps be explained by changes in attendance habits and the content of movies. Moviegoing frequency reached its pinnacle in 1947, and by 1968 (the last year included in the first study) had plummeted to one-sixth of that. The proportion of evaluative agreement between critics and audiences peaked in 1954 and steadily declined thereafter. The implication is that reduced attendance meant reduced agreement between audiences and critics.

Equally important are changes in the content of movies. Until the early 1950s, movies could be characterized as "family films." But a 1952 Supreme Court decision granting movies First Amendment protection and the advent of television, which offered family programming, changed movie content. Thus the earlier study may actually document a fairly homogeneous evaluation by critics and audiences to an essentially homogeneous product. The liberating effect of the Court's decision and the competition of TV engendered a broader, more diverse range of movie topics and themes, and critics' and audiences' evaluations began to diverge. The renaissance of movie content was assisted by the introduction of the MPAA's film rating system in late 1968. With clas-

Table 4.3

Comparison of Professional Critics' and Audiences' Evaluation of 636 Films

	Evaluation		
	Excellent	Fair	Poor
Critics	28.0%	36.4%	35.6%
Audiences	33.6	57.5	8.9

SOURCE: Bruce Austin, "Critics' and Consumers' Evaluation of Motion Pictures," *Journal of Popular Film and Television* 10 (Winter 1983):163. Scores listed under each of the three types of evaluation represent percentages of the numbers of "votes" by individual audience members and critics in each category. The critics cast a total of 5,330 votes and audiences 209,880 votes.

sification replacing censorship, still greater diversity of screen content became possible.

A reason for recent audiences' apparent reluctance to evaluate films extremely negatively could be financial. Having paid for admission to a film ($7 in New York in 1987, compared to 44 cents in 1948), in addition to other ancillary expenses, audiences may be determined to enjoy themselves. For critics, going to the movies is a job.

With the results of these two studies in mind, the question of the impact critics have on attendance can be addressed. Armchair observations generally suggest that critics in general have little influence on audiences. *Rolling Stone's* David Marsh wrote, "All one has to do is glance at the charts to see that the effect of rock critics on the American record buyer is about equal to [communist] Gus Hall's sway on the American presidential elections."[35] David Shaw of the *Los Angeles Times* believes that movie critics' influence is limited: "Generally speaking, critics are far more likely to confirm and crystallize existing predispositions than to actually change anyone's mind."[36]

Research generally confirms Marsh and Shaw's observations. A 1965 study of British filmgoers found that 85 percent of the respondents cited reviews as their source of information about films; however, the critics' recommendation played only a minor role in attendance decisions.[37] In a 1975 U.S. survey, only 37 percent of the respondents reported that reviews were either "very" or "somewhat" important in their decision about going to a movie.[38] Research in 1981 and 1982 found that reviews were what drew the attention of only 5 percent of college students and 2 percent of high school students surveyed to the film they had most recently attended.[39]

Several studies suggest that reviews play an important role in alerting audiences to films. In another context, Walter Lippmann called this the "signal function" of the media. Another possible use audiences have for movie reviews is to gather information about the film's story or plot. In short, movie reviews may augment data gathered in the other phases of the selection process.

Personal Influence

Personal influence refers to the impact of other people's comments on an individual's movie attendance decision. These comments may range from very direct, clearly intentional attempts at persuading the individual to see a particular film to less direct, more casual kinds of influence. An example of the former is when one of your friends tells you that you *must* see *Switching Channels.* An example of a more casual kind of personal influence is listening to your friends' lunchtime discussion of a film they have seen.

As noted in Chapter 1, word of mouth is viewed by the movie industry as an especially potent variable affecting the success of a film. Distribution and release strategies are often constructed with a critical eye toward what the word of mouth on a film will be; studio publicity and advertising attempt to maximize exposure of people's positive comments about a film. For instance, radio ads for *Porky's* (1982) featured the "vox pop" (man in the street) format of radio news interviews: A series of responses from theater lobby interviews proclaiming how funny the movie was were played back to back.

The film industry's concern with personal influence is well founded. By the time of World War II, communication scholars were drastically revising their theories and research approaches on the effects of the mass media. Until then, the dominant mode of thinking had emphasized what might be called a "powerful effects" model, in which the media were thought to have fairly direct and uniform effects on audiences. The shift to a model of more limited effects was prompted by the results of several studies that emphasized the part the audience played in the flow of mass communications. The impact of media messages on audiences was now regarded as diluted, diminished, or at least filtered through psychological (beliefs, values, attitudes) and sociological (primary and reference groups) variables. This "two-step flow" theory viewed information as moving from the media to relatively well informed people who, in turn, would pass along not only the information but also their interpretations to others.[40]

Elihu Katz and Paul Lazarsfeld's classic study, *Personal Influence,* documented the role of opinion leaders in four areas: marketing, fashion, public affairs, and movies.[41] An opinion leader was defined as someone who, through his or her day-to-day contact with others, helped shape their opinions and behaviors. For movies, the opinion leaders were younger than those for other issues. They not only attended movies more often than nonleaders, they were also especially attentive to things and events related to motion pictures. More frequently than "regular" moviegoers, the opinion leaders reported being influenced by promotional activities of the film industry and seeking specific information about movies in newspapers and magazines.

At about the same time as Katz and Lazarsfeld's research in the 1950s, Leo Handel's Motion Picture Research Bureau was also seeking to determine how

audiences learned about new movies and what sources of information influenced attendance at a specific film.[42] To answer these two questions, personal
interviews with a national sample of 1,500 people were conducted. As Table
4.4 indicates, personal contacts and reviews shared the greatest influence among
specific sources mentioned. Table 4.4 also demonstrates that while in-theater
advertising helped generate awareness about movies, its impact on attendance
decisions was slight.

The findings from the 1950s about the influence of personal advice on
attendance decisions are generally supported by subsequent reports.[43] A 1978
study by the Newspaper Advertising Bureau found U.S. movie opinion leaders
to be younger, single, better-educated people who attended movies more often
than others. The NAB study also found that movie opinion leaders were more
likely to see movies soon after they were released, did not seem to mind having
to travel a long distance to see a movie they were interested in, and paid
particular attention to information and advertising about movies that the media
presented.[44]

The uniformity of research findings on the influence of personal contacts
in movie attendance decisions has raised this variable to near omnipotent
status. But the precise *content* of such personal communication, its *emotional*
dimension or tone, and the exact *manner* in which personal communication
interacts with other variables in the attendance decision process remain unex-

Table 4.4

Sources of Information and Their Degree of Influence on Movie Attendance
Decisions

Source of Information	Sources from Which Respondent Learned About Last Picture Attended[1]	Most Influential Source
Hearsay	39%	17%
Advertising in newspapers and magazines	44	12
Reviews	36	17
Trailer	27	8
Advertising in/on theater	20	3
Radio	12	2
Outdoor advertising	3	1
Other	5	. . .
None	. . .	40

SOURCE: Leo Handel, *Hollywood Looks at Its Audience* (Urbana: University of Illinois Press, 1950), p. 89.
Reprinted by permission.
1. Percentages total more than 100 because of multiple mentions.

plored. For instance, if the conversation focuses on a movie's stars, then perhaps we should attribute the influence to the Production Elements focus ring. Or if opinion leaders disagree with professional critics' assessment of a movie, the Reviews focus ring needs to be reexamined. In short, we know little of *what* is talked about by opinion leaders and how it interacts with the other attendance focus rings.

The influence of strangers' opinions was noted by two researchers studying conformity, who sought to learn whether people's appreciation of a movie could be affected by overhearing the comments of those leaving an earlier screening.[45] The study subjects waited behind a retaining rope at a public theater as patrons from a screening of Steven Spielberg's *Sugarland Express* (1974) walked past. Among the exiting patrons were three pairs of research confederates. On separate occasions, three experimental conditions were created: (1) The confederates engaged in easily overheard conversations reporting their favorable reaction to the movie, saying things like "I wouldn't mind seeing this one again" or "The acting was fantastic, but the plot was even better." (2) Comments such as "You couldn't pay me to see that thing again" and "Well, another two bucks shot" were voiced. (3) No comments were made in the subjects' presence by the confederates.

To assess the effect of these comments, a theater employee distributed questionnaires to the subjects after they had watched the movie, asking them to rate it on a ten-point scale. The subjects were led to believe that the questionnaire was designed to help the theater management better choose movies their patrons would like. Subjects who had been exposed to the negative comments rated the movie significantly more negatively than those who had heard the positive comments (and vice versa). Because the confederates were strangers to the subjects, we may need to reevaluate the influence of movie critics on attendance decisions; most of us are not personally acquainted with critics.

Story and Type

Research has consistently demonstrated that people cite a film's plot or story and its genre as both their most important reason for moviegoing in general and as their reason for attending a specific film.[46] How do audiences come to learn the plot or genre of a movie so that they can then use this information to decide whether to see it? If you say you prefer adventure films, do you associate the same qualities with adventure as I do? Aesthetically oriented film scholars have discussed at length distinguishing characteristics among genres.[47] While such exegeses no doubt advance the "science of cinema" among specialists, they do little to suggest how lay audiences approach the question. As one scholar noted, "testing [genre] preferences is difficult because there are no established categories [that] are scientifically useful."[48] Many movies are hyphenates: comedy-drama, comedy-adventure, adventure-romance, and so forth. How, for instance, should a film like *Romancing the Stone* be classified? Is it a comedy? Or an adventure? A romance? A little of each, perhaps? A

British study in 1949 stated that because "few films conform exactly to any category, it is difficult to assess what it is in a particular film [that] makes an appeal."[49] When attempting to measure genre preferences, it is necessary to sort the genres into meaningful, mutually exclusive, and exhaustive categories.

A related problem concerns the *meaning* of genre labels. In a 1955 study of the audiences for first-run movies, the researchers asked their sample an open-ended question about film type preferences; respondents used labels and terminology of their own choosing. The research team reported a "fuzziness . . . in the meaning of names given the program types by the respondents."[50] Closed-ended questions, which provide a set of responses to choose from, are not necessarily the cure, either. "If we ask, 'What type of movie do you like best?' the answers depend upon the way the movie types are classified and upon the respondents' understanding of the terms we are using."[51]

In an effort to get around the problems of genre labels and their meaning, researchers have used box office or rental data as the means to measure genre preference. An attempted predictive model for movie financial success used domestic exhibitor rental data, coding films into one of five genres.[52] But this method has problems of its own: (1) Exhibitor rentals are not equivalent to the number of admissions (people attending a particular film). (2) Rental data are often inaccurate, incomplete, unreported, or not accessible to and verifiable by independent (nonindustry) researchers. (3) Film rental revenues represent only attendance, not necessarily preference, motivation for attendance, or enjoyment. (4) Box office data may be more of a measure of the menu (what films are offered at any given time) than actual audience preferences; similarly, variations in distribution patterns and advertising support for different movies affect availability and hence the breadth of the menu.

Even if a predictive model could be constructed, its usefulness would be short-lived. Film producers, distributors, and exhibitors alike have at various points in the cinema's history anointed various genres as attractive and appealing and others as box office poison.

It is clear that audiences do have film type preferences and can articulate their preferences, frequently by employing commonly used genre labels. However, several aspects of the issue remain unclear, including the relationship between expressed preference and actual behavior and how audiences come to perceive the film's plot and genre before actually seeing the picture. Regarding the last point, advertising and publicity, along with critical reviews, undoubtedly help form the audience's image of what films are about. The Story and Type focus ring, then, is much more complex than it might appear at first glance. Given its importance in affecting attendance decisions, much is yet to be learned about this focus ring.

Production Elements

The disparate components of the Production Elements focus ring are organized here in three groups: offscreen personnel, onscreen personnel, and production values.

Offscreen production personnel are the editors, cinematographers, costume designers, grips, gaffers, best boys, and so forth. Here we focus attention on the three positions that represent the most significant proportion of a film's above-the-line costs (with the possible exception of acting talent) and whose name recognition can affect attendance decisions: producer, director, and writer. (Above-the-line costs refer to contractual agreements arranged before filming begins; below-the-line costs are typically organized as expenses (for people and objects) incurred during the shooting and the completion period.)

Onscreen production personnel are the actors. Production values include a film's music and photography (color versus black and white as well as visual effects).

The director.   Although a few directors, such as D. W. Griffith, gained critical if not public recognition early in film history, directors didn't really come into their own until the mid-1950s. Francois Truffaut, later a director himself, wrote of the "politiques des auteurs" in a 1954 issue of the French film journal *Cahiers du Cinema*. Truffaut's auteur (author) theory had the effect of apotheosizing the director as film's artistic guiding hand. Filmmakers who had for years worked in relative obscurity suddenly found themselves in the limelight. The importance of film directors to attendance decisions is implied in the introduction to a book titled *The Film Director as Superstar*: "Over half the movie tickets sold today are bought by moviegoers between the ages of sixteen and twenty-five. They know what a director is, what he does, and what he's done."[53] The director's box office value has been further certified by studio executives. Producer Milton Sperling, for instance, stated, "The director has become a key ingredient in ensuring the studio of its investment."[54] On the other hand, film scholar Michael Mayer maintains that the box office records of most directors are "erratic" and that few have demonstrated "a continued box office appeal." He concludes that "the mere hiring of an outstanding or competent director is obviously no assurance of popularity, particularly in these days when directors' services come high."[55]

The producer and screenwriter.   Although a handful of producers may gain name recognition by virtue of an iconoclastic or flamboyant reputation, such as Otto Preminger, few find themselves the subject of any prominent and sustained attention; perhaps even fewer are portrayed in a positive light. The producer has been characterized as often acting in an adversarial role to the director and having to heel obediently to the studio money managers. A producer, wrote British director Bryan Forbes, "generates about as much artistic excitement as a sackful of dead mice and the total sum of his cinematic knowhow is his ability to read the balance sheet of his last picture."[56] Axel Madsen, in his book about Hollywood in the 1970s, discussed film producers in a chapter entitled "Producers and Other Vices."

Screenwriters rarely receive any notice at all, good or bad, outside of the Hollywood colony; as one observer states, "Perhaps the greatest ignominy the screenwriter endures is anonymity."[57]

Despite the critical attention paid to directors, producers, and writers, audience surveys do not support the contention that they make a difference at the box office. A British survey conducted in the mid-1960s identified one-third of its sample as interested in "the technical side of filmmaking." When these individuals, who tended to be more frequent moviegoers, were asked what attracted them to the film they had seen most recently, only 10 percent reported that it was the producer or director; a mere 3 percent of the remaining sample offered the same reason.[58]

More recent research with American students found that the producer, director, and screenwriter were rated uniformly unimportant to attendance decisions. In these studies, respondents were asked to assess the importance of 28 variables in regard to the film they had seen most recently. The three offscreen production personnel were consistently ranked lowest and least important in affecting attendance decisions.[59]

The actors. In the early days of motion pictures, actors received no onscreen credits. Still, audiences quickly identified favorite performers, often giving them nicknames such as "Little Mary" (Mary Pickford) or "The Biograph Girl" (Florence Lawrence). Carl Laemmle was reputedly the first to feature acting credits as a means to exploit public attraction to movie stars; this attraction continues unabated today. Their names fill the headlines of supermarket tabloids, their photographs are prominently featured on the covers of national magazines, and their advice is sought on diverse topics ranging from diet and nutrition to politics and policymaking. But do stars sell tickets? Do audiences make attendance decisions based on them?

George Gallup's Audience Research Inc. conducted bimonthly interviews from 1940 to 1948 to determine the box office appeal of various stars. A later analysis of the relationship between the star power reported by this "Continuing Audit of Marquee Values" and ticket sales found that the marquee values generally failed to predict success and concluded that top-grossing films predicted high marquee values, rather than the other way around.[60] A researcher concluded in 1971 that "it would appear that the money spent on highly inflated salaries for stars was not productive."[61] And a 1980 study of key production personnel's track records found that the performers' records were weak and insignificant predictors of box office success.[62]

That audiences find some stars more attractive than others is unquestionable. However, few individuals indicate that stars alone are very important to movie attendance decisions.[63] However, in terms of diffusion theory, the actors no doubt contribute much to the audiences' awareness and knowledge about a film by virtue of publicity, in contrast to offscreen personnel, who are less likely to attract press attention.

Production values.   The visual look of a film, including black-and-white versus color photography as well as special effects, has rarely been investigated.
We can speculate that at least for contemporary moviegoers, color photography is simply expected, and hence the issue as a whole is today moot; exceptions, of course, do occur: Mel Brooks's *Young Frankenstein* (1974), Woody
Allen's *Manhattan* (1979), David Lynch's *Elephant Man* (1980), and Prince's
Under the Cherry Moon (1986) were all produced in black and white. No
doubt the exciting visual effects of films like *Star Wars* and *Close Encounters
of the Third Kind* enhanced audience enjoyment.[64]

The influence of a film's musical sound track on attendance decisions has
likewise rarely been researched. No doubt one reason for this is that audiences
go to *see* a movie, not hear it. Like film editing, music in movies is often
designed to enhance the visuals without attracting attention to itself.

In the genre of musicals, however, the score is in the spotlight. Musicals
have existed as long as sound in the cinema. It is plausible that MGM's reputation as the premiere producer of musical films in the '30s and '40s enhanced
attendance. But many filmed musicals were adaptations from the stage, so
determining whether it was the music, the play, the studio's reputation, or
some combination of these that formed attendance decisions is impossible.
Failed film adaptations of hit Broadway musicals (*The Wiz, The Pirates of Penzance*) are as easy to name as the successes (*West Side Story, The Sound of
Music, Grease*).

A recent and interesting trend is the increased symbiosis between the popular music industry and film. Rockumentaries such as *Woodstock, The Last
Waltz,* and *Stop Making Sense* achieved popular success. Filmed biographies
of popular recording artists have flourished: *Coal Miner's Daughter* (Loretta
Lynn), *Sweet Dreams* (Patsy Cline), *La Bamba* (Ritchie Valens).

Most intriguing are those films that apparently rely on their music to attract
young audiences. *Saturday Night Fever* was a hugely successful film and soundtrack album in 1977; *Sgt. Pepper's Lonely Hearts Club Band* failed dismally
one year later. Playing to nostalgia worked well for *American Graffiti* and
Grease, but not so well for *American Hot Wax* or *Grease II.* Ray Parker Jr.'s
theme song for *Ghostbusters* purportedly added $20 million to the box office
take of the film; apparently no number of hit songs and popular artists could
save *FM* from failure. In short, the results of introducing and promoting pop
music as a key element to movies are uneven and await rigorous research.
What can be said, however, is that hit records drawn from or created for movies
that are promoted on radio stations and music video outlets certainly boost
publicity for the film.[65]

If we were to rank the importance of the three components in the Production Elements focus ring according to available audience research, onscreen
personnel would take first place, followed by offscreen personnel and then
production values. Taken as a whole, however, this focus ring by itself does
not appear to have much influence on attendance decisions. Nevertheless,
production elements represent the primary resource material from which
advertising and publicity draw and thus affect attendance decisions indirectly.

SUMMARY

Movies, like other innovations, may be adopted by audiences through a process of gaining information about a film, forming evaluative judgments about it, and then deciding whether to attend it based on the information gathered and judgments made. A five-part model of elements in the attendance decision was developed that mirrored the steps in the innovation adoption process: advertising and publicity, reviews, personal influence, story and type, and production elements.

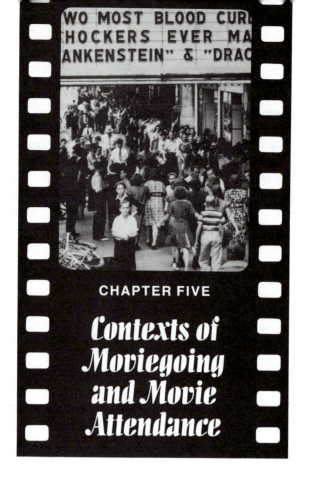

CHAPTER FIVE

Contexts of Moviegoing and Movie Attendance

S o far we have considered the moviegoing public as a whole. But this audience is really many audiences. This chapter examines three distinct audiences in some detail: the art film audience, the cult film audience, and the drive-in audience. These three case studies present divergent, yet connected, insights to the many ways that film as experiential consumption might be understood. They clarify the unique and shared characteristics of film audiences.

The art film audience exemplifies the trend toward specialization that exhibitors are increasingly adopting; the cult film audience may be the most contemporary of the three discussed; and the drive-in movie audience has perhaps the longest history. The portraits of the three audiences include historical, technological, and social details.

THE ART FILM AUDIENCE

The audience for the arts in the United States has long been a topic for scholarly investigation.[1] But unlike the audience for such traditionally acknowledged "high culture" art forms as ballet, opera, and theater, the audience for films that might fit in this category—the so-called art films—have received little research attention.[2] That the audience for art films is a special segment of the moviegoing public is demonstrated by the unique methods used by the major film distributors to market such films. Autonomous or semi-autonomous units such as Triumph Films (Columbia Pictures), Universal Classics, United Artists Classics, and 20th Century-Fox International Classics have all been recently established. These specialized distribution operations, along with specialized theaters ("art houses"), represent an attempt by the film industry to attract one particular segment of their market.

The art house offers "films from other countries, reissues of old-time Hollywood 'classics,' documentaries, and independently made films on offbeat themes" to a selective (as opposed to general or mass) audience.[3]

Development of the Art Theater and Audience

In the late '40s, only about a dozen theaters, half of them in New York, regularly screened art films.[4] The dearth of domestic product and restrictive trade practices that effectively blocked the importing of foreign films account for this paltry number; both were a function of the U.S. film industry oligopoly, which was not broken until the 1948 *Paramount* decision.

Most film historians agree that the *Paramount* decision was a key factor in the rise of the art theater.[5] The Supreme Court declared that the major studios had illegally fixed prices and engaged in block booking. (Block booking refers to a distributor's requirement that exhibitors rent a package, or block, of several films under one agreement; usually some of the films are not expected to perform well.) The Justice Department mandated that the major producer-distributors get rid of the theaters they owned, effectively breaking the oligopoly. Because the studios had lost their guaranteed markets, domestic production declined by 28 percent between 1946 and 1956, while the number of imported foreign films increased by 132 percent.[6] With fewer American-made movies to choose from and increased competition among exhibitors for the U.S. pictures available, as well as the divestiture of the majors' exhibition branch, "movie theaters compensated by filling their screen time with independent and foreign films and reissues"—the program material of the art house.[7]

In the decade following the consent decree, the number of art theaters increased. By 1956, 226 U.S. theaters devoted all their screen time to art films; in 1964 there were 500 such theaters, and in 1980 an estimated 1,000, or about 8 percent of all indoor theaters.[8] Two effects of the *Paramount* decision might account for the increase in art houses: the boom in independent production and exhibition and the diminished power and effectiveness of the Production Code Administration (PCA) to control the content of domestic production.[9]

Virtually concurrent with the *Paramount* decision was the debut of television, which usurped much of Hollywood's audience. In response to the resulting fragmentation of the film audience, producers and exhibitors specialized. Three additional reasons for the growth of the art film have been cited: "the establishment of film libraries and the study of film appreciation in colleges and universities, . . . the widespread wartime use of documentary film . . . [which] helped create audience interest in new film themes and techniques," and the emergence of "many 16-mm. movie societies."[10]

The foreign film.   The foreign film has been the staple of art houses. Foreign filmmakers have typically been viewed as innovators. The feature-length film was first popularized when Adolph Zukor imported the four-reel *Queen Elizabeth,* starring Sarah Bernhardt, to the United States from France in 1912. At the time, American exhibitors were of the opinion that audiences simply would not sit still for any film longer than 10 or 15 minutes.

But "after the initial flurry of interest before 1920, American audiences showed a definite distaste for 'foreign' films, including those from Britain."[11] Interest in foreign films in the United States revived following the end of World War II, due in part to "the vast number of Americans who traveled abroad during and since World War II." Other explanations offered: increased sophistication of audience tastes, "the trend away from isolation," and the presence of the United States in the United Nations, which "created a broader interest in foreign customs and practices."[12] According to another scholar, "two events [were] largely responsible for the foreign film's quick gain of a faithful and expanding audience": British producer J. Arthur Rank's deal to have his "prestige pictures" distributed by Universal-International and the widespread publicity for and critical endorsement of Rossellini's *Open City* (1945).[13]

A look at the future.   The myriad new (especially television-related) technologies may result in movies that are still further specialized and "heightened" to do what theatrical film can do best—movies that are defined "more clearly as an art form."[14] Given the increasing segmentation of the film audience, a reasonable expectation is that an increasing number of screens will be devoted to art films.

The Art Audience Profile

Informal reports have tended to paint an elitist and occasionally unflattering portrait of art film patrons. Movie critic Pauline Kael wrote that

> the educated audience often uses "art" films in much the same self-indulgent way as the mass audience uses Hollywood "product," finding wish-fulfillment in the form of cheap and easy congratulation on their sensitivities and their liberalism.[15]

According to several studies of art film patrons, they do tend to be highly educated. One researcher noted that compared to mainstream moviegoers, his sample held more prestigious occupations, were a more mobile group, and were heavier consumers of other cultural activities.[16] Another found that although mainstream and art audiences differed little demographically, their media use behaviors differed significantly: Art film patrons were more print-oriented; mainstream patrons were more television-oriented. In general, mainstream audiences were more likely to attend movies for emotional stimulation; they rated reasons such as "to cheer up," "to cry," "to be excited," and "to laugh" higher.[17]

Art film audiences are more frequent moviegoers. "The art-film devotee probably goes to everything that sounds halfway promising," one researcher concluded.[18] Similarly, a 1959 study found that the type of picture was "relatively unimportant to the art-film addict" when deciding which film to attend.[19] Influences on attendance that have been cited include the recommendations of friends and reviewers, the reputation of the producer or director, and the descriptions in film series brochures.[20]

THE CULT FILM AUDIENCE

Unlike the art film, the cult film is a fairly recent occurrence. One film historian traces the phenomenon to the late 1960s "as camp interest developed in Roger Corman's various monster and motorcycle movies."[21] Many movies predating 1960 have since become the object of cults.

Defining the Cult Film

Cult films are the "private genre" of "the privileged children of the middle class." The movies are "generally offered at Friday and Saturday midnight screenings in college towns" to a young audience; a "general trend [of the film content] has been toward what we might call a trash esthetic" laced with sadomasochism; the films are populated by "egregiously eccentric characters," are inexpensively produced using on-location settings, and are given poor distribution ("dumped") by their studios.[22]

Cult films are not *made* (as, for example, a producer sets out to *make* a musical or Western) as much as they *happen* or *become*. It is doubtful that a filmmaker *could* consciously contrive to make a cult film; rather, it is the audience that turns a film into a cult film. This implies that cult films are not genre-bound.

Two elements clearly define the cult film: the nature of its exhibition and the nature of its audience. First, the film must be screened at an unconventional hour (usually around midnight) and these screenings must play on a regular and continuing (minimally once a month) basis. Occasionally rereleased movies (such as *Fiddler on the Roof, Gone with the Wind,* and most of the Disney catalog) and films that are shown regularly on television, such as *The Wizard of Oz,* are therefore excluded. Thus is the true cult film movie distinguished from the popular one-shot revival often presented at film festivals. A film can have a cult following and not be a true cult film.

The second defining aspect of the cult film is the audience. Cult films are uniquely characterized by repeat attendance. The cult film veteran is typically young, single, and a high school or college student. Cult films find an audience, for one reason or another, on the college circuit and in repertory movie houses, whose audiences are heavily populated with students.

Numerous films meet the definition of cult film: *Reefer Madness* (1936), *Night of the Living Dead* (1968), *El Topo* (1971), *Pink Flamingos* (1973), and, especially following Ronald Reagan's election as president, *Bedtime for Bonzo* (1951). At least three book-length treatments of the cult film phenomenon have been published since 1980.[23]

A Case Study of the Cult Film Audience

The Rocky Horror Picture Show, if not the most popular, is certainly the best-known cult film. Although the following case study is clearly limited and certainly not definitive, it paints a portrait of the audience for one enormously successful cult movie.

When *Rocky Horror* was previewed before a Santa Barbara, California, audience in July 1975, the initial response was generally poor. The movie premiered in Westwood September 26, 1975, with a normal exhibition schedule. Although the film did brisk business in Los Angeles, this was atypical. Tim Deegan, 20th Century-Fox's director of advertising, noted that in most theaters "the movie bombed the first time out. It was a disaster."[24] It was subsequently distributed poorly and promoted unenthusiastically.

The movie "officially broke into the midnight circuit at the Waverly Theater in New York City on April 1, 1976. . . . Around Halloween 1976, an anonymous group of people, largely unknown to each other, began to dress up when they went to see *Rocky Horror* at the Waverly Theater."[25] Thus slightly more than one year after its unpromising release, *Rocky Horror* began to gather an ardent following. Attendance at the midnight shows picked up so dramatically that at least one theater instituted reserved-seat sales.

Fox's marketing strategy for *Rocky Horror* at this point was decidedly low-key; marketing vice president Ashley Boon stated:

> We are only supporting one engagement in the whole United States, and that's in New York, and it's a one inch by one column ad in "The Village Voice," once a week, and that is it. Our total advertising is fourteen thousand dollars [over a four-year period].[26]

The studio's *initial* limited promotional efforts were premised on the belief that the film was an esoteric, sure-fire flop. Upon attaining cult status, the promotional strategy was designed to be relatively subtle so that the audience would feel that they were discovering something rather than being hyped.[27]

Audience participation. The audience's response while viewing *Rocky Horror* is by now well known. In addition to news media reports, the 1980 film *Fame* portrayed the audience response. During its heyday, lines began forming more than two hours before the show. A good deal of noisy, amiable socializing still takes place outside theaters. Inside, though, is where the patrons truly go into action.

"Movie-going is essentially a social activity ... and young people are more likely to band together for the purpose of entertainment," a sociologist wrote in 1947.[28] But the social activity that occurs during *Rocky Horror* is quite different from what goes on at other pictures. Throughout the film the devotees call out for camera cuts and character actions, ask questions of the characters (appropriately timed to the film's dialogue), respond to the characters' comments, and provide a plethora of addenda to the film's dialogue. Not only do the viewers verbally respond to the picture, they also "help" the characters by such acts as providing flashlights to show the way to Brad and Janet as they trudge through the dark, rainy night and add their own special effects, hurling slices of toast when a toast is proposed in the film and squirting one another with water pistols in the rain sequence.[29]

Audience response to the images projected before them is nothing new. At nickelodeons, "the crowd went expecting to interact volubly with the screen, and each other, and this they did—sometimes to excess."[30] Anecdotes of early film audiences who physically reacted *to* the new medium are numerous: At a screening of the Lumière brothers' *L'Arrivée d'un Train en Gare* in 1895, the audience shrieked and ducked when they saw the train approach a railroad station; at the 1896 debut of Edison's Vitascope in New York City Music Hall, "patrons in the front rows ran screaming from their seats, afraid they were about to be drenched" when shown R. W. Paul's *Beach at Dover,* which depicted waves lapping up on the shore. As one film historian notes, "Audiences would have to learn how to watch movies."[31] In the 1950s, cinematic gimmicks such as Cinerama, 3-D, Smell-O-Vision and AromaRama were designed to get the audience to react *to* the screen.

For *Rocky Horror,* the audience participation is *with* (as opposed to a reaction *to*) the film; the viewers interact as much with each other as they do with the characters and action on the screen. A 1950 study of popular films states: "Where these productions gain the sympathetic response of a wide audience, it is likely that their producers have tapped within themselves a reservoir of common daydreams."[32] Several contemporary observers of the *Rocky Horror* phenomenon maintain that the film and the audience participation serve a cathartic function.[33] Whatever the reasons for the behavior, audience participation appears to be a key motivation for first-time *Rocky Horror* attendance and for repeat attendance.

An audience study. A total of 562 *Rocky Horror* patrons were interviewed while waiting in line for the movie in Rochester, New York, on Friday and Saturday evenings one weekend in October 1979 and one in November 1979. The audience was divided into three groups: "virgins," who had not seen *Rocky Horror* before; "veterans," who had seen it 1 to 12 times; and "regulars," who had seen it 13 or more times. Nearly two-thirds (61.7 percent) of those interviewed had seen *Rocky Horror* at least once previously. The number of times the respondents had seen it ranged from 0 to 200. The mean number of viewings was 7.03. Excluding the virgins, the mean number was 11.39. By way of comparison, a national telephone survey for 20th Century-Fox of 750 people in the top 30 film markets found the mean number of *Rocky Horror* viewings per person to be 2.37.[34]

The size of the attendance unit ranged from 1 to 60. (Only 2 virgins, 4 veterans, and 4 regulars reported attending alone.) Overall, the mean size of the attendance unit was 4.67. The most common attendance unit was the male-female group (more than two persons), followed respectively by the all-male group, an opposite-sex friend, the all-female group, and attendance with a spouse.

Males made up a greater proportion of the *Rocky Horror* audience. Only within the virgins group did females outnumber males, and then by just a few. Significantly more males than females were regulars. The range of ages reported was from 13 to 50, but most individuals were between 17 and 22. Veterans tended to be the youngest and regulars the oldest audience groups. More than half the audience reported their occupation as either high school or college students. For those not enrolled in school, the largest segment were blue-collar workers.

How did the audience learn about *Rocky Horror* and what prompted them to attend? Word of mouth was by far the largest initial source of information about *Rocky Horror*: Nearly three-quarters of the sample reported learning about the film from various personal contacts.

Is going to see *Rocky Horror* a planned or a spontaneous behavior? More than three-fourths of the respondents stated that their attendance had been planned.

A distinguishing feature of *Rocky Horror* audience members is their level and frequency of interaction with both the movie and each other. Slightly more than half (51 percent) of the respondents brought props with them.

By far the most popular prop was rice (to be thrown during the wedding scene, early in the picture). A variety of water sprayers (for the rain sequence) and newspapers (to imitate Janet as she walks through the rain holding one over her and perhaps to protect against the other audience members' water spraying and rice throwing) were also favored. Less frequently mentioned props included marshmallows, eggs, potatoes, balloons, bird seed, noisemakers, teddy bears, and ears and nose masks. Thus while not everyone brought a prop to the theater, those who did came well prepared.

Costuming oneself like one of the film's characters is a more extreme form of participation, a form of public commitment. Overall, relatively few (8.6 percent) in this sample indicated that they had ever dressed up. Nearly half (41.4 percent) of the regulars, though, reported such behavior. Among those audience members who had dressed up, *Rocky Horror*'s leading character, Frank N. Furter, was the most popular model.

The most common reason virgins gave for attending *Rocky Horror* was the reputed unique nature of the film and the audience. Word-of-mouth "advertising" played a large part in their attendance decision. Few first-timers mentioned the quality of the film as the factor that attracted them. (In fact, respondents in the Fox phone survey reported "a very average rating" for the film; people generally thought it was "not a terrific film.") The social experience promised by *Rocky Horror*'s reputation and satisfying their curiosity are potent drawing cards for first-time viewers.

By definition, veterans and regulars are devoted *Rocky* followers. The reasons for repeat attendance that they reported were largely social rather than related to qualities of the film itself.

This study suggests, then, that the preparation, the waiting, and finally the active participation in the viewing of the film appear to be part of a group ritual. Many questions remain to be answered. Why does audience participation occur? What are the social and psychological needs of the audience that the *Rocky Horror* experience gratifies? How are these needs met? What determines how and why an individual becomes a *Rocky Horror* regular? Why don't all veterans go on to become regulars? To what extent is the content of the cult film an important element in drawing repeat attendance, and what are the most salient components? Finally, why are these components important to the audience?

THE DRIVE-IN AUDIENCE

Although the innovation of indoor film exhibition occurred virtually simultaneously around much of the globe, the development and exploitation of the outdoor form were uniquely American. This section examines the development of the drive-in and reviews the research on its audience.

Development of the Drive-in

Anecdotal reports, often touting Yankee ingenuity, cite farmers who stretched bed sheets between telephone poles on which to project movies as the first drive-in entrepreneurs. Such stories no doubt contain elements of truth, but represent only isolated, unorganized novelties, not the development of an industry. The first true drive-in movie theater is credited to a chemical manufacturer named Richard Milton Hollingshead, Jr., who opened it in Camden, New Jersey, in early June, 1933. This modest initial effort contained seven semicircular rows of parking spaces with 50-foot-wide aisles, which accommodated some 400 cars, each parked on a 5 percent grade. Early press reports called the drive-in "a colosseum for movie-minded motorists," but it was not an instant success, at least not in terms of widespread adoption or diffusion.[35] By the end of World War II, one author estimated, there were "only some 60" drive-ins nationwide; another source placed the number at 300.[36] Following the war, however, the drive-in form of exhibition experienced rapid growth. Wartime curtailment of consumer automobile production and gas rationing had slowed the drive-in's development; when these restrictions were lifted, though, Americans enthusiastically took to the road. By 1948, there were some

800 U.S. "ozoners" accounting for 4.5 percent of all theaters and 2.9 percent of all U.S. film revenues.

Postwar prosperity brought population migration from the cities to the developing suburbs. Because even a modest-sized drive-in requires some 10 to 15 acres of land, building them in densely populated urban centers was impossible. The suburbs offered both space and customers. Investors found construction and operating costs relatively low, damage to the physical plant minimal, and high concession sales possible.[37] In 1954, the Council of Motion Picture Organizations reported that drive-ins "accounted for almost half of the weekly motion picture attendance during the months of July and August for the years from 1952 through 1954."[38] Undeterred by zoning squabbles, allegations that they caused traffic hazards, and charges by moralists of contributing to the delinquency of minors, drive-ins were thriving.

Some observers contended that the drive-in was, in fact, what saved movies from annihilation by TV. Motion Picture Association of America president Eric Johnston said in 1952 that "drive-ins more than make up for the total seats lost through the closedown of theaters." TV undeniably hurt movie attendance with but "one shining exception," the drive-in, according to *Business Week.*[39]

In 1967, drive-in operations accounted for slightly more than one-quarter (27.4 percent) of all U.S. theaters and slightly less than one-quarter (24.4 percent) of all film revenues. These figures represent the peak of popularity for drive-ins. Since 1967, the number of theaters and revenues have steadily slipped. Factors contributing to the slow demise of the drive-in include high operating expenses, increased competition from multiplexes (which offer types of films formerly limited to drive-ins), VCRs, and cable television, and the tremendous appreciation in real estate value of the land on which drive-ins are situated. Today drive-in operators find that either selling their land outright or developing it for shopping malls or industrial locations are powerful incentives to get out of the film exhibition business.

Legal actions have also hurt business. Local public-nuisance laws have required theaters to close by a specified time, which reduces the number of times a film might be shown and the number of films on the bill and eliminates dusk-to-dawn movie marathons. More serious are the nuisance actions affecting drive-in theaters that show R- and X-rated films and whose screens are visible to nonpatrons.

The most optimistic forecast suggests that the drive-in has hit a plateau. New construction will be extremely limited and may balance the number of closings.

The Drive-in Audience Profile

Many observers feel that the drive-in audience is somehow special and different. As far back as 1949, Hollywood moviemakers were reported as believing that drive-ins appealed to a distinctly different audience than walk-ins.[40]

The drive-in was thought to appeal to the overweight, the elderly, the infirm, and the disabled. Such individuals, some believed, might not normally attend walk-in movies because of inconveniece or their discomfort in conventional theater seats. The outdoor theater, some speculated, also attracted "people who are extremely health conscious." The informality of drive-ins, it was said, made them attractive to individuals who disliked having to get dressed up to go to the movies.[41]

But the largest proportion of the drive-in's first audience was the family, in particular young, moderate-income, non–white-collar families with small children. More than half the drive-in audience was composed of the family group—two adults plus a child or children—according to research conducted in 1949, 1950, 1957, and 1959. A 1953 study reported that "the principal appeal of the Drive-in is to dating couples, family groups with small children, and to vacationists."[42] In 1966, one West Coast exhibitor noted that his chain drew "a double, a twin audience": One part was composed of teens and the other was the lower-middle-class family. This exhibitor's sense of his audience's composition affected his booking policy. Since he felt "the drive-in audience is comparatively an unsophisticated audience," he avoided screening "class pictures," "nudies," or "so-called art pictures."[43]

According to one study, the family as the predominant attendance unit for drive-ins may be even more pronounced today than it was 30 years ago. A recent survey commissioned by one of the largest U.S. drive-in circuits, Pacific Theatres, indicated that fully 72 percent of those attending California drive-ins "were classified as young married couples with two or more children who couldn't afford to go out and pay for a babysitter."[44]

The 1950s drive-in audience went to the movies quite frequently; average attendance ranged from 2.3 to 5.2 times a month. At least half of those surveyed reported they attended drive-ins a majority of the time and one-third said they attended no other type of theater during the summer.[45]

Not everyone loved drive-ins, of course. Females surveyed in the early '50s consistently reported a preference for conventional theaters over drive-ins.[46] And 60 percent of a 1951 sample believed that movies at drive-ins "were either not as good, or were less desirable because they were older than those pictures available at conventional theaters."[47]

A Case Study of a Contemporary Drive-in Audience

Personal interviews were conducted with 607 patrons at a Rochester, New York, drive-in theater on weekends (Friday, Saturday, and Sunday) during October 1981 and April, May, and June 1982. The respondents' mean (and median) drive-in attendance was once a month. The sample was divided into three groups: "Infrequent" drive-in goers reported attendance of once in two to six months or fewer; "occasional" drive-in goers reported attendance of once or twice a month; "frequent" drive-in goers reported attendance of three times a month or greater.

The respondents were asked, "Suppose there were a movie you wanted to see and it was playing at both a drive-in and a walk-in theater. Which type of theater would you go to, all things equal?" Overall, 76.5 percent selected the drive-in.

The size of the drive-in attendance unit ranged from 1 to 14. The mean size of the attendance unit was 2.66 persons (including the respondent). Contrary to results of research in the '50s, the family group accounted for only a small part (16.7 percent) of those interviewed. The most common relationship of the respondents' companion was an opposite-sex friend, followed by the family, spouse, male-female group (more than two persons), same-sex friend, same-sex group, and alone. The sample's average age was 24 years, 57.9 percent were male, and 33 percent were married.

More than one-third of the sample was employed in blue-collar (factory, production-line work) or pink-collar (secretarial, waitress) jobs. More of the frequent drive-in goers held less prestigious jobs or were unemployed than those who attended the drive-in less often. Table 5.1 displays data on the drive-in audience's occupation from 1955, 1959, and this 1982 study.

People who attend movies at least once a month constitute only 23 percent of the U.S. public over 12 years of age, and these same individuals account for 85 percent of all movie admissions.[48] Previous research has indicated that the drive-in audience attends movies frequently. For this sample, attendance at walk-in theaters for the sample averaged once a month; total movie attendance averaged twice a month. Thus these respondents were, indeed, heavy moviegoers.

Table 5.1

Occupational Profile of the Drive-in Moviegoer

	1955	1959	1982
Service, sales, clerical, and unskilled	15.7%	13%	37.4%
Students	16.0	*	25.8
White collar	8.9	*	10.9
Skilled and semi-skilled	16.3	21	9.5
Unemployed	2.7	*	7.6
Housewives/homemaker	19.3	*	3.6
Professional and semi-professional	3.8	11	3.6
Manager, proprietor	3.5	21	*
Farmer, farm managers	14.5	14	*

SOURCE: For 1955, Sindlinger and Company, *An Analysis of the Motion Picture Industry 1946–1953, Volume 1*. For 1959, Steuart Henderson Britt, "What Is the Nature of the Drive-in Theater Audience?" *Media/scope* 4 (June 1960): 100–02, 104. For 1982, Bruce A. Austin, "The Development and Decline of the Drive-in Movie Theater," in *Current Research in Film: Audiences, Economics, and Law*, vol. 1, ed. Bruce A. Austin (Norwood, N.J.: Ablex, 1985), p. 80.

A series of questions was asked concerning the respondents' decision-making process for their moviegoing on the evening they were interviewed. First they were asked whether they had planned to go to the drive-in on the evening they were interviewed or whether their attendance was a spur-of-the-moment decision. The sample divided nearly equally on this question. A follow-up question asked whether they had decided to see the particular movie playing before deciding when to go see it, or whether they first decided to go to the movies and then selected a film. Again the sample divided nearly evenly in their response.

More than half the sample used the newspaper as their source of information about the movie they were attending; word of mouth accounted for almost one-fifth of the responses. Two questions probed the reasons for going to the drive-in as a leisure activity. The respondents' most important reasons for going to drive-ins are presented in Table 5.2. "To see the movie" ranked only 6th out of 14 reasons. This study suggests that drive-in attendance is motivated by the low cost, the comfort and privacy afforded by one's car, and the opportunity to socialize. For many, the movie apparently serves as merely a backdrop.

Over the course of a half-century, the U.S. drive-in moved from a novelty

Table 5.2

Most Important Reason for Drive-In Attendance

	Infrequents	Occasionals	Frequents	Total
Less expensive than walk-ins	17.2%	18.0%	20.2%	18.1%
More comfortable than walk-ins	13.2	17.1	24.6	17.0
Privacy	14.5	20.3	8.8	15.6
Can have fun (party, drink, smoke)	13.2	18.0	15.8	15.6
To be outdoors	8.8	6.5	8.8	7.9
To see the movie	8.8	6.0	7.9	7.5
Convenience (can take the baby)	5.7	5.5	4.4	5.4
Entertainment	3.5	1.4	1.8	2.3
Casual; don't have to dress up	2.2	2.8	1.8	2.3
To get out of the house	2.6	1.8	1.8	2.2
Change of pace; a different movie experience	3.1	0.9	1.8	2.0
Nothing else to do	3.1	0.9	1.8	2.0
Quieter than walk-ins	2.6	0.0	0.9	1.3
Romance; to "make out"	1.3	0.9	0.0	0.9

SOURCE: Austin, 1985, p. 84.

to a prospering form of exhibition to a now declining industry. The drive-in helped create an outlet for the exploitation movies of such film producers as New World Pictures, and aroused the ire of indoor exhibitors, moralists, and local legislators.

SUMMARY

Three specific types of movie audience were examined, providing an overview of moviegoing specialization in terms of film types, exhibition forms, and film experiences. The art film audience is a devoted one. Also passionate is the cult film audience. Relatively recent in development, the cult film is not the kind of movie one can set out to make. The audience identifies and determines which films will or will not attain cult status. Compared to the two other audiences analyzed in this chapter, drive-in moviegoers seem to be less *film* fans than fans of the form of movie consumption.

CHAPTER SIX

Movies and Attitudes

his chapter discusses people's attitudes toward movies and the effect of movies on attitudes toward a variety of referents. An understanding of people's attitudes toward movies helps advance our knowledge of why people go to them and what accounts for shifting (or stable) patterns of attendance. A social responsibility perspective argues that understanding effects of movies on viewers' attitudes toward various social groups, for instance, is a necessary prerequisite to formulating policy to regulate movies.

THE CONCEPT OF ATTITUDE

Writers as early as 1918 have defined social psychology as the scientific study of attitudes.[1] Our everyday conversation is filled with direct and indirect references to the concept of attitude. We speak of having a negative attitude toward work or school, for example. The expression of attitude is pervasive.

Attitudes are learned through direct and indirect experience.[2] In other words, our attitudes are not innate—we are not born with them. An understanding of an individual's attitudes helps explain the individual's behavior.

Because attitudes can be measured and articulated, we are able to move beyond such spurious and meaningless concepts as "instinct" as an explanation for behavior.[3] An attitude's influence is not simply a direction to respond in some way; rather, the attitude provides order, coherence, and consistency of response.

Because they are acquired through experience, attitudes are relatively persistent and enduring. This does not mean, of course, that change is never possible. But it rarely occurs as the result of a single stimulus. The practical consequence of this attribute of attitudes is that "by changing people's underlying attitudes, it should be possible to produce long-lasting rather than transient changes in behavior."[4]

Attitudes vary in direction and intensity, which can be thought of as two interrelated continua.[5] *Direction* can be thought of as a line with the endpoints labeled "like" and "dislike" or "favorable" and "unfavorable." *Intensity* can be viewed as a continuum with endpoints labeled "strong" and "weak." The concepts interact with each other. Hence, we speak of being moderately (intensity) in favor (direction) of cigar smoking.

Attitudes develop and change because they function as the means to satisfy an individual's needs and/or to achieve a goal.[6] Attitudes that help achieve desired goals and avoid undesirable ones are viewed as serving the adjustment, instrumental, utilitarian, or adaptive function; attitudes that help preserve the self in relation to others from unacceptable or intolerable thoughts, experiences, or desires are viewed as serving the ego-defensive function. A contrasting position, preservation of self-identity and self-image without regard to others, is the value-expressive or self-realizing function of attitudes. Lastly, the knowledge or economy function of attitudes serves to satisfy needs for understanding, consistency, stability, organization, and clarity.

Three other dimensions are involved: affect, cognition, and behavior. *Affect* refers to the individual's emotional response (feeling) to the attitude referent; *cognition* refers to beliefs or factual knowledge (thinking) about the referent; and *behavior* concerns the individual's overt actions (acting) toward the referent. The consistency attribute of attitudes suggests that for any given attitude referent, these three dimensions are likely to be in alignment. Of course, this is not always so, as we know but perhaps don't like to acknowledge.

Of these three, the relationship between attitude and behavior is the most controversial. Does attitude cause behavior or does behavior cause attitude? If, for instance, you have ever purchased a product, had second thoughts about the purchase afterward, and then rationalized why your choice was a good one, you have experienced the behavior-causes-attitude approach. To further complicate things, a third contingent of scientists posits a reciprocal-causation hypothesis.[7]

The attitude-behavior discrepancy is nearly as old as the study of attitudes itself. A classic study that purports to demonstrate that attitudes do not always predict behaviors is the one done in 1934 by Richard LaPiere. LaPiere accompanied a young Chinese couple on a lengthy trip in the United States to see how the proprietors and staff of restaurants and hotels would respond to the couple's request for food and lodging. At the time of the study, sentiment toward Chinese in the United States was not favorable. The couple stopped at 251 establishments and was refused service only once. Several months after the trip, LaPiere wrote to the managers of the places the Chinese couple had visited, asking them whether they would accept Asians as guests: 92 percent said they would *not.* LaPiere concluded that because the actual behavior of the managers had differed remarkably and consistently from their written responses, the prediction that attitude governs behavior was flawed.[8]

Does such research as LaPiere's invalidate the hypothesis that attitudes cause behavior? Donald Campbell argues that it does not, maintaining that attitudes should be related to *patterns* of behavior rather than to one particular instance. Expressing negative responses by mail, as in LePiere's study, is easy, while rejecting the Chinese couple who stand before you is difficult. Inconsistency, according to Campbell, would be demonstrated only if the managers had responded in their letters that they would accept Asians at their establishments but had refused them in person. Campbell suggests that rather than measuring one instance of attitude–behavior, researchers should study the trends and patterns of attitude–behavior over time.[9]

ATTITUDE TOWARD MOVIES

Measuring and understanding people's attitudes toward movies presents challenges on several levels. Attitudes are abstractions; we cannot physically observe attitudes themselves. Variables of attitude measurement include the design, method, and interpretation of attitudinal data. Assuming that accurate quantitative measurement is possible, a second problem is the attitude referent—in this case, movies, which come in a multitude of forms. When asking about people's attitudes toward movies, we need to consider the many ways that movies might be conceptualized: as an art form (elite or popular), as an entertainment medium, as a pastime, and so forth. And we need to consider the many film genres and their specialized audiences.

The Censorship Movement

Interest in people's attitudes toward movies influenced the conduct and direction of the broader study of mass communication. Attempts to restrict and control movies and their content began virtually with the first frame. A tide of concern and moral outrage over the alleged evils perpetrated by this menace to the masses swelled as the medium moved into its second quarter-century. But what kept the advocates of censorship from achieving their goal was the lack of evidence for their arguments. Emotionally loaded, experiential, anecdotal, and idiosyncratic expressions of opinion about the harmful effects of movies were not enough to compel or justify such decisive action as censorship.

One person who recognized the evidential shortcomings of the arguments for censorship was the Reverend William H. Short, the executive director of the pro-censorship National Committee for Study of Social Values in Motion

Pictures, later renamed the Motion Picture Research Council.[10] In 1928, Short created a 400-page document filled with seemingly every statement ever written or uttered that pointed out the evils of movies. However, he recognized that these denunciations lacked the "adequate and well-authenticated basis in fact" necessary to promulgate policy to control movies. To realize his goal of national censorship of the movies, Short petitioned for and received a $200,000 grant from the Payne Fund, a private philanthropic foundation, to sponsor research supervised by the Motion Picture Research Council and conducted by prominent scientists.

The research addressed two aspects: the content of movies along with the size and composition of their audiences and, second, the effects of movie content on audiences. The initial purpose of the Payne Fund studies was "the development of a national policy concerning motion pictures." The caution exercised by most of the scientists when reporting their results was for naught, since the entire project had been initiated and shaped by Short's "special needs and goals: to get the goods on the movies, to nail them to the wall." Mark A. May, one Payne Fund researcher, verified this observation, stating that Short had "threatened to withhold [May's] study from publication" because it did not come out strongly against the film industry and that Short "was really out to damn the movies straight away to hell!"[11]

A popular summary volume to the Payne Fund research, written by journalist Henry James Forman and titled *Our Movie Made Children,* can be seen as William Short's final attempt to sharpen the ax he was grinding. Forman focused selectively on portions of the attitude research to draw his conclusions. At several points he introduced the tabula rasa argument: that children entered the theater as clean slates ready to be marked by movies.[12] Short and Forman were successful; the film industry progressively strengthened its self-regulatory policies.

Development of an Attitude-Toward-Movies Scale

A scale for measuring attitudes toward movies resulted from the work of L. L. Thurstone, one of the researchers on the Payne Fund project.[13] How he constructed the scale is important to an understanding of its validity and precision.

Thurstone first gathered opinion statements about movies from the existing literature on movies and by questioning students. Then 25 people who had been trained in Thurstone's method for attitude measurement evaluated each opinion statement individually as to its degree of favorableness or unfavorableness toward movies. The raters placed each statement in one of 11 piles ranging from "most strongly in favor of the movies," through "neutral," to "most strongly against the movies." The next steps in the process involved 200 people, who further sorted the statements using the same 11-pile procedure. Eventually the initially large number of statements was reduced to a set of 40 that made up the final attitude scale. Respondents indicated their agreement with each of the 40 items with a check mark, their disagreement with an X.

The scale offered the advantage of mathematical precision. By tabulating a person's responses and using the weighted scale values, the individual's attitude toward movies could be summarized. Though other approaches to measurement have been developed for attitudes toward things other than movies, Thurstone's scale has remained the standard for motion pictures.[14]

Research on Attitude Toward Movies

A frequently cited study titled "The Attitude of High School Students Toward Motion Pictures," sponsored by the National Committee for Better Films and published in 1923, is actually quite a bit more (as well as quite a bit less) than strictly an attitude analysis. A questionnaire distributed in 200 schools as part of an English exercise sought such data as frequency of movie attendance, preferences for various story types and performers, and when and with whom attendance occurred. A *Survey* magazine article stated that the researcher had studied the attitude of high school students "forwards, backwards and criss-cross" and concluded: "The current motion picture has not carried high school pupils off their feet—indeed it apparently must show considerable advance in art, taste, and wholesomeness before it can command their unqualified appreciation and support."[15] This conclusion is not really supported by the data.

The study's sponsor, which later became known as the Better Film National Council, had been established by the National Board of Review, itself a film industry–sponsored organization, which may suggest at least the possibility of biased results.[16] We might suspect, for instance, that the industry would not welcome study results indicating a mania for movies among young people, for fear of further fanning the calls for control. This statement suggests a powerful-effects model of mass communication at a time when mass-communication theory and research had shifted to a limited-effects posture. The key findings reported were a favorable, "but not very favorable" (approaching the neutral position), attitude toward movies; older students were more favorably disposed than younger ones; and males held a more favorable attitude toward movies than females, especially at the college level.

Since that 1923 study, not many researchers have tried to measure audience attitude toward movies.[17] The few who have found that males express a more favorable attitude toward movies than females. All but one of the studies, however, used samples composed of more males than females. In this instance the attitude-behavior link is clear: The literature on moviegoing has long reported that men attend movies somewhat more often than women. However, we cannot conclude that such attitude differences exist for all men and all women, because all the attitude studies involved students.[18]

Perhaps more important than attitude differences by gender is the apparent shift in attitude toward movies over time. The word *apparent* must be stressed, for several reasons: (1) Only a few such studies have been conducted. (2) They are rather widely separated in time. (3) The samples responding are extremely homogeneous. Attitude toward film has shifted from a favorable (1933) to a more tepid (1952 and 1962), and, finally, a slightly unfavorable

(1977 and 1982) position. In 1930, the United States had a population of 123 million and weekly movie attendance averaged 90 million; by 1970, the population was 203 million and movie attendance had dropped to 15 million.[19] But we cannot be certain whether an increasingly unfavorable attitude toward movies resulted in diminished attendance or the other way around. Certainly attitudes are influenced by a variety of factors, as is frequency of moviegoing. Disenchantment with movies may have resulted from the rise in competing leisure activities. The increased costs of moviegoing may have affected behavior and attitudes. People may go less and expect more from movies when they have to pay more, and if their expectations are not met, a less favorable attitude may result.

One attempt to link people's attitudes toward movies with their behaviors was a 1965 study that sought to determine how the attitudes of a group of parents related to how they monitored and controlled their children's exposure to movies and TV. The parents expressed positive evaluations for movie and TV fare that reinforced "traditional" moral and ethical values; most parents also expressed concern about and an unfavorable attitude toward horror, crime, and adult drama. But a negative attitude did not necessarily translate to parental action. Despite their concerns about certain kinds of movie and TV fare and their attempts to supervise their own children's exposure to it, the parents expressed a sense of helplessness in promoting any change in the industry. Government intervention was viewed by the parents as the means to bring about changes in programming. The parents especially favored the establishment and legal enforcement of a movie classification system (which did go into effect three years later).[20]

MOVIES' IMPACT ON ATTITUDE AND BEHAVIOR

As we have seen, various reformers argued that movies, with their captivating power, were capable of injuring innocent, unsuspecting viewers; movies could pervert people's thoughts and behavior. But a second group turned this negative-effects argument on its head, asserting that if, indeed, movies were so powerful, why not channel that power in a positive direction? Why not use movies as the means to achieve socially desirable ends?

Around the time of the Payne Fund research, reports from scientists and educators from around the world were being published attesting to motion pictures' instructional value.[21] In particular, scientists argued that films in the classroom had beneficial educational outcomes. Later researchers conducted examinations of the attitudinal impact of motion pictures on various facets of education.[22]

The Movies' Special Capacity for Harm

The very newness of the medium at the turn of the century served as a source of apprehension for many. The question of attitude change as a result of exposure to movies was raised almost immediately. (As virtually every mass medium was introduced and became widely adopted, similar fears were expressed; usually such fears are not allayed until a new "villain" arrives.) Certain qualities of the medium were identified that endowed films with persuasive powers unmatched by the other media of the time.

In general, those who believed that movies had a special capacity for harm relied on two perspectives: (1) the physical context of the viewing experience and the associated screen images and (2) the motives people have for movie attendance and their expectations about movies. A scenario from 1942 about the expectations radio listeners bring with them to that experience is instructive:

> In return for whatever satisfaction you seek in each [radio] program, you specifically agree to give the broadcaster a shot at influencing you. You don't tune in a station to be sold a White Owl cigar or a Lucky Strike cigarette. But you do agree to let the broadcasters try to sell you for so many minutes, in return for so many more minutes of Raymond Gram Swing or Clifton Fadiman.[23]

Radio audiences expected the sales pitch and could muster their defenses against this form of persuasion. The same cannot be said for moviegoers. The persuasion process for film is sneaky. We may attend movies expecting to be entertained or to appreciate an artist's work. That we do not expect to be persuaded and go through a change of mind makes us especially susceptible to those effects.

The expectations involved in moviegoing also guarantee the essential prerequisite for persuasion and attitude change: attention. Moviegoers' aural and visual attention is directed at the screen. Moreover, distractions are also minimized when viewing movies. Thus involvement in the image-message is heightened while distractions and the opportunity for counterarguing are diminished.

The physical context of movie viewing also enhanced the opportunity for persuasion, or so it was argued. That the movie theater in and of itself might provoke unacceptable behaviors is illustrated by a 1913 report on Cleveland movie theaters commissioned by the mayor to investigate the "certain evils which seem to be attendant upon motion picture exhibitions." The moral tone of theaters was found to run the gamut, with at least one-fifth of the Cleveland theaters possessing a "bad moral condition." A call for adequate lighting was supported by this example:

> A young girl, 16 years of age, frequented a certain very poorly lighted motion picture theater in this city. A flirtation with a strange man considerably her senior soon sprang up. Soon they were daily attending the theater sitting in the dark recesses of the room and embracing each other. Later an illegitimate child resulting from this association was thrown over the back fence by the irate [grandmother] and the case became a court record. The girl, who had always been known as decent up to the time she started on her downward path, became incorrigible and is now detained in one of our

public institutions because of her gross immorality, which she claims she cannot live without. She says that her present feelings have resulted from the associations above referred to.[24]

The implication, of course, was that the movie environment itself was immoral. The screen images, according to critics, could only enhance an already dangerous environment.

Other elements of the cinema raised apprehension about the influence of movies on attitudes and behavior. Besides the darkened theater were the contrasting brightly projected images that portrayed life in a highly believable and often glamorous fashion, creating a "monopoly of the individual's senses"[25] and sounding the alarm of persuasibility.

One argument advanced for the special harmfulness of cinema concerned the social context. It was paradoxically argued that moviegoing was harmful because it was both an individual and a social experience. Moviegoers' isolation in the darkness of the theater, some critics posited, made them all the more susceptible to the evil influence of movies. At the same time, even the presence of others would not mitigate the effects of movies and might, in fact, simply add fuel to the fire. One of the harshest critics among the Payne Fund researchers, Herbert Blumer, argued that audience members were detached, alienated, and unconnected with the other people in the audience, communicating little with one another, forming a social aggregate that "has certain features of the mob."[26] In the context of the time, it seemed clear that the effect of movies on attitude could be no less than immense; the mid-1930s were an era when sociological and mass-communication thinking focused on notions of social organization as gesellschaft-oriented and the media were conceptualized as having a hypodermic and uniform effect on their audiences.[27]

Despite the numerous flaws, excesses, and inaccuracies of these theories about movies' effects, they found considerable popular support. One Payne Fund researcher, Frank K. Shuttleworth, wrote: "The complaint against the movies is not that specific films influence specific conducts and attitudes, but rather that the general run of movies has a generally unfavorable influence."[28] More vociferous was Blumer, who in his article titled "Moulding of Mass Behavior Through the Motion Picture" stated, "Where the objects of concern are presented vividly and distinctly, where they are brought into intimate and close touch with the spectator, and where they share the impelling movement of drama, they arrest attention, check intrusion, and acquire control. The individual loses himself in the picture."[29]

Senate hearings on motion pictures and juvenile delinquency in 1956 reaffirmed these fears. Despite the lower "attainability" of movies relative to other media, especially comics and television, the Committee on the Judiciary concluded that "in terms of the total impact it [movies] may be said to be much greater" because of the superior technical means of production and presentation.[30] Although TV would soon take on the "special capacity for harm" mantle, until then intuition suggested the more powerful potential of movies.

Testing the "special capacity for harm" hypothesis. None of the early studies of movie audiences explicitly sought to validate or refute the assertion that movies were especially capable of injury. The uniqueness of movies was simply accepted without supporting evidence. Not until the 1950s was some systematic testing of the "special qualities" undertaken.

One special quality of movies was that they presented moving images and hence closely approximated real-life activity. Thus movies were expected to have more powerful and more harmful effects than would comic books, dime and pulp novels, scandal sheets, and other printed matter. A 1967 experiment gathered four groups of individuals to compare the effect of film motion on affective response to a 12-minute movie as well as the effects of moving images on information recall and various attitudes concerning aspects of the film stimulus. The results showed that compared to still images of the same stimulus, moving images were more likely to produce attitude change. When more complex and true-to-life conditions were present, however, the "power" of motion washed out.[31]

Among other studies that have been conducted, the evidence does not overwhelmingly endorse the specialness of movies as a means for attitude change.[32] Further, to argue the *special* capacity for harm implies a comparison among media. But no such comparison has been made.

Research on Movies' Impact on Attitudes

No doubt the most systematic, extensive, and long-term analyses of movies' effect on attitude were those conducted for the Army during World War II, published as a four-volume set titled *Studies in Social Psychology in World War II.* The third volume reports the results of research on two kinds of movies: instructional films designed to teach particular skills to servicemen and orientation films that attempted to modify various attitudes and beliefs of soldiers and motivate them for fighting. Among the movies used were the seven-part *Why We Fight* series directed by Frank Capra, the successful Hollywood director of *It Happened One Night* and *Mr. Smith Goes to Washington.* Results of extensive testing indicated that movies were quite effective in conveying factual information and that the nuts-and-bolts films, together with in-person instruction, were useful in imparting skills. Less successful, however, were the films designed to affect attitudes and stimulate motivation.

But this series of studies involved captive audiences exposed to generally nontheatrical films in nontheatrical situations.[33] What do we know about the effect of theatrical films shown to theatrical audiences on audience attitudes?

As part of the Payne Fund research, Ruth Peterson and L. L. Thurstone conducted nearly two dozen studies of movies' effect on attitude change from 1929 through 1931.[34] Attitudes toward various nationalities, races, crime, war, capital punishment, prohibition, and the treatment of criminals were examined. In general, the procedure involved administering an attitude scale to students in the 4th through 12th grades in school, inviting the students to attend a feature film at a theater about two weeks later, and administering the same attitude scale the day after the screening. For instance, to study attitudes toward war, *All Quiet on the Western Front* was shown; *The Jazz Singer* and *The Birth of a Nation* were employed to study attitudes toward Jews and blacks respectively. Scores from before and after the screening were compared to determine attitude change. Of 14 such studies involving students' single exposure to one film, only 4 showed changes in attitude that were statistically significant; in the remaining 10, changes were in the direction predicted but failed to reach better than chance levels. Attitudes toward Chinese, war, the punishment of criminals, and blacks all changed as a result of seeing a movie.

Peterson and Thurstone also looked at the cumulative effect of movies on attitude and the persistence of that effect. When the children viewed two movies about war that separately had resulted in nonsignificant findings, there was an indication of significant changes in attitude; after seeing three movies on separate occasions about crime and the punishment of criminals, changes in attitude were significant. To test the persistence of attitude change, the researchers administered attitude scales before showing films, the day after, and from 2½ to 19 months after exposure. For the most part, the findings indicated that attitude scores regressed toward the pupils' pre-exposure position, but that the changes in attitude remained significant. One exception was found that perplexed the researchers and that they could not explain: For attitude toward war, the movies had the predicted effect of changing attitude to a more pacifist state, but after 9 months, the students' attitude not only reverted to its initial position, their attitude became more favorable to war than it had been originally. In other words, there was a boomerang effect.

Hollywood traditionally avoided "message pictures"; one movie mogul reputedly said "If I want to send a message, I'll call Western Union." But during World War II, Hollywood produced a number of films designed to muster support for our allies: Favorable treatment of the Russians appeared in *Mission to Moscow, North Star,* and *Song of Russia*; for Great Britain there were *Mrs. Miniver* and *The White Cliffs of Dover.* Antipathy to Nazi policies resulted in several films that examined the issue of anti-Semitism.[35]

Attitudes toward Jews. Two studies examined the impact on attitude of one such film, *Gentleman's Agreement* (1947), in which journalist Gregory Peck poses as a Jew to expose high-society bigotry. The first study, published in 1948, involved a standard pretest-posttest design as well as essay questions. Although the sample was small, those who were Jewish and/or had already seen the movie were screened out. The results indicated a significantly increased tolerance toward Jews, which diminished only slightly when the attitude scale was administered a third time, three days after seeing the film. Responses to the essay questions revealed that respondents "projected the direction of their own change in attitude into their predictions of the way in which the public would receive future pictures like *Gentleman's Agreement.*" Interestingly, this study noted a boomerang effect: Fully one-quarter of the sample became *more* prejudiced toward Jews after seeing the film.[36]

A 1960 study of the same film sought to discover not only how the movie affected attitude toward Jews but whether the attitudinal impact would transfer to other social groups. As was found in the 1948 study, the film was effective in improving attitudes toward Jews and, unlike the earlier report, this one showed little evidence of any boomerang effect. It also found some evidence that viewers generalized the film's message about tolerance to other groups. Though the results were not as dramatic as were those for Jews, a noticeable improvement in attitudes toward blacks was found.[37]

Attitudes toward blacks. Among all the issues investigated by the Payne researchers in 1933, shifts in attitude toward blacks following exposure to *The Birth of a Nation* were the most pronounced. The movie is extremely sympathetic toward (indeed it glorifies) the Ku Klux Klan and is clearly anti-black. Thirty years later, a researcher returned to the same school where the earlier data had been gathered but made substantial modifications to the method: A control group and a revised attitude scale were employed, and only three hours intervened between pretest and posttest (compared to nine days in the earlier study).[38] No statistically significant changes in attitude were found; in fact, the data revealed a slight shift toward favorability, opposite that which would be predicted.

A 1972 study using three Sidney Poitier films—*Lilies of the Field, To Sir, with Love,* and *Guess Who's Coming to Dinner*—found that viewing all three films resulted in more positive attitudes toward blacks among white students as compared to white students who did not view the three movies.[39]

Both the second *Birth of a Nation* study and the study of the Poitier films must be viewed in their historical context. Each took place in the early 1970s, following the civil rights movement. People would be unlikely to express unfavorable attitudes toward blacks in that social climate.

Attitudes toward mental illness. A 1958 study found that exposure to a single film had no effect, but viewing a series of three films significantly shifted adults' attitude toward mental illness. The movies employed, however, were not theatrical films.[40] A 1983 study found that theatrical viewing of the 1975 movie *One Flew Over the Cuckoo's Nest* resulted in *less* favorable attitudes toward the mentally ill. Pretest scores were obtained prior to the release of the film; attitude differences were compared between those who saw the film and those who saw the film and a 90-minute PBS documentary designed to balance the effect of *Cuckoo's Nest.* The attitudinal impact of the TV documentary "was nil" both by itself and in combination with seeing the film. In other words, counterpersuasion was not effective in diminishing or altering attitudes presumably shaped by a theatrical movie.[41]

Social issues and propaganda. The effects of a silent "radical labor news reel" that compared the worst aspects of the capitalist world with the best conditions of the USSR were examined in 1934. Despite the excesses of the film and a presumably intelligent and resistant sample of college students, the film was indeed effective in shifting attitudes toward a socialist position on a wide range of socioeconomic issues.[42]

A study 17 years later contradicted these findings. A film produced by the German Propaganda Ministry titled *Blitzkrieg im Westen* was shown in a theater to about 1,300 Americans in April 1941—before the United States entered the war. Clearly a radical terror propaganda movie, it failed to shift viewers' attitudes appreciably toward German Nazis. No doubt these results are confounded by the composition of the audience ("a cross section of Harvard and Radcliffe faculty and students") and the introductory talks by the researchers about "some general principles of war propaganda."[43]

The effect of two Works Progress Administration documentaries on attitudes toward the WPA and the issue of government assistance in soil erosion programs was tested in 1938. *The Plow That Broke the Plains* and *The River* were exhibited theatrically and today are often screened in college courses on documentary films. The films were found to be effective in changing attitudes in the predicted direction.[44]

The effect of movies on attitudes toward due process of law was studied in 1954 and 1968. The first study used edited versions of *The Ox-Bow Incident* (1943), about a lynching, and *Boomerang* (1947), a murder story in which the culprit gets away.[45] The second study employed a film especially produced for it.[46] Both studies used printed material to be read by the respondents before seeing the movie. Neither found significant changes in attitude as a result of exposure to films.

Summarizing the Research Results

In general, the research on movies' impact on attitudes has had mixed results. Despite the fears and concerns of many observers, it would be inaccurate to conclude that either children or adults have "minds made by the movies." Nor, in most cases, do they have their minds changed by the movies.

The Payne Fund research by Peterson and Thurstone demonstrated more often than not that movies did not affect attitudes. A companion volume likewise showed no significant difference between two extremes: Nonmoviegoing children did not differ from moviegoing children with regard to their moral knowledge or social attitudes.[47] Overall, the Payne Fund researchers carefully tempered the presentation of their data with the caveat that movies were but one factor in a child's life. The influence of the movies on children was necessarily filtered by other salient factors in their social milieu.

Implicit in early attitude research was the acceptance of the hypodermic-needle theory of mass communication: The powerful, pervasive, and credible mass media conveyed a uniform message to passive, uncritical audience members, resulting in a uniform response. Other mediating influences were ignored. Consideration of the various ways that people are resistant to persuasion and attitude change was likewise missing from research on movies' effect on attitude.

Contemporary work by communications scholars Sandra Ball-Rokeach and Melvin DeFleur provides a useful theoretical approach to understanding how movies might affect audience attitudes. Their dependency model of mass media effects stresses the interactive relationships between society and media, media and audience, and society and audience. This model posits that the nature and extent of media influence on audiences depend on these interactions. As society becomes more complex, as direct experience with social structures decreases, and as access to media systems increases, audiences may come to rely on the media to fulfill various intellectual and emotional needs. Attitude formation and attitude change may be among the kinds of media effects generated under certain conditions, according to this model.[48]

The effectiveness of movies as a means for attitude change depends on their credibility. How trustworthy and believable are specific films? The process of adult discount ("It's only a movie") no doubt functions as a means for diminishing impact on attitudes.

A final consideration is the way people receive and internalize information. While attention may in fact be assured in the movie-viewing situation, attention guarantees neither retention nor what is retained. The social psychology and communication literature provides numerous examples of selective perception. One is a study of the effect of *Home of the Brave* (a 1949 film about a black soldier) on racial attitudes, which found evidence of systematic distortion of the film's message among prejudiced individuals so that they would interpret the movie's message as confirming and reaffirming their beliefs.[49]

SUMMARY

Two sides of the study of movies and attitudes were examined: people's attitudes toward the medium and the medium's potential to change people's attitudes on social issues. A common thread was the concern about the social harm movies were believed capable of inflicting. The few studies on attitude toward movies indicates that favorability has diminished over the years. The research on movies' impact on social attitudes reports several instances in which movies seemed to have a clear effect.

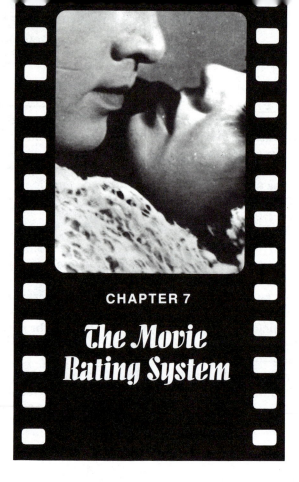

CHAPTER 7

The Movie Rating System

he model for movie attendance presented in Chapter 4 is composed of five focus rings that represent sources of influence on movie attendance decisions. The Production Elements focus ring includes a movie's rating: G, PG, PG-13, R, X. This chapter analyzes movie ratings from two perspectives. First, does a movie's rating affect people's attendance decisions? Second, are movie ratings an appropriate way of achieving the purpose of the film industry's self-regulatory policy? We begin with an overview of movie censorship, followed by an evaluative analysis of the movie ratings as a policy and their impact on attendance behavior.

MOVIES AND CENSORSHIP

Private ordering refers to censorship, regulation, or control by an industry itself or by other nongovernment organizations. *Public ordering* refers to regulations promulgated and enforced by government agencies.[1] Virtually since their inception, motion pictures have been subjected to both public and private ordering. The earliest known instance of movie censorship occurred within weeks of the medium's debut. *Dolorita in the Passion Dance* (1896), "an Americanized version of the 'Ouled Nail' girls' dance from North Africa," was condemned and removed from peep-show exhibition in Atlantic City for its daring display of the star's uncovered ankles and provocative posturing.[2]

Some municipal and state film censorship boards were established by 1910. The Supreme Court affirmed the *absence* of First Amendment protection for movies in a 1915 decision.[3] Numerous attempts at federal regulation were made; though ostensibly pertaining to economic issues of interstate commerce, these laws were usually a thin disguise for control over the content of films.

The film industry's response to the cries for censorship typically took the form of pious statements solemnly recognizing the medium's social obligations and resolving to self-regulate. On both rhetorical and pragmatic levels, this strategy proved enormously successful in averting public ordering. Rhetorically, the industry appeased all but the most radical censorship advocates by arguing that self-regulation was in everyone's best interest. The industry's self-regulation not only demonstrated its sense of public responsibility but also relieved others of the financial and logistical burdens of the continued monitoring of films. Pragmatically, self-regulation presented the veneer of restraint, preserved industry sovereignty, and avoided the economic hardships that might be imposed by external agencies. For instance, if censorship boards were instituted in every state, conceivably any given movie would have to be separately edited for each state—an intolerable economic burden.

The genesis of industry self-regulation can be traced to March 1909, when industry representatives approached Dr. Charles Sprague Smith, founder and director of the People's Institute of New York, requesting that he organize a committee composed of like-minded citizens to "preview" movies prior to their New York exhibition. Within a few months the committee, named the National Board of Censorship of Motion Pictures, expanded its coverage to encompass all of the United States. Later renamed the National Board of Review, it was the first of several industry plans designed to squelch the mounting cries for censorship.

By the 1920s, the industry itself undertook the burden of regulation. Through the work of Will Hays, president of the Motion Picture Producers and Distributors of America (MPPDA), the industry majors agreed to follow a strict code of filmmaking called the "Formula," adopted in 1924. The MPPDA reviewed synopses of proposed motion pictures. Two years later, the Studio Relations Department was formed to review scripts and finished films in an attempt to circumvent the scissoring by state and municipal censorship boards. Then in 1927, a set of regulations known as the "Don'ts and Be Carefuls" were implemented. This list of 36 items instructed producers on the themes and scenes that would either be forbidden or that deserved "special care."

In 1930, these regulations were replaced by the Motion Picture Production Code, which, in 1934, also introduced the Production Code Administration (PCA). The PCA proved to be the self-regulatory mechanism that largely quelled the qualms of nonindustry advocates of censorship; it had censorial powers, including the right to review and demand changes in films before issuing a seal of approval and to levy a $25,000 penalty on those who failed to comply with the review procedures. Thus after two decades of intra-industry turbulence and outside pressure, self-regulatory equilibrium had finally arrived. For the following two decades, little would disturb the censorial stability established by the PCA.

A major assessment of the industry's self-regulatory policy by an outside agency took place in 1947. The Commission on Freedom of the Press, or the Hutchins Commission, as it is more popularly known, was funded by Time Inc. and the *Encyclopaedia Britannica* in order "to consider the freedom, functions, and responsibilities of the major agencies of mass communication." Under its aegis, Ruth Inglis wrote *Freedom of the Movies,* which presented qualified support for the industry's methods for self-regulation. In the preface to her book, the commission offered six recommendations; the first was that "the Constitutional guarantees of freedom of the press should be recognized as including motion pictures." The final recommendation sought to address problems Inglis had identified in her study: "The public should sponsor a national advisory board to review and propose changes [in the movie code] from time to time [because the code's] regulations were devised at an early stage of the movies, and, however useful they may be, they do not encourage the screen in attaining its full stature as a civic and artistic medium."[4]

Still, the movie industry's self-regulatory efforts were headed for difficulty. In part, the trouble that would ensue can be traced to 1943, when Howard Hughes distributed *The Outlaw*, starring Jane Russell, without a seal of approval.[5] More important than such blatant acts of code defiance, however, were the effects of television, which proved to be perhaps the most significant reason for the eventual demise of self-censorship by the movie industry. Because the electromagnetic spectrum was designated as a public resource (and hence amenable to government regulation) and because TV was a "guest in the home," its content was family-oriented. Filmmakers sought to reclaim their lost audience by showing them those things that television could not. Otto Preminger's *The Moon is Blue* (1953), a sex comedy, and *The Man With the Golden Arm* (1955), a drama focusing on heroin addiction, were both distributed without a code seal of approval. Both quite clearly violated code tenets, and both performed well at the box office. Elia Kazan's 1955 film *Baby Doll*, which *did* earn PCA approval, was met with ferocious opposition by the Catholic Legion of Decency and other organizations. In short, the era of discreet films and censorial stability faded out as a directly competitive medium faded in.

The "mammary madness" and social-problem films of the '50s proved to be the mildest of harbingers. Hollywood increasingly turned to more explicit treatments of topics that television would not dare touch: premarital sex in *Happy Anniversary* (1959), homosexuality in *Suddenly Last Summer* (1959).

While the MPPDA and its successor, the Motion Picture Association of America (MPAA), had steadfastly refused all schemes for film classification, United

Artists imposed its own "adults only" label on its *Elmer Gantry* in 1961. The move toward classification instead of censorship was strengthened by the release of *The Pawnbroker* in 1965, which contained frontal nudity, *Who's Afraid of Virginia Woolf?* in 1966, which included numerous instances of profanity, and *Alfie* (1966), which concerned abortion. All three films were distributed with the MPAA-authorized label "suggested for mature audiences."[6]

Who's Afraid of Virginia Woolf? proved to be the last straw. The film went into national release with a "mature audiences" tag *and* a code seal. MPAA president Jack Valenti apparently recognized that classification was inevitable. In the case of *Virginia Woolf,* Valenti's comments in the press release announcing the decision to grant a seal emphasized that this exemption to the code was only for "a specific important film." Nonetheless, within two weeks he advocated the "adoption of a 'revised Code,' actually a new Production Code."

Following the *Virginia Woolf* episode, the MPAA and NATO (National Association of Theatre Owners) actively began discussing alternatives to the antiquated PCA method of self-regulation. According to Valenti, the rating system that went into effect November 1, 1968, resulted primarily from two factors: "an avalanching revision of American mores and customs" and two 1968 Supreme Court decisions that upheld "the constitutional power of states and cities to prevent exposure of children to books and films which could not be denied to adults." A third reason for the development of the rating system, mentioned in passing by Valenti, was Hollywood's historic fear of "intrusion of government into the movie arena."[7] A consequence of the two Court cases was that various film classification schemes came under consideration by several state and municipal legislatures, among them one in Hollywood's own front yard, California.

The events leading to film classification follow the general developmental model of industrial self-regulation. As articulated in a 1941 article, this model "is enlightened industrial self-interest": It serves both the industry's economic interests and forestalls other forms of regulation.[8]

Regardless of the self-interest that motivated its adoption, the film rating system represents a radical shift in industry philosophy related to self-regulation. The MPAA saw the classification system's purpose as to provide

> *advance information to enable parents* to make judgments on the movies they want their children to see or not to see. Basic to the program was and is the *responsibility of the parent to make the decision.* ... The only objective of the ratings is to advise the parent in advance so he may determine the suitability or unsuitability of viewing by his children.[9]

Thus, according to the MPAA, no judgment is made as to approval or disapproval of films, nor is any prior restraint exercised, as when the PCA provided self-regulation.

The *reasoning* implied in creating a classification system was that not all films are appropriate for all viewers. Underlying this assertion is the presumption that if certain age groups viewed certain kinds of films, they would suffer harm. Thus the social *purpose* of the rating system was to provide advance information about the content of movies with the *goal* of protecting individuals in this age group from exposure to these certain kinds of films. The *method for implementing* the system was to establish attendance restrictions by classifying films, according to their content, into age-specific categories.

On the face of it, the process by which movies receive a rating is fairly straightforward. First, movies are voluntarily submitted to the MPAA by their producer. There is no requirement that a film be rated, although in practice virtually all pictures produced and/or distributed by the major studios are submitted. (Some distributors don't submit films that they think would get an X rating, releasing these films with various warning tags such as "adults only" or "This picture contains scenes of a violent nature.") Using five criteria—theme, language, nudity and sex, violence, and, since 1986, drug use—a seven-person board, the Classification and Rating Administration (CARA), assigns a rating by majority vote: G for general audiences, all ages admitted; PG for parental guidance suggested; PG-13 for special parental guidance for attendance of children under 13 years; R for restricted, under-17-year-olds require accompanying parent or adult guardian; and X for no one under 17 years admitted.[10] The PG rating symbol was originally to have been simply P. However, its first public presentation was as M (mature audiences), followed by GP, before finally becoming PG. The PG-13 rating, initiated July 1, 1984, is sometimes referred to as "the Indiana Jones rating," because it came into being following the brouhaha over what was perceived as excessive violence in the PG-rated *Indiana Jones and the Temple of Doom.*[11] The precise age restrictions specified for the R and X ratings have varied over the years from 16 to 17 for R and 16 to 18 for X.

Producers can appeal a rating or re-edit their film or both in order to qualify for a different (usually less restrictive) rating. Fearing that an X rating "would have meant a financial kiss of death," director Brian DePalma resubmitted *Dressed to Kill* (1980) three times before it qualified for an R.[12] Alan Parker trimmed 10 seconds from *Angel Heart* (1987) to win an R. The composition and character of CARA have provoked criticism and concern, as has the apparent inconsistency of the appeal process; there are both an official and an informal method of appealing a rating.[13]

The move to film classification in the United States had been a long time coming. Compared to other nations, the American film industry remained one of the few holdouts in this regard, often vehemently opposed to the idea of classification on the grounds of free speech and the dangers of censorship. In Great Britain, for example, the British Board of Film Censors began classifying movies virtually at the medium's birth. Likewise, in Australia the Commonwealth Film Censorship Board was established in 1917.[14]

Since 1970, the British Board has issued certificates to films in one of four categories that are roughly equivalent to those established by the MPAA: U, passed for general audiences; A, passed for general audiences, but parents are warned that a film so rated may have material not suitable for under-14-year-olds; AA, passed as suitable for persons 14 years and over; and X, no one under 18 years admitted. Freiwillige Selbstcontrolle (Voluntary Self-Control) in West

Germany classifies films as suitable to all those over 6 years, those over 12, those over 16, and those over 18; all children under 6 years are prohibited from attending movies.

REACTANCE THEORY AND MPAA RATINGS

The five movie rating symbols were designed as warnings about various aspects of film content. According to one psychological theory, such warnings may increase the attractiveness of those films.

Reactance theory is concerned with the numerous freedoms involved in daily experience and response an individual elects when a freedom is threatened or eliminated. Its originator, Jack Brehm, states that reactance is "a motivational state with a specific direction, namely, the recovery of freedom."[15]

Empirical support for reactance theory has been widely reported under a variety of conditions. One study, for instance, took its cue from a popular country and western song, "The Girls Look Better at Closing Time." People in three bars were interviewed as to their perception of the attractiveness of certain individuals of the opposite sex. Results revealed that the individuals became more attractive to those interviewed as the amount of time available for interacting with them (before the bar's closing time) decreased. Using reactance theory as an explanation, the author wrote: "In the bars we studied, the freedom of each person to meet someone else was threatened by the imminence of closing time. Thus the threatened options—members of the opposite sex—looked more attractive at midnight than they had earlier."[16]

A study that predates the articulation of reactance theory by nearly 20 years supports it. In 1947, a representative sample of Californians was polled on their attitude toward movie censorship and how censorship might affect their moviegoing. Recall that in 1947 the PCA exercised strict censorial restraint on movies. Nearly half of those polled felt that the extent of movie censorship exercised at the time was "about right," almost one-third said it was "not strict enough," and 10 percent reported it was "too strict." Table 7.1 reports the cross-tabulation of responses from this survey concerning the respondents' likelihood of seeing a movie that had "trouble with the censors" (such as *The Outlaw* and *Duel in the Sun*) and their attitude toward the strictness of censorship. As may be seen, 58 percent of those who felt censorship was too strict were more likely to see a film that had trouble with censors. But even among those respondents who felt censorship was not strict enough, fully one-quarter also expressed greater likelihood of attendance at films that had trouble with the censors.

A 1977 study examined the impact of viewer advisories about movies on Belgian television. The advisories cover three kinds of movie content: violence, sex, and other (for example, depressing or tense theme). In addition, there are three levels of advisories, ranging from the implicit to the explicit. The authors found that the advisories "make the movies more desirable [and,] as

Table 7.1

Attitude Toward Censorship and Likelihood of Seeing a Risqué Movie

	Movie Censorship Is:		
Likelihood of Attendance	Too Strict	About Right	Not Strict Enough
More likely to see movie	58%	46%	25%
Less likely to see movie	15	14	31
No difference	27	39	39
No opinion		1	5

SOURCE: Leo Handel, *Hollywood Looks At Its Audience* (Urbana: University of Illinois Press, 1950), p. 129. Reprinted by permission of the publisher.

a result, the movies with advisories are watched more than the movies without them."

Reactance theory does not predict that the increased attraction of the restricted object necessarily means greater enjoyment of it. In fact, the Belgian study found that films without warnings were enjoyed more than films with warnings. The level (implicit to explicit) appeared to make no difference.[17]

Reactance theory predicts greater attraction (and hence attendance) among under-17-year-olds to R- and X-rated movies than to G, PG, or PG-13 films. The theory suggests that the MPAA film rating system is faced with a paradoxical dilemma, because its classification scheme may produce an effect exactly opposite to what it was designed to achieve.

AUDIENCE RESEARCH FOR POLICY EVALUATION

In general, mass communication policy is made in response to or in anticipation of a particular effect that a particular medium has or might have on either the public at large or some significant group within that public. It follows, therefore, that policy decisions for movies, or any communications medium, must be developed with an eye toward their behavioral implications. The behavioral outcomes must be periodically assessed so that policymakers and others can understand the full range of effects (both intentional and unintentional) that the policies may have.

Awareness, Information Value, and Use of the Ratings

The public's awareness of the rating system, the information value of the ratings, and parental use of the ratings as a guide for their children's movie attendance are all concepts directly related to the success of the MPAA's policy. The research results on these three concepts are a means to evaluate whether the policy has realized its purpose.

Annual studies commissioned by the MPAA have found that public awareness of the rating system has virtually reached the saturation point. The pervasiveness of simple awareness of the system's existence has also been confirmed by independent research as early as 1970.[18] But awareness does not necessarily imply understanding.

Comments challenging the information value of the ratings have been long and loudly voiced. Film exhibitors have been particularly critical about the cloudiness of meaning of the PG and R ratings. A Kansas exhibitor stated in 1980: "In the selection process for films for our screen, I find the current rating system wholly inadequate. G, I understand, that's simple. X, likewise, and R are clear. But, that vast wonderland called PG is beyond my comprehension."[19] Filmmakers have also stated their complaints on this matter.[20]

Sources outside the movie industry have been equally critical of the informational haziness of the rating symbols. *Consumers' Research* magazine reported, "The industry's PG rating has proved quite unsatisfactory to careful parents since films so designated have often been a cause of embarrassment."[21] And the chairman of the Classification and Rating Administration has had to warn that "PG does not mean 'pretty good'" (or, as some wags have noted, "pretty gamy").[22]

The rating symbol itself offers no clue to a film's content. For example, the R symbol will be displayed in an ad or on a poster along with the notation that under-17-year-olds cannot attend unless accompanied by an adult; no statement about *why* the film is R-rated is offered—which of the five criteria used by CARA is the reason for the R rating. Moreover, the public is unlikely to know about the five criteria; neither the MPAA nor CARA publicizes this information.

By way of comparison, the British Board of Film Censors does make this kind of information available. In 1979, the board's secretary stated: "Three years ago the Board decided it had no right to carry on a secret censorship of public entertainment in Britain. As a result we began publishing monthly reports of all decisions taken by the Board, with reasons for classification and for cuts, and with our justification for refusing films altogether."[23]

By 1980, various proposals for more explanatory ratings in the United States were advanced, and some were actually tested in Kansas and Missouri. In these two states, interested individuals could find out whether a rating was due to explicit sex, language, or the level of physical violence.[24] In 1984, MPAA president Valenti professed that he had "always favored the information extension of the system." By 1986, however, when proposals for an SA (substance abuse) rating symbol (to be attached to the five existing symbols) were being advanced, he had apparently modified his posture, arguing that the SA label would open the floodgate to other special-interest groups.[25]

Studies commissioned by the MPAA of the usefulness of the system to parents have found that about two-thirds of those surveyed consider the system "very useful" or "fairly useful" as a guide for deciding what movies children should see. But the surveys ask respondents about how useful they *perceived* the ratings to be, not about their *actual use* of the ratings. Thus the validity of the results as a means to judge the utility of the ratings is, at best, questionable.

Independent research on the information value and, especially, the usefulness of the rating system, though scarce, has tended to disagree with the MPAA-commissioned polls' results, noting that parents had unfavorable reactions to the rating system, only half the parents actually used the ratings as a guide to their children's movie attendance, and teenagers reported that, for the most part, their parents rarely exerted an influence on their movie attendance.[26]

Movie Ratings and Movie Attendance

Even before the rating system began in 1968, and continuing to the present, observers have ruminated about the influence of the ratings on movie attendance. Some movie distributors and exhibitors, for instance, view the R and X ratings as handicaps, because they directly limit potential audience size (assuming the age restrictions are enforced). Others view these same ratings as symbols of forbidden fruit, which might increase the attractiveness, and hence revenues, of these films. Similarly, the G and PG ratings alternately have been predicted to affect box office returns positively ("safe") and negatively ("childish").

One observer asserts that so many producers believe the G rating to be box office poison, they "try to ensure a PG or R rating by the gratuitous addition of 'strong' language or nudity or violence."[27] Jennings Lang, producer of Universal's 1980 remake of *Little Miss Marker*, stated: " 'G' can be a problem. Kids are attracted to a 'PG' because they think something exciting is happening." Lang notes that to qualify his film for a PG, he included some "strong language."[28]

The MPAA has always maintained that no relationship exists between a film's rating and its box office return. In 1978, MPAA director of research Michael Linden wrote: "There have been high-grossing pictures with each of the ratings and conversely financial failures with each, in sufficient quantities to reveal no patterns whatsoever."[29] Jack Valenti has gone so far as to advance "Valenti's Law of Ratings: If you have a movie that a lot of people want to see, no rating will hurt it. If you have a movie that few people want to see, no rating will help it."[30]

One approximate measure of differential attendance at films by MPAA rating is the film rental revenues earned by rating symbol. Three studies that used film rentals all suggest the popularity of the PG symbol. Moreover, all three studies found that G and PG accounted for two-thirds of the successful films; the remaining one-third was, by and large, accounted for by R-rated films.[31] These reports do not appear to support reactance theory's prediction of greater attractiveness of restricted films. However, the limitations of rental revenues as a data base from which to draw conclusions about behavior qualify this conclusion (see Chapter 4, "Story and Type").

But a 1973 study reported that more of the teenagers in the sample preferred R-rated films to films with the other ratings. Further, "teenagers have little problem when it comes to seeing R-rated films": 86 percent of this sample had seen R pictures and 53 percent had seen X-rated movies.[32]

Three studies have used an experimental procedure to test whether or not the ratings affect attendance. Generally, the results indicated that the ratings did not produce a boomerang effect among under-17-year-olds. Reactance theory, in other words, was not supported.[33] The Commission on Obscenity and Pornography's 1970 report made specific mention of "the weakest element in the rating procedure": local enforcement of age restrictions for admission.[34] The National Association of Theatre Owners claims only 15 percent "slippage" in age enforcement, but other reports have indicated a much higher percentage. In 1979, a television station used six children ages 8 to 13 to test enforcement of age restrictions by theaters in Chicago. The underage children were admitted to R-rated movies three-fourths of the time.[35]

SUMMARY

This chapter has attempted to answer the following question: Has the MPAA's self-regulatory policy fulfilled its purpose, and is the policy's method for implementation an appropriate one? The MPAA's stated purpose for its self-regulatory policy is to provide "advance information to enable parents to make judgments on the movies they want their children to see or not to see." But the rating symbols carry little informational value, and research suggests that parents do not hold the ratings in high regard.

The MPAA's method for implementing its policy to protect under-17s from exposure to certain kinds of material has "worked" insofar as film classification has not served to create or promote a desire for "forbidden fruit" (R- and X-rated films) among the age group it was designed to protect.

At the same time, the evidence also suggests that ratings do have an impact on attendance decisions. However, it seems unlikely that a film's rating, *by itself*, would cause an attendance decision; on the other hand, the data suggest that ratings may very well cause a *non*-attendance decision. It can be suggested that the X rating carries with it a substantial social stigma and that therefore under-17-year-olds "self-enforce" the age restriction for this rating. In terms of the under-17s' *desire* to attend R-rated movies, the literature shows no significant difference between desire to attend R-, PG-, and G-rated movies; further, G, PG, and R films were all significantly preferred to X.

Although we find the method for implementing the policy an appropriate one, enforcement of the age restrictions imposed by the rating system has been, at best, remiss. Apparently, if under-17-year-olds want to see an R-rated movie unaccompanied by an adult, they have at least a 50 percent chance of being admitted. Clearly, the MPAA's policy is meaningful and effective only to the extent that it is enforced.

In short, on only one count is the MPAA's self-regulatory policy judged adequate. The method of attendance restrictions is appropriate: Ratings, in and of themselves, have not fostered a desire for restricted films over nonrestricted films among under-17-year-olds. But the literature does not endorse the conclusion that the MPAA's purpose for establishing its policy has been fulfilled. Finally, policy decisions and policymaking that affect or are directed at people must be developed and evaluated in terms of their behavioral implications, and the study of behavior outcomes vis-à-vis mass communications policy must be periodically assessed; without such continual measurement and observation, the policy may become outmoded and inappropriate simply by virtue of social change.

CHAPTER EIGHT

Film Audiences and the Future

"No one ever bought a ticket to watch technology."[1]
—Syd Silverman, publisher of *Variety*

Since the mid-1970s, the popular press has been rife with reports about new communications technologies. *New* is a relative term. Often what we mean by *new* is "new to *us.*" What is new about the new media is their entrepreneurial development, exploitation, diffusion, and audience adoption. These factors change not only how we define film but how we experience it. In 1930 *film* meant celluloid images, viewed in a theater. This definition has given way to a broader conceptualization. Today we have to articulate more carefully what we mean when we say that we saw a movie. Was it on videotape, disc, broadcast television, pay TV, made-for-TV, or at a theater?

This chapter concludes the discussion of movie audience research by examining audiences as they enter what has been variously labeled as an explosion, a wave, a new age, or a communications revolution. Some see the interaction between movies (as traditionally defined) and the new media as confrontational. But confrontation can be viewed as an early stage in a longer process that eventually results in cooperation and symbiosis among media forms. *Sym-*

biosis, a term drawn from biology, refers to the mutually beneficial coexistence of two dissimilar organisms. The confrontational model of new *versus* old media forms is rejected in favor of an adjustment and accommodation process of new *and* old media forms.[2] Broadly, this chapter attempts to sort out what we know to have occurred, what we suspect is occurring, and what we might expect to occur.

MOVIES AND THEIR EARLY RIVALS

At two points in film history the economic structure of the industry was seemingly threatened by competing media. First radio and then a quarter-century later television provoked consternation among the Hollywood moguls, who feared these new forms of entertainment would siphon off audiences. To be sure, the broadcast media resulted in adjustments by the movie industry. But dire predictions of doom and gloom went unrealized. Radio and television proved to be economic allies of movies, spurring their technological development. Consider first the case of radio.

Radio

On August 16, 1922, radio station WEAF in New York broadcast the first paid advertisement.[3] The profit-generating possibilities of the medium brought investors and entrepreneurs out of the woodwork; the number of U.S. radio stations jumped from 30 in 1922 to 556 one year later. Radio served as the technological impetus that forced Hollywood to hasten the introduction of sound to the screen.

Lee De Forest's invention of the audion or triode vacuum tube made both radio and sound film possible. De Forest had begun work on developing a sound-on-film process as early as 1913. At virtually the same time as WEAF broadcast its first commercial, De Forest was producing and exhibiting short, synchronized sound films called "Phonofilms," which featured such performers as the vaudeville team of Weaver and Fields. By 1923, Phonofilm musicals were being produced.[4] Other experiments included the first "music video," produced in 1907, a clumsy attempt to lip-synch a record by Enrico Caruso with a filmed image of him. D. W. Griffith filmed several sequences of *Dream Street,* released with great success as a silent film in 1921, using a sound-on-disc process. Neither the audience's nor Griffith's response to the sound version was encouraging.[5] Despite the technological capacity to produce sound movies, actual implementation was several years away.

For movie producers, a clear consequence of adopting sound technology was the loss of universal accessibility; silent films offered no language barrier, thereby making them understandable by all. These early experiments served to reinforce Hollywood's belief that talkies would never work.

The introduction of network radio, however, renewed interest in talkies. Network radio broadcasting was inaugurated November 15, 1926, with WEAF's

"Big Broadcast," a $50,000, four-hour live program originating in the Grand Ballroom of the Waldorf-Astoria Hotel and carried by 25 radio stations. Movie business was down to 20 to 30 percent that night. "Just to fight back, the cinema would have to use the human voice as part of their entertainment."[6]

The concept of network made moviemakers sit up and take notice. Networks removed radio from its parochial and technical ties to any one community; networks were a sign that radio was here to stay. They meant that radio content could (and would) be standardized: The same content could be delivered the same way at the same time across the country. Furthermore, unlike movies, radio was free and effortlessly available in the home, a particularly attractive feature during the Great Depression; network radio broadcasting became an important part of people's lives as they sought less costly forms of entertainment.

Radio was said to have been "a serious competitor of the cinema in the early 1920s."[7] In 1939, a survey asked respondents "If you had to give up either going to the movies or listening to the radio, which one would you give up?"; 79.3 percent said the movies, only 13.9 percent said radio.[8]

Other sources, however, suggest a more modest impact. One observer wrote in 1931 that "for a while radio did affect theater attendance adversely, but not seriously."[9] *Variety* also was more sanguine, reporting that it was "only in the smaller towns" that radio hurt attendance.[10]

Instead of reacting in panic to the "threat of radio," some moviemakers sought peaceful coexistence. Some, like Warner Bros., purchased radio stations. Others viewed radio as a means to promote movies and movie stars. Some took heart in conclusions about the limited social effects of radio published in a 1927 issue of the *American Journal of Sociology*: "Broadcasting cannot compete with other amusements. Broadcasting does not encourage association or herding, and can, therefore, never compete injuriously with the theater, the concert, the church, or the motion picture."[11]

Radio and movies symbiotically shared not only audiences but technology and talent. Radio stars became movie stars and movie stars proved extremely popular among radio audiences.[12] Despite the initial fears, the film industry not only survived but thrived following the introduction of radio broadcasting.

Television

As Chapter 2 noted, the adoption of television was not the sole cause of the decline in movie attendance in the '50s. Other factors included the restricted entry of U.S. films to European markets (and hence diminished revenues) combined with increased domestic competition from European films (further fractionalizing the audience); unionization and strikes by the Hollywood labor pool; the U.S. government's antitrust case (*Paramount*); and congressional inquiries about Communist infiltration in and propagandizing by the film industry.

The film industry's early reactions to the introduction of television can be characterized as hand-wringing concern by some and casual complacency by others. Harry P. Warner asserted that "television constitutes a long-range threat to the motion picture business." Another studio head, Samuel Goldwyn, argued that TV was not the cause of the industry's woes: "Good pictures on television do not keep people away from the theaters. It's bad pictures [in theaters] that keep them away."[13] With the clarity of hindsight, we can see that Hollywood's response to the challenge of television followed a three-stage process beginning with complacency, then competition, and finally cooperation.[14]

The film industry largely conceptualized the challenge in terms of *audience* and *behavior* as opposed to a threat to *a way of doing business.* Hollywood launched a publicity campaign whose slogans included "Movies are better than ever!" and, more directly targeted to televiewers, "Get more out of life—Go *out* to a movie!" and "Don't be a living room captive: Step out and see a great movie!"

In addition to hoopla, the film industry also tried a strategy that had worked well when radio was the threat: fighting technology with technology. Existing technologies were dragged out of hiding and pressed into the service of movies. Among these were wide-screen processes, such as Cinerama and the less costly CinemaScope, stereo sound, full-color productions, and 3-D—none of which could be duplicated by television.[15] Moreover, the technological strategy was often tied to film content that television was either financially unable or too timid to offer. Thus "big pictures" ("Blue Chip Pix," in *Variety*ese) such as *The Robe, The Ten Commandments,* and *Around the World in Eighty Days,* featuring top-name stars, the wide screen, and sumptuous production values, became the order of the day. At the same time, Hollywood took to presenting movies that addressed controversial themes (such as *Gentleman's Agreement* and *Home of the Brave*) or exploited the "talents" (principally the breasts) of female stars such as Jayne Mansfield, Marilyn Monroe, and Anita Ekberg. Because TV, like radio, had to behave like a guest in the home, it could not compete with movies on this level either.

Eventually Hollywood recognized that the fight with television was futile; it was a war of attrition, and the film industry would end up economically drained. The final stage in the development of a symbiotic relationship between the two media was cooperation. A report prepared for the Theatre Owners of America identified the autumn of 1955 as the "courtship of movies and TV." Such shows as *Warner Brothers Presents, The 20th Century-Fox Hour, Disneyland,* and *M-G-M Parade* made their network debuts that season. The report noted that movie attendance dropped 17 to 20 percent in areas where the programs were shown; attendance increased 3 to 7 percent over the same time period the year before in areas where the shows were not broadcast. The consummation of the courtship, "the wedding of the movies and TV," occurred in October 1957, when TV began airing the pre-1948 movies it had acquired from most of the major studios.[16]

POST-TELEVISION SYMBIOSIS

Symbiosis between film and other media forms occurs on four important levels: technology, economics, society and culture, and art.

New Technologies

The introduction of radio and television demonstrated the film industry's elastic ability to bounce back from the threat of new technologies. But what of today's challenges? Some say that today the film industry is facing a full frontal assault by myriad new video technologies, each vying for the same slice of leisure time cut for moviegoing. The earlier competitors conveniently arrived one at a time, with a 25-year breathing spell in between. Now the industry faces a confluence of multiple technological innovations: MDS, LPTV, VCR, HDTV, DBS, STV, SMATV.[17] Will merely tinkering with technology do the trick for Hollywood this time? Will the outcome be a symbiotic union or some other formulation?

Some observers insist that moviegoing is here to stay. Claims one study: "Every innovation in communications technology has turned out to be less overwhelming in its impact than was initially predicted, with the exception of printing."[18] Milos Forman, director of *Amadeus* and *One Flew Over the Cuckoo's Nest*, states: "The radio didn't kill theater, and records didn't kill live concerts, and I think it will always be exciting to go and see a good movie on a big screen."[19]

But the doomsayers have persuasive arguments. In 1972 it was predicted that with the development of new technologies, "mass communication will no longer mean the simultaneous diffusion of identical messages to mass audiences"; instead, it will be marked by "increasing fragmentation and individualization."[20] A decade later, the new technologies were thought to threaten the "established 'media order,' . . . challenge many of the ground rules . . . , take away or redistribute audiences . . . [and] undermine some of the established purposes assigned to media in society."[21] The disappearance of today's movie theater has been predicted: "Obsolescence is a natural counterpart to innovation."[22]

Whereas the symbiosis approach suggests mutual accommodation among media forms, some compelling evidence makes us wonder whether this will continue to be the case. One factor to consider is the rate of innovation adoption. This rate in consumer markets has been found to be increasing over time.[23] The adoption of cable TV took a relatively long time, but increasingly rapid rates of adoption for other in-home video alternatives (such as VCRs) and delivery systems (such as pay-per-view) do not bode well for the future of theatrical film exhibition.

Another reason VCRs, cable TV, and premium cable services are all formidable competition for theaters is the trend toward multiplexes. Their diminishing screen size has nurtured an audience accustomed to the movie experience as virtually identical in form to television.

Subscription television.   The oldest of the new media is subscription television (STV), which scrambles its signal to prevent free viewing. Signal scrambling was first done in 1947 by Zenith for its Phonevision system in Chicago, which used telephone lines rather than over-the-air transmission.[24] Samuel Goldwyn championed this system as having the greatest potential for generating revenues for the movie industry. Here was a technology that moved the box office from Main Street to the living room.[25] The technological and economic benefits of STV were tested by Paramount when, in 1953, it implemented a system called Telemeter in Palm Springs. This experiment, and others, failed. Best known among the STV entrepreneurs is former NBC president Sylvester L. (Pat) Weaver. Heavily financed, supported by several major corporations and a number of entertainment industry personalities, Weaver's Subscription Television company was introduced to Los Angeles, and, briefly, San Francisco in mid-1964. It too was a failure, in large part because of an emotional campaign launched by movie exhibitors that placed the STV issue on the California ballot in a public referendum.[26]

Cable.   Like STV's, cable television's history is lengthy. Community antenna television (CATV), as it was then known, was designed in the 1940s primarily to deliver broadcast TV signals to areas that until then had been unable to receive TV clearly because of signal interference or their distance from TV transmitters. In its early development, cable simply involved the relatively unsophisticated technology of placing a master antenna on the highest elevation possible and running wires to individual homes. Later, inventive amateurs and enterprising electronics experts designed methods to extend the web of wires by developing booster transmitters to ensure signal strength.

Until 1975, cable TV was more or less an earthbound means of retransmitting ordinary TV signals. Then Time Inc.'s Home Box Office (HBO) began using a *Satcom I* transponder to deliver programming. The decision to lease space on a satellite and, on September 30, 1975, offer the Ali-Frazier "Thriller in Manila" fight was profound. The coupling of satellite technology and earth-station distribution via cable systems created a new two-tiered system of pay television: basic and premium.

By 1988, half of all U.S. households had cable: more than 44 million homes served by some 6,200 cable systems. It is estimated that by 1993, 60 million homes in the United States will have cable.[27]

Home video.   Two forms of home video exist: video discs and videocassettes. Development of video discs began in the late 1960s. Initial interest and sales were promising, but after taking a $580 million loss, RCA announced in 1984 that it was dropping its disc system, and today the home video disc market has all but evaporated. The disc system is hampered by three incompatible formats, a high price for both the player and the software, and its commercial restriction to a playback-only format.

Far more popular than discs are videocassette recorders (VCRs). Since November 1975, when Sony introduced its Betamax, sales of VCRs for home use have soared. Like video discs, VCRs are available in two incompatible formats, Beta and Video Home System (VHS). Today the VHS format has captured fully three-quarters of the market. By 1986, a third format, 8 millimeter, had been developed and introduced. In addition, vast improvements in image quality and stereo sound capability have been made.

Other new media.   Though cable and home video predominate, other new media have also attempted to find and develop audiences. "Drop-ins" and low-power television (LPTV) represent additional broadcast outlets available to TV viewers. Multipoint distribution service (MDS), begun in 1975, is hampered by its limited range (also true of LPTV) and easy signal disturbance; it requires an unbroken line of sight between sending and receiving units. A spin-off of MDS is multichannel MDS (MMDS), which provides for four or more channels by one operator, in contrast to MDS's one-channel capacity.

Satellite technology not only played an essential role in cable development, it is also a means for other forms of information delivery. Since 1962, when the first communications satellite (AT&T's *Telstar*) was launched, this mode of transmission has helped make possible direct broadcast satellite (DBS) and satellite master antenna TV (SMATV). Although DBS's pay-per-view potential is formidable, its high start-up cost has prevented its adoption in the United States as of 1986. SMATV couples satellite technology with hard-wire cables to distribute information within one limited location, such as an apartment complex. In general, SMATV finds itself in head-to-head competition with cable systems.

The Economics

Typically, Hollywood's response to the influx of newer media has been to view such changes in its economic environment as revolutionary rather than evolutionary. Nevertheless, Hollywood managed to adapt and adjust to radio and television, remaining prolific, prosperous, and profitable. Today it is clear that the film and television industries have melded into one; each medium is economically dependent on the other.[28] Filmmakers rely on TV to generate additional revenues for their theatrical releases and to ensure that their sound stages and production facilities are kept busy. Broadcast television relies on Hollywood for product. On the business level, the symbiotic union between the two media is virtually complete: Rather than being economically mutually exclusive, they are mutually nourishing.

The new media are essentially distribution systems, and as such they compel the movie companies to become producers for them in much the same way broadcast TV has done. This creates a business environment of economic interdependence between the new media and Hollywood. As distribution services, the new media have significantly changed the pattern of film exhibition. In 1965, movies generally opened with a theatrical run, followed by airing on network television, and, finally, release to the syndicated and local TV markets. By 1985, the new media had interposed themselves between the theatrical and network TV showings; now movies begin their exhibition in movie theaters, then travel to home video (primarily cassettes), pay television, network television, and finally syndication/local TV. The irony of these developments is that the markets once thought of as "ancillary" to the theatrical market have become primary in their revenue potential.

One clear impact of the new media is that the period between theatrical and nontheatrical release is getting shorter. Thus films have less opportunity to demonstrate their "legs," or box office strength. A movie that needs time to generate positive word of mouth may never find a theatrical audience. Anything short of a blockbuster may well be relegated to "marginal" or "failure" status.

In December 1980 20th Century-Fox decided to release *Nine to Five* on videocassette the same day it opened the picture theatrically. Exhibitors managed to "persuade" Fox not to by threatening to pull the film from their theaters. Just a couple of years later, however, emboldened by premium TV's increasing audience attraction, Universal became the first studio to release a film theatrically and on pay TV simultaneously. Although the film was financially disappointing in both venues, the February 18, 1983, release of *The Pirates of Penzance* was an ominous sign to theater owners of what may become at least one possible pattern of film releasing. Should the strategy prove successful, the product-value criterion of theatrical returns will, of course, go by the wayside, and exhibitors will be left with fewer and fewer films and patrons.

In 1980, a movies-only pay TV service named Premiere, designed to compete with HBO, was formed by the Getty Oil Company, Columbia Pictures, MCA (parent to Universal Studios), Paramount Pictures, and 20th Century-Fox. Although this venture ultimately failed, it was a clear sign of things to come.

Premium cable services now participate in the production of theatrical movies. HBO, which buys some 200 movies annually, began its close symbiotic link with Hollywood with $3.5 million in "participation" money for *On Golden Pond* (1981). Without HBO's funding, the picture may not have been produced; with the money, HBO was guaranteed sole pay-TV rights for the film over a specified period of time (the equivalent of the theatrical "exclusive run"). By mid-1983, Tri-Star Pictures, formed by HBO, Columbia, and CBS, was in operation; it released its first important feature, *The Natural,* in early 1984. (CBS dropped out of Tri-Star in 1986.) While such developments may raise eyebrows among antitrust scholars and hark back to the days before the 1948 consent decree, when the film industry was a vertically integrated oligopoly, the trend toward increased concentration and the formal or informal merger of new and old technologies continues unabated.[29] The broadcast TV networks have found that because of cable's competition, it is economically advantageous to produce made-for-TV films rather than leasing TV rights to theatrical pictures.

In short, the Hollywood studios have seen increased use of their facilities in order to produce theatrical, made-for-cable, and made-for-broadcast films. And in addition to their demands for current product, the pay-TV and videocassette industries have also increased the value of the movie studios' extensive film libraries.

In generating revenue once a film has been produced, home video now rivals the theater. In 1980, sales of videocassettes accounted for 1 percent of a film's total earnings, or about $20 million in worldwide sales. By 1985, sales had rocketed to 34 percent of total revenues, or almost $2 billion. Pay cable's contribution to a film's coffers is similarly impressive. In 1978, pay cable revenues represented about 2 percent of a film's total earnings. Five years later, the figure had increased to 12 percent. In 1982, cable fees amounted to 17.4 percent of all movie studio revenues, for the first time exceeding revenues from foreign sales.[30]

If the past is even a modestly accurate predictor for the future, the new communications technologies can be seen as sources of increased profitability for parts of the film industry. Radio and television did not replace motion pictures. Instead, the new forms served as the impetus for realignment, reassessment, and redistribution of effort and energy for the film industry.

The Audiences

Although the film industry is in no immediate danger of having to fold up shop because of new media, will audiences continue to go to theaters to see movies? An absolute answer to the question is elusive. For instance, *Variety* readers were greeted with this headline on January 15, 1986: "Say VCR Effect on Tix Sales Peaking: Study Suggests Homevid a Phase." Six weeks later, the same publication reported the results of a study that offered a gloomy forecast: "Teens Leaving Theaters for Homevid: New Study Gives Exhibs Bad News."[31] However, Harmetz noted in 1988 that "ticket sales reached $4.2 billion last year, making the 1987 box office the best in Hollywood's history."[32] Let's look at the relationship between pay cable and VCRs and theatrical film audiences.

Cable. In 1983, premium cable subscribers paid out some $2.4 billion to watch movies at home; the entire population spent $3.5 billion to watch movies in theaters.[33] The relationship between cable and theatrical film audiences can be investigated from three perspectives: demographics, motives for cable adoption, and cable's effect on movie attendance. For comparative purposes, four groups have been constructed: nonsubscribers, basic cable subscribers, premium cable subscribers, and frequent moviegoers (at least one film a month).

Frequent moviegoers tend to be under 30 years old; so do premium subscribers.[34] Education and income levels are similar among the premium cable and moviegoer groups: Most fall in the "some college" or "graduated college" categories.[35]

Why do people subscribe to cable and premium cable television? Several studies have confirmed that the most important reason was "for more movies."[36] As symbiosis suggests, audiences are not so much giving up movies as they are moviegoing.

Although research focusing specifically on the impact of cable and pay cable adoption on movie attendance is sparse, some studies find that after cable is installed subscribers go out to the movies less often. (Nevertheless, these reports do not indicate that a majority of the people questioned say this.)[37] But another study found that "regular viewers of HBO, The Movie Channel, and Showtime attended motion picture theaters some 9.4 percent more frequently than the public at large."[38]

Table 8.1

Preference for Seeing Movies in Theaters Vs. Waiting to See on TV

	Frequency of Attendance			
Preference	Frequent (once/mo. or more)	Infrequent (3 or 4 times in past 6 mo.)	Nonattending	Total
Prefer to go to theater	77%	52%	18%	43%
Prefer to wait for TV showing	22	48	82	57
No answer	1	*	*	*

SOURCE: Newspaper Advertising Bureau, 1986, p. 31. Reprinted by permission.

*Less than 0.5%

A 1982 study found that the most frequent moviegoers did not subscribe to cable television.[39] And in the 1986 study summarized in Table 8.1, three-quarters of the frequent moviegoers preferred to see movies in a theater; only half the infrequent moviegoers did.

The conclusion to be drawn from the foregoing is that cable television has had a detrimental effect on frequency of moviegoing. Cable TV and theatrical movies share a similar target audience, and a key motive for cable subscription is to see movies. Although some subscribers have expressed dissatisfaction with cable, at present their number is small. Given the growth projections for cable and premium cable, further shrinking of the theatrical movie audience can be expected.

Home video.   If the adoption rate for cable is remarkable, it is even more so for videocassette recorders. The rate of VCR adoption has paralleled the growth of color TV "almost unit for unit."[40] In 1987, half of all American households had a VCR.[41] They seem to complement each other.

As with cable, demographic profiles of VCR owners show a clear overlap with the frequent moviegoer: VCR households are better educated, have higher incomes, are more likely to hold professional or managerial jobs, tend to be urban, and are younger.[42] Further, VCR ownership is related to cable subscription and ownership of other home-entertainment technologies. Thus cable TV and VCRs seem to pose a two-pronged threat to moviegoing.

Research on owners' use of their VCRs shows that recording movies is the most frequent activity. Movies and cultural programs form the core for much videotape library-building. And a large majority of VCR owners rent or purchase prerecorded tapes: some $7 billion worth in 1987.[43] By 1986, some observers were noting that the number of movie cassettes rented exceeded the number of books borrowed from libraries.

The film industry views the issue of tape rentals as problematic on several levels besides the competition with theatrical exhibition. According to copyright law, once retailers have purchased a movie videotape, they can rent out that tape repeatedly without any additional payment to the movie's copyright owner. This differs from cable or broadcast TV arrangements, which involve straight rental of a film or rental on a per-subscriber basis. Another concern is the illegal duplication of films. When one manufacturer announced in 1986 the possible availability of a two-tape VCR, the film industry responded that such a machine would further ease the already relatively simple process by which videotapes could be duplicated.

The actual effect of VCR ownership on moviegoing has yet to be determined. One position holds that theatrical release of a film helps strengthen its legs in the ancillary markets. Communications consultant Morton D. Wax asserted that "theatrical exhibition anoints, endorses, and awards any picture with commercial value."[44] Moreover,

> a feature's value in ancillary markets is increased by even an unsuccessful theatrical release. Exposure of the film in theaters appears to serve as a "quality signal" to later patrons by distinguishing it, for example, from "made-for-TV" movies, which generally cost less and have inferior reputations.[45]

Nevertheless, such common industry wisdom did not deter HBO from producing *The Terry Fox Story* and offering it to subscribers. On May 22, 1983, this movie became the first major feature film ever produced for initial release on pay television.[46]

Paramount Pictures reported that the videocassette release of *Flashdance* did the opposite of what many expected, boosting theatrical receipts.[47] However, a study for Paramount in 1982 reported that 48 percent of VCR owners went to the movies less often than nonowners, as did pay TV subscribers.[48] And by 1986, the initial glosses of optimism about the symbiotic effect of theatrical film and VCR industries had begun to dull. A study that year found that among VCR owners, 32 percent of the frequent and 43 percent of the infrequent moviegoers reported they went out to the movies less often than before they owned a VCR.[49] Still worse news came from a three-year national survey commissioned by Columbia Pictures: "Many times more films are being seen on rented videocassettes than in motion picture theaters, and the gap is widening at an explosive rate."[50]

To summarize, pay TV and home video are the dominant new media. For both technologies, movies make up much of the "software." On the level of business and economics, it is clear that the new media will easily replace any money lost at the theater box office. The greatest impact on moviegoing by these technologies will be among less frequent, or occasional, moviegoers. They will fill their leisure hours by increasing the already high percentage of time devoted to media use with these technologies. Less severely affected by the new media, but affected nonetheless, will be the frequent moviegoers. This group has the most leisure time and, like all other social groups, is finding its leisure time expanding. But more than others, this group spends most of its leisure time outside of the home.

Industry Responses

Moviemakers have eagerly adopted technology in the face of competitive innovations as a means for either mimicking or outdoing them. Thus today videotape is used for rehearsals side by side with film for instant playback, thereby reducing the number of takes printed, and for editing. Other examples of Hollywood's turn to new technologies include wireless microphones, use of radio to synchronize camera and audiotape recording, the Steadicam and Skycam, computer-assisted special effects generators, and improved film stocks and lens optics. And as they learned to do with broadcast TV, moviemakers use the new media to promote and sell their pictures, offering music videos derived from them to MTV, VH-1, and Night Tracks, for example. The exhibition branch of the industry, at the time of this writing, appears to be breaking from its traditional, hesitant posture and actively seeking technological means to maintain its competitive edge.[51]

Perhaps the most interesting development among exhibitors is "electronic cinema," which includes the production of theatrical films on videotape, as well as their distribution (by satellite, for example) and exhibition.[52] Satellite-fed video distribution of movies is predicted by 1990.[53]

Another innovation waiting in the wings is large-screen film. It differs from wide screen in that it utilizes nearly all of an individual's field of vision. Imax, Omnivision, Dynavision, Envirovision, and Showscan are all large-screen processes that are either currently or nearly available. Showscan, for instance, which is available and has been tested on audiences, uses 70-millimeter film projected at 60 frames a second, more than double the standard frame size and projection speed. But Showscan's developer has reported the studios' reluctance to commit the money to produce Showscan movies and exhibitors' reluctance to purchase the new equipment necessary to show the movies.[54]

Another response by the theatrical branch of the industry is to encourage a return to the theater of yesteryear. Larger, more comfortable, and architecturally compelling theaters are thought to be one way of seducing patrons back to the movies.

Another response to the competition from new media is publicity. During the first quarter of 1986, Peter Sealey, president of Columbia Pictures domestic marketing and distribution, proposed a $22 million "Go Out and See a Movie" campaign to attract audiences back to the theater. Sealey's plan involved a cooperative effort between U.S. exhibitors and distributors: Funding for the project would derive from taking a penny each from the ticket price normally given to distributor and exhibitor.[55]

The history of mass communications shows that the introduction of new media forms forces existing media to specialize as a result of the "demassification" of their audiences. For example, the introduction of television killed general-circulation magazines and prompted the development of special-interest periodicals. Thus we might expect film exhibitors to begin narrowing their range of offerings. A few distinct genres already have their own theaters; perhaps most obvious are theaters that show sexually explicit movies exclusively. Other types of specialty theaters may evolve, including an increase in the number of houses that screen only art or classic films, martial arts movies, and so on.

To summarize: Exhibitors are faced with declining admissions; producers and distributors with a greater number of venues for their product, but not necessarily a greater number of independent buyers, because of oligopolistic control of the market; audiences with more technological gadgetry but diminished quality of content, because of the increased demands made on the production sector.

Thus the production and distribution branches of the industry are certain to endure. The outlook for exhibitors, while less optimistic, is still largely positive. In 1983, an industry reporter predicted that "while some marginal theaters may close, by the end of the century, even if the sky falls in, there will be an irreducible minimum of 10,000 to 12,000 screens" in the United States.[56]

SUMMARY

This chapter reviewed the interaction among competing media, motion pictures, and movie audiences. It was argued that radio and television, although at first viewed by the film industry as competitors, proved to be the impetus for technological advancement. The symbiotic relationships among these media were stressed, and a similar result was predicted as newer forms of media delivery systems are introduced. These new media were discussed in terms of how they might affect the size and structure of theatrical movie audiences.

Notes

Chapter 1

1. Quoted in Lydgate, 1944, p. 90.

2. Babbie, 1979, p. 7; Selltiz et al., 1976, p. 2.

3. Thomas, 1967, pp. 141–42. The denouement to this anecdote was screenwriter Herman J. Mankiewicz's riposte: "Imagine—the whole world wired to Harry Cohn's ass." Mankiewicz never worked again for Columbia.

4. Harmetz, 1988, p. 1 (Arts & Leisure).

5. Quoted in Daly, 1980, p. 90.

6. Quoted in Daly, 1980, p. 130.

7. Daly, 1980, pp. 78–84.

8. Handel, 1946 (*THR*). For a more complete treatment of the reasons for the lack of film evidence research, see Austin, 1983, pp. xvii–xlii.

9. Bob Rehme, for instance, a respected movie marketing veteran, had this to say in 1981: At Avco-Embassy "we do market research, but there's nothing like being in the audience in person. Many companies rely totally on research, on what the computer says, and I think it's wrong. You need to be personally involved." Quoted in Yakir, 1981, p. 76.

10. Ramsaye, 1926, p. 450. As Ramsaye describes it (p. 429), Hale's Tours and Scenes of the World was "a kind of theatre." Patrons entered a railway coach replica, complete with a ticket taker attired in a conductor's uniform, and viewed a movie of trackside scenery. Adding to the effect, the car swayed and bells rang.

11. Hampton, 1970, p. 46.

12. Palmer, 1954, p. 9.

13. Handel, 1953, p. 304; Powdermaker, 1950, pp.43–47. More recently, MacCann, 1976, p. 5, notes: "the urge to construct scientific explanations for art naturally turns attention away from questions of quality." He goes on to ask: "Why don't the euphoric young semiologists who want to codify 'every square research of the screen image' settle down and do a little honest audience research on what those codes really mean to various living viewers?"

14. Lazarsfeld, 1950, p. xii; Handel, 1953, p. 304.

15. Handel, 1953, p. 305.

16. Lindquist, 1969, pp. 54–55.

17. Marx, 1975, pp. 14–15. The question concerning whether movies are a product or a service is discussed in Chapter 3.

18. Musun, 1969, p. 2.

19. *Los Angeles Times*, 1972, pp. 31, 36–37.

20. Earnest, 1985, p. 4; see pp. 3–6 for further discussion of related issues.

21. See Earnest, 1985, pp. 3–6, and Handel, 1950, pp. 12–14, 74–78.

22. Hollinger, 1983, p. 36.

23. Paul K. Perry, 1968, p. 4.

24. See Grant, 1983.

25. George Miller, 1967.

26. Waterman and Glass, 1983, p. 9.

27. Lewis, 1933, p. 39.

28. Information on casting tests and the Audit of Marquee Values was drawn from "Gallup Looks at the Movies," 1981; Handel, 1950, pp. 32–34; Kindem, April 1981 and 1982; Paul K. Perry, 1968.

29. Simonet, March 1978, and Simonet, untitled, no date. See also Lydgate, 1944, and Wolff, 1947.

30. Information on ERIS drawn from Jowett and Linton, 1980, pp. 28, 96–98; and "NATO Demo Promise," 1968.

31. Information on Sunn drawn from "Computer-Testing," 1975; Jowett and Linton, 1980, pp. 96–97; and Morrisroe, 1980.

32. Information on title testing from Earnest, 1985, p. 9; Handel, 1950, pp. 14, 35–45; and Simonet, untitled, no date.

33. See Beaupre and Thompson, 1983; DuVall, 1982–83; Earnest, 1985, pp. 9–12; and Simonet, untitled, no date.

34. See Fiske and Handel, 1947; Merton and Kendall, 1946; Wimmer and Dominick, 1983, pp. 100–103; and Simonet, untitled, no date.

35. Information on sneaks drawn from Garner, 1983; Gold, February 1985; Handel, 1950, pp. 8–9, 61–67; Harmetz, 1983, "The Anatomy of the Sneak Preview," pp. 219–29; Kearney, 1985; and Pryor, 1983.

36. Everson, 1984.

37. Handel, 1950, pp. 46–60.

38. See Cirlin and Peterman, 1947; "Electric Movie 'Reviewers,'" 1947; Fiske and Handel, 1947, pp. 391–93; "Gallup Gadget," 1945; "Gallup Gadget Charts Movie Appeal," 1945; Hollonquist and Suchman, 1944; Levy, 1982; Mabie, 1952; Rivkin, 1946; and Sturmthal and Curtis, 1944.

39. Kantor, 1955; Nicholas Rose, 1954. Kantor details at great length and precision the means for installing and using this method; Rose presents an analysis of its practical application.

40. For a discussion of "preview house" methods, see "Market Research for Film Sell," 1976.

41. See Farber, 1981.

42. See "Columbia Working to Manage Word of Mouth on Pictures," 1978, and Lentz, 1979. For related information on the interactive effect of word of mouth and marketing efforts, see Bayus, 1985.

43. Rumors may be understood as a special kind of word of mouth. Although the causes of rumor certainly differ from negative word of mouth about a film, the consequences are to some extent similar: anxiety versus deterrence to attend a movie. For

discussion of rumor see: Allport and Postman, 1947; Rosnow, 1980; Rosnow and Kimmel, 1979; and Watzlawick, 1976, pp. 74–83.

44. Bogart, 1984, pp. 1, 2, 131, 139.

45. Handel, 1950, pp. 72–73.

46. Spake, 1982.

Chapter 2

1. For an interesting narrative on the history of leisure in the United States, see Dulles, 1965, and Norman P. Miller and Duane M. Robinson, 1963, pp. 22–102. See also Larrabee and Meyersohn, 1958, who collected more than three dozen articles on various aspects of the topic. For a useful bibliography of various leisure issues, see Crandall et al., 1977. My colleague Stanley McKenzie provided me with an interesting example of how leisure was viewed during the last quarter of the 16th century. Shakespeare's plays were all performed outside London city limits because the Puritans controlling London had banned all forms of public entertainment as breeding grounds for crime, sedition, and idleness (see Craig, 1961, pp. 26–28).

2. Parker, 1976, pp. 17–18. The "free time" concept is related to the economic approach to time. As an economic variable, time is viewed as a scarce resource and is analyzed in terms of its allocation and consumption. Another way of thinking about time is as a social construct. In this sense time is used as a means for understanding social change, or as a factor that influences social interaction, or as imbued with social meaning as it refers to specific moments such as holidays. See Block, 1979, pp. 30–34, for further discussion on these viewpoints. On defining leisure, see Max Kaplan, 1960, p. 4; Kando, 1980, pp. 18–19; Miller and Robinson, 1963, pp. 5–8.

3. Miller and Robinson, 1963, pp. 107–38, 164–73. See also Witt and Bishop, 1970.

4. Joffre Dumazadier, reported in Roberts, 1970, p. 19.

5. Beard and Ragheb, 1983. See also Crandall, 1980. Tinsley and Kass, 1978, and Tinsley et al., 1977, offer analyses of need satisfaction as a correlate to motivation.

6. United Media Enterprises, 1983. UME is a subsidiary of Scripps-Howard, a large media firm that owns 6 radio stations, 6 television stations, and 15 daily newspapers with a total daily circulation of 1,515,000 (see Compaine, 1982, pp. 42, 53). Research for the study was conducted by Research & Forecasts Inc.

7. Curran and Tunstall, 1973, p. 199. This theme is developed on pp. 207–11. See Dimmick et al., 1979, for an analysis of media use and life span.

8. Max Kaplan, 1960, p. 6; see also Parker, 1976, pp. 39–41.

9. Kando, 1980, p. 93. The first occurred in England during the 1770s as water and steam were employed to power manufacturing plants. About one century later, again in England, the use of electric power created the second revolution. The last two revolutions occurred much closer together: in the first part of the 20th century, changes in the form of production in the United States constituted the third revolution, and after World War II the use of automation and nuclear power characterized the fourth industrial revolution.

10. Roberts, 1970, p. 23.

11. Data for this section are from Joseph Zeisel, 1958.

12. Ware, 1935, p. 101.

13. Ewen, 1976, p. 25.

14. A most useful source of pre-1930 data is the *Report of the President's Research Committee on Social Trends*. Commissioned in September, 1929, by Herbert Hoover, the Committee was charged with the task of charting changing social trends in the United States. The summary volume of the *Report*, published in 1934, was the product of more than two dozen researchers' efforts and totaled 29 chapters in just under 1,600 pages of text; there were an additional 13 volumes of supporting studies. See also Thompson and Whelpton, 1934, pp. 6–8. On the trend toward metropolitanism see also McKenzie, 1934, pp. 443–96; Sydenstricker, 1934, p 605.

15. Hurlin and Givens, 1934, p. 282.

16. Somers, 1971.

17. Fry and Jessup, 1934, p. 1012.

18. Ogburn and Tibbitts, 1934, p. 674.

19. "The Moving Picture and the National Character," 1910. As an extreme comparison, Hibben (1925) reported that there were approximately 2,000 movie theaters in Russia by 1925; mainland China had only 276 movie theaters in 1934, of which only 157 were equipped for sound, and the total seating capacity of the silent theaters was a mere 85,000. See also Burton, 1934.

20. Haynes, 1912.

21. California State Recreational Inquiry Committee, 1914. Knight, 1915.

22. Lynd and Lynd, 1929, p. 263 especially, and 1937, pp. 260–62.

23. Steiner, 1934, p. 941.

24. May, 1980. Information on cost of operation is reported on p. 36; May discusses the class and gender division on p. 18. The reader may be interested in other historical aspects of the movie industry that are beyond the scope of the present work. The standard social and economic histories include the following: Hampton, 1931; Jacobs, 1939; Lewis, 1933; and Ramsaye, 1926. Two especially useful social histories are Jowett, 1976, and Sklar, 1975.

25. Davis, 1911, pp. 4, 44–45.

26. See also May's (1980) chapter titled "Rescuing the Family: Urban Progressivism and Modern Leisure," pp. 43–59. Roberts called the emergence of mass leisure "the most radical change that had affected the lives of the working class in the twentieth century" (1970, p. 1). The effects of the growth of commercial amusements were not limited to the working class, however; people of all social and economic classes embraced commercial amusements. A 1931 study of annual expenditures among San Francisco Bay region families (reported in Lynd and Hanson, 1934, p. 895) found that professional-class families spent twice what working- and middle-class families spent on commercial amusements exclusive of movies; for movies the pattern of expenditures was reversed.

27. Howe, January 1914. May (1980) provides a thumbnail biography of Howe on pp. 46–47.

28. "Eye Strain in Motion Picture Theaters," 1921.

29. Troland, 1926.

30. Kleitman, 1945.

31. Brock, 1945.

32. Mitchell, 1929, pp. 4–5.

33. Weigall, 1921, p. 672.

34. Wells, 1932, p. 540.

35. Fulk, 1912, pp. 460–61.

36. Collier, 1908, pp. 74–75. Collier's report is apparently related to Davis's 1911 study.

37. Censorship and self-regulation are covered more fully in Chapter 7. See Czitrom, 1984; *The Community and the Motion Picture*, 1929; Howe, June 1914; and "How Children Are Entertained," 1915, in which the unnamed author writes, "It seems probable that a Board of Praise might be more helpful than a Board of Censorship" (p. 212). Richard Randall's 1968 book is perhaps the most exhaustive source on the topic of movie censorship.

38. *Fortune* Survey, 1949.

39. Editors of *Fortune, The Changing American Market*, 1955. Unless otherwise noted, all references and quotations in this section are drawn from the *Fortune* book.

40. See Austin, 1985, for a discussion of drive-ins.

41. See Doherty, 1986, for a discussion of teenpics and exploitation filmmaking between 1955–57.

42. See, for instance, "The Do-It-Yourself Market," 1958; Havighurst and Feigenbaum, 1959; Mead, 1957; Riesman, 1957.

43. "Hours and Earnings," 1983.

44. United States, Bureau of the Census, 1970, pp. 399–401.

45. "Youth Barometer," 1985.

46. See United Media Enterprises, 1983.

47. See "Leisure Times Activities," 1977, and Segers, 1977.

Chapter 3

1. For a discussion of "media talk" in everyday life, see Irving Allen, 1982.

2. Pryluck, 1981, p. 1.

3. For additional discussion on consumer behavior, see Bettman, 1979; Howard and Sheth, 1969; and Punj and Stewart, 1983.

4. Warshow, 1970, p. 26, emphasis in original. See also Stephenson, 1978.

5. Cited in Stephenson, 1978, p. 113.

6. An interesting report on the concept of adult discount is Brodbeck, 1961. To study this concept he used a 1955 French film entitled *Wages of Fear* (remade in 1977 by William Friedkin as *Sorcerer*) about men who drove trucks loaded with nitroglycerine over rugged South American terrain. Brodbeck found that the perceived reality

of the film *increased* with the age of the viewer, contrary to the "discounting" theory of cognitive maturity. But at the same time, this cognitive development should also permit a more complex and thorough understanding of the subtlety and nuance of screen narrative, resulting in greater involvement. See also Freidson, 1953, in which he sought to explain the change in children's film-type preferences and the notion of adult discount as a function of maturity.

7. Munsterberg, 1916, p. 95.

8. Mauerhofer, 1966, p. 232.

9. Holbrook and Hirschman, 1982, p. 132. For a discussion of the subjective experience of television, see Csikszentmihalyi and Kubey, 1981. Empirical support for this view was reported in a study that sought to understand the subjective experience of leisure. The authors (Unger and Kernan, 1983) stated that a dimension they labeled "intrinsic satisfaction" represented the essence of leisure. This dimension referred to three statements pertaining to various leisure activities: "I enjoy it for its own sake, not for what it will get me"; "pure enjoyment is the only thing in it for me"; "it is its own reward."

10. A full treatment of motivation is, of course, beyond the scope of this chapter. For a discussion of broader issues of motivation, see Atkinson, 1964; Britt, 1950, p. 670; K. B. Madsen, 1968; Weiner, 1972; and Paul T. Young, 1961.

11. Franklin's moral algebra is noted in Kozielecki, 1981, p. 96. Still earlier than Franklin's formulation was that of French mathematician and philosopher Blaise Pascal, who created a theorem for decision making in gambling situations (see Heckhausen, 1977, p. 285). John Dewey's problem-solving format is also roughly analogous, although it does not possess the mathematical procedures advocated by Franklin or Pascal. Somewhat more formally, expectancy-value theory is derived from research by Tolman (1932) on the expectancy concept, Lewin's (1935) work on valence, Atkinson's (1964) achievement motivation theory, and Vroom's (1964) research on worker motivation theory.

12. However, one might well decide to select a less valued but more certain alternative rather than risk the more valued but less certain outcome, even though the multiplicative factor of the first is slightly lower than that of the second.

13. Fishbein and Ajzen, 1975. See also Babrow and Swanson, 1984.

14. Heckhausen, 1977, pp. 285, 288.

15. See, for example, Ajzen and Fishbein, 1980, pp. 65–68, 153–71, and Hansen, no date. For a critique of the discrepancy between theory and practice in the use of expectancy-value, see Towriss, 1984.

16. Katz (1959) cited a study written by Berelson himself a decade earlier, entitled "What Missing the Newspaper Means," which offered insight on the value of one mass medium to people, rather than on the medium's impact upon them. See Berelson, 1949 and 1959. Some cite Lasswell, 1948, as first articulating the approach. The Kennedy paraphrase is presented in Palmgreen, Wenner, and Rosengren, 1984. Other examples of early uses-and-gratifications research include Herzog, 1944; Maccoby, 1954; Riley and Riley, 1951; and Wolfe and Fiske, 1949.

17. Bauer, 1964, offers a related view of an active or obstinate audience. The discussion of assumptions underlying the uses-and-gratifications approach is drawn from Katz, Blumler, and Gurevitch, 1974, pp. 21–22, and Palmgreen et al., 1984.

18. Katz et al., 1974, p. 20. We should note that the concept of gratifications itself has been criticized. Babrow, 1985, offers a useful discussion of the various, varying, and often inconsistent meanings of "gratifications." He examines this problem from the perspective of how the concept has been operationalized and the problem's impact on conceptual and theoretical clarity. Palmgreen and Rayburn, 1985, echo Babrow's concern and offer a clear explanation set in expectancy-value terms.

19. See Greenberg, 1974, p. 89; Van Leuven, 1981, p. 430; Galloway and Meek, 1981, p. 439; and Palmgreen and Rayburn, 1982, pp. 574–575. Theoretical elaboration of media use and satisfaction has resulted in two models (see McLeod, Bybee, and Durall, 1982, and Garramone, 1984). The drive-reduction model holds that people have clearly articulated needs as well as firm expectations about the ability of various media/content's ability to satisfy those needs. The extent of GO can be assessed by the "fit" or discrepancy between GS and GO. The exposure-learning model posits that the GS-GO relationship may differ from that described above in terms of "fit." GO may be different from the gratifications originally sought. Audiences have prior expectations of need fulfillment by media/content but these expectations are "fluid" and susceptible to change as a result of continued use, exposure, and the satisfactions obtained may thus differ from those originally sought.

20. Haley, 1952, p. 374.

21. Deshaies, 1951.

22. Wozniacki, 1977; O'Brien, 1977.

23. Winick, 1970. For a brief overview of movie motivation research, see Garrison, 1972.

24. Low, 1948, p. 108.

25. Rosten, 1939, p. 315, emphasis in original.

26. Dennis Rook states that "Rituals and behavioral habits represent overlapping sets: not all habits involve rituals, nor do all rituals necessarily represent habitual activity. . . . Typically, a ritual is a larger, plural experience, while habits tend to be singular behaviors" (1985, p. 252). Alan Rubin has written extensively on the ritualistic and instrumental uses of media; see, for instance, Rubin, 1983. On the concept of "escape," see Katz and Foulkes, 1962.

27. Lassner, 1944.

28. This study is discussed in Gaer, 1974.

29. Moller and Karppinen, 1983. As would be expected given the positive relationship between age and education, under-21-year-olds scored high on the relaxation motive and low on the information and aesthetic motives.

30. Opinion Research Corporation, 1957, pp. 78–81.

31. Projective measures are frequently employed when sensitive topics are investigated. Little evidence exists attesting to the accuracy, efficacy, validity, or reliability of projective measures; see Julian Simon, 1978, pp. 306–7 and Selltiz et al., 1976, pp. 332–70.

32. Newspaper Advertising Bureau, 1978.

33. Kaufman, 1973. Alternately, Dolf Zillmann's review (1980) of the television-viewing literature reports fairly consistent findings that anxious people watch suspenseful drama to reduce their anxiety.

34. Deanna Robinson, 1974.

35. Austin, October 1984 and Spring 1986.

Chapter 4

1. Rogers, 1983, discusses the details of this history on pp. 38–86. See too Katz, Levin, and Hamilton, 1963, for additional information.

2. Ryan and Gross, 1943.

3. Rogers calls this an "invisible college" comprised of researchers whose work focused on a common topic. For a discussion of invisible colleges, see Crane, 1972.

4. Rogers, 1983, p. 11.

5. Ibid., p. 5. For a more detailed and elaborate definition, see Katz et al., 1963, p. 240.

6. Rogers, 1983, pp. 20–22, 163–209. Here we use as the adoption agent one individual. As Rogers points out, the adoption agent can be several people and involve an entire organization. Rogers's model of innovation diffusion closely mirrors the sequence in which persuasion occurs (see McGuire, 1973, p. 182).

7. Ostlund, 1974.

8. Rogers, 1983, discussed "people" attributes in the innovation adoption process on pp. 241–70; he analyzes the five characteristics of innovations on pp. 210–40.

9. Gatignon and Robertson, 1985, especially pp. 854, 859, 862–63.

10. See Kozielecki, 1981, pp. 195–96, 289–91, as he discusses it with reference to psychological decision theory.

11. Handel, 1950, pp. 151–54.

12. Opinion Research Corporation, 1957, p. 21. My research with college students ("Film Attendance," Spring 1981) found that three-fourths indicated they were most likely to go to a movie when there was "a picture that especially interests" them. Whether similar patterns of behavior are followed for viewing televised movies or those rented on videocassette awaits further research.

13. Musun, 1969, pp. 241–50.

14. Karp, 1985.

15. For information on sequels, see Graham, 1985; Richard, 1985; and Stephen Silverman, 1978. The 1985 release of *Remo Williams: The Adventure Begins* was interesting because the title portended a sequel even before the release of the original.

16. See Dominick, 1987 and Simonet, 1987.

17. For a discussion of merchandising, see Lees and Berkowitz, 1981; Blum, 1983; analysis of more recent trends is presented in Gold, June 1985. A relatively recent phenomenon is "casting" products in movies: A product's manufacturer pays the filmmaker to include the product in a film. Sometimes controversial, the practice has resulted in such product placements as Hershey's Reese's Pieces in *E.T.* (after the manufacturers of Milk Duds turned down the "part"). See Gluckson, 1985; Linck, 1982; Marich, 1984; and Rotkin, 1982.

18. See Austin, Spring 1981 ("Film Attendance"), February 1982, and February 1984; *Los Angeles Times,* 1972; Real, 1985; Simonet, 1980, pp. 169–70. Litman's research

(1983, p. 173), however, found that earning nominations in the Best Actor, Best Actress, or Best Picture categories generated $7.34 million in additional revenues; actually winning one of these three awards accounted for another $9 million (among films released from 1972 to 1978). A problem with Litman's study is that he was compelled by the lack of available information to assign an arbitrary rental value of $500,000 to the many films that did not earn the $1 million in rentals to qualify for inclusion in *Variety's* published list of exhibitor rentals.

19. DeBauche, 1982, p. 8.

20. To control the excesses of overly enthusiastic or unethical film advertisers, the industry adopted a self-regulated advertising code in 1930. For discussion of the history of movie advertising, see especially DeBauche, 1982, and also Musun, 1969, pp. 216–31. Haralovich, 1985, offers an interesting analysis of film advertising in the 1940s.

21. Lipton, 1972, p. 227.

22. Ardnt and May, 1981.

23. Faber and O'Guinn, 1984.

24. Quoted in Wilson, June 1977. See also Francis, 1979, and Matthews, March 1986, for additional background on trailers.

25. Faber and O'Guinn, 1984. See also Austin, Spring 1981 ("Film Attendance"), February 1982, February 1984; Gutman, 1982; and Steve Ryan, 1977, for discussions of audience response to trailers.

26. Austin, Spring 1981 ("Film Attendance"), February 1982, February 1984; Faber and O'Guinn, 1984.

27. See Newspaper Advertising Bureau, 1981, pp. 46–48; *Los Angeles Times,* 1976, p. 13, and 1972, p. 47; "Papers Outscore TV," 1975; "Survey in Syracuse," 1985; and "Trib-Star Checks Out Film Fans," 1976.

28. For information on movies and market segmentation, see Knapp, 1983, and Knapp and Sherman, 1986. For an overview of market segmentation, see Atlas, 1984. Dwight Williams, 1971, presents information on media preferences, and Elliott and Quattlebaum, 1979, offer data on media use. Arnold Mitchell, 1983, provides specific discussion of perhaps the best-known market segmentation approach, Stanford Research Institute's "Values and Lifestyles" (VALS) program.

29. Berry, 1985.

30. Ramsaye, 1926, pp. 680–81. John W. English wrote, "While early movies were regularly reported and reviewed, film criticism only became an accepted practice in 1924 when *The New York Times* named Mordaunt Hall as its first regular, full-time critic" (1979, p. 11). Lounsbury, 1973, offers a detailed discussion and analysis of the growth of serious film criticism from 1909 to 1939. A number of writers have discussed and dissected the distinction between reviewers and critics. For stylistic purposes the two terms are used interchangably here. The conceptual validity of the distinctions is acknowledged and discussion of this issue may be found in English, 1979, pp. 17–18; Koch, 1970; and Brown, 1978. Much of the material presented in this section is drawn from Austin, Winter 1983, in which a more detailed analysis of movie critics may be found.

31. DeLaurot, 1955, pp. 4, 11, emphasis in original. Likewise, James Monaco wrote that critics "serve as authoritative evaluators" (1980, p. 36); Robert Albert stated that

a critic " more than reflects interests and values; he helps fashion and express them for others" (1958, p. 271); and John Winge, himself a film critic, asserted "I am a moralist trying to teach according to my ethical ideas" (1949, p. 70). For an interesting discussion of the relationship between film criticism and the economic success of films, see Hillwig, 1980, and Simonet and Harwood, 1977. On the consensus between critics and audiences, see Champlin, April 1980, p. 41; England, 1951, pp. 43–44; Farber, 1975; and Steinberg, 1972, p. 244. On the lack of consensus, see Gillette, 1972; Koch, 1970; McGilligan, 1979; and "Replies to a Questionnaire," 1953.

32. English, 1979, pp. 45, 62. See also Albert and Whitelam, 1963; Callenbach, 1951, p. 356. Brown's 1978 study of 452 newspaper critics of all art forms reports that more critics felt that a function of reviewing was "to educate readers, to raise their taste appreciation" than "to represent in [their] reaction to the work the tastes and standards of the majority of [their] readers." Caldecott, 1982, found that newspaper movie critics viewed one of their primary duties as that of being a kind of consumer advocate.

33. Wanderer, 1970.

34. Austin, Winter 1983.

35. Quoted in Berendt, 1977, p. 31.

36. Shaw, 1977, p. 139.

37. Silvey and Kenyon, 1965.

38. National Research Center of the Arts, 1975, pp. 41–42.

39. Austin, Spring 1981 ("Film Attendance") and February 1982. See also Caldecott, 1982. For additional research on reviews, see Litman, 1983; Wyatt and Badger, 1984.

40. Numerous textbook summaries and reviews of the two-step flow theory are available. See, for instance, DeFleur and Ball-Rokeach, 1982, pp. 192–94, and Lowery and DeFleur, 1983, pp. 176–203. Revisionist interpretations of this theory and its development are instructive: See Gitlin, 1978, and Rowland, 1983. Interestingly, despite the purported abandonment of the "hypodermic needle" theory, which posited the direct effect of the media, attention to the impact of subliminal advertising persists. Wilson Bryan Key's writing (1973, 1976) perhaps best exemplifies the return of the hypodermic theory. For related information on the indirect effects of marketing efforts on word of mouth, see Bayus, 1985.

41. Katz and Lazarsfeld, 1955 (movies and movie opinion leaders are discussed on pp. 296–308); see also Lazarsfeld, 1947. The Opinion Research Corporation's 1957 study for the MPAA also found that movie opinion leaders were younger and attended movies more frequently (pp. 84–87).

42. Handel, 1950, pp. 88–90.

43. See Austin, Spring 1981 ("Film Attendance"), February 1982, and February 1984; for non-U.S. studies, see Gaer, 1974, pp. 66–68; Bose, 1963, pp. 85–87; and Falewicz, 1964.

44. Newspaper Advertising Bureau, 1978, pp. 28–35.

45. Burzynski and Bayer, 1977.

46. A review of this literature is presented in Austin and Gordon, 1987. See also Austin, Spring 1981 ("Film Attendance"), February 1982, and February 1984; "It's Film's Plot," 1958; *Los Angeles Times,* 1972; Mayer, 1978; Owens and Rollin, 1979; and Silvey and Kenyon, 1965.

47. See, for instance, Kaminsky, 1974; Schatz, 1981; and Solomon, 1976.

48. Peck, 1980, p. 44.

49. Wall and Smith, 1949, p. 122.

50. Smythe et al., 1955, p. 398.

51. Lazarsfeld, 1947, p. 166. See also Ford, 1939, p. 107. For an example of content analytic procedures as applied to movies, see D. Jones, 1942.

52. Litman, 1983.

53. Gelmis, 1970, p. xvii.

54. Quoted in Fadiman, 1972, pp. 66–67.

55. Mayer, 1978, p. 44.

56. Quoted in A. Madsen, 1975, p. 130. On the "rehabilitation" of the producer's reputation and role in the 1980s, see Ansen and McAlevey, 1985.

57. Fadiman, 1972, p. 118.

58. Reported by Silvey and Kenyon, 1965.

59. Reported by Austin, Spring 1981 ("Film Attendance"), and February 1982.

60. Simonet, 1980, pp. 164–69.

61. Garrison, 1971, p. 306.

62. Simonet, March 1978. Litman's 1983 study also found that stars had little measurable impact on exhibitor rentals (see p. 170). See also Kindem, 1982, for additional discussion of the Audit.

63. See Silvey and Kenyon, 1965; Austin, Spring 1981 ("Film Attendance") and February 1982. The Opinion Research Corporation's 1957 study also reported the diminished importance of stars. Other reports of interest include Bose, 1963; Carlson, 1963; and "It's Film's Plot," 1958. On the preference for stars of the same sex as the respondent, see Handel, 1948, and "Movies and Movie Stars," 1937.

64. For an excellent discussion of special effects, see Brosnan, 1976.

65. For recent discussions of popular music and films, see McGuigan and McAlevey, 1985; Ressner, 1985 and 1986; and Tannenbaum, 1985.

Chapter 5

1. Much of the material for this section is drawn from Austin, Winter 1984.

2. Tocqueville, 1956; Veblen, 1899. For additional information on the audience for the arts, see National Research Center of the Arts, 1975, which reports the results of a national survey of 3,005 people, and DiMaggio and Useem, 1978.

3. Twomey, 1956, p. 240.

4. Toffler, 1964, p. 21. The importance of a New York release for art films remains to the present. How a film performs in New York is seen by other exhibitors as a barometer for judging its commercial viability in other venues. See Matthews, May 1986.

5. See Balio, 1976; Guback, 1976; Mayer, 1978, pp. 66–73; and Twomey, 1956, pp. 239–47. For additional information on the *Paramount* decision, see Conant, 1960, and Cassady, 1958.

6. Computed from data reported by Jowett, 1976, p. 346.

7. Ibid. See also Twomey, 1956, p. 242.

8. A fivefold increase in the number of theaters was reported by Adler, 1959, p. 7; the 1956 figure is cited by Twomey, 1956, p. 240; the 1964 figure by Toffler, 1964, p. 21; and the 1980 figure by Kando, 1980, p. 149. At the end of 1984 there were an estimated 20,200 theater screens in the United States, of which 17,368 were indoor screens (see Gertner, 1986, p. 32A).

9. Balio, 1976, pp. 318–19. See also Guback, 1976, p. 398. Because the majors no longer owned theaters, their enforcement of the PCA's rules was eliminated. The PCA's power was further weakened by the 1952 *Miracle* decision (*Burstyn* v. *Wilson*, 303 N.Y. 242, 101 N.E. 2d 665 [1951]; 343 U.S. 495 [1952]; see also Randall, 1968).

10. Twomey, 1956, pp. 240–41. See also Adler, 1959, p. 7, and Diamond, 1977, p. 2.

11. Jowett, 1976, pp. 57, 204–5.

12. Mayer, 1978, pp. 67–69, 70–72. Adler, 1959, p. 7.

13. Twomey, 1956, pp. 245–46.

14. Kando, 1980, p. 149.

15. Kael, 1961–62, p. 5.

16. Adler, 1959.

17. Faber et al., in press.

18. Chamberlin, 1960, p. 39.

19. Adler, 1959, p. 10.

20. Adler, 1959; Smythe et al., 1953; Austin, Winter 1984.

21. Monaco, 1979, p. 66. The material for this section is drawn from Austin, Spring 1981.

22. Monaco, 1979; the quotations may be found on pp. 66, 276, 167, and 163 respectively.

23. See Hoberman and Rosenbaum, 1983; Peary, 1981; and Samuels, 1983. Peary's book is especially valuable for the film credits it reports.

24. Quoted in Henkin, 1979, p. 25. See also VonGunden, 1979.

25. Henkin, 1979, pp. 26 and 106.

26. National Broadcasting Company, 1979, p. 22.

27. Henkin, 1979, p. 123. See also Sayre, 1979, p. 64.

28. Lazarsfeld, 1947, p. 163.

29. For additional examples of audience participation at *Rocky Horror*, see Sayre, 1979, and VonGunden, 1979, among others.

30. Jowett, 1976, p. 41.

31. Mast, 1976, pp. 19 and 29.

32. Wolfenstein and Leites, 1950, p. 13.

33. See Mano, 1978, p. 1494, and Bold, 1979, p. 860.

34. Earnest, 1985.

35. "Camden's Drive-In Theater," 1933. The material for this section is drawn from Austin, 1985.

36. Luther, 1951, p. 401; Sindlinger and Company, p. 41.

37. "Drive-In Film Business Burns Up the Prairies," 1951.

38. Council of Motion Picture Organizations, 1954, p. 2.

39. "Hollywood Learns How to Live with TV," 1952, pp. 46–47. On theater closings between 1946 and 1953, see Sindlinger and Company, p. 39.

40. See "Twice as Many Drive-In Theaters?", 1949, p. 44.

41. See Cullman, 1950, p. 68.

42. The 1949 study is reported by Luther, 1950, p. 45; the 1950 study by Luther, 1951, p. 409; the 1957 study by the Opinion Research Corporation, 1957, pp. 10, 104; and the 1959 study by Britt, 1960. The 1953 study is Sindlinger and Company, p. 43.

43. Paletz and Noonan, 1965–66, pp. 15, 17.

44. "Selig Nixes Drive-In Doomcriers," 1983.

45. Luther, 1950, p. 45.

46. Sindlinger and Company, p. 17.

47. Luther, 1951, p. 409.

48. Cited in Gertner, 1986, p. 33A.

Chapter 6

1. Allport, 1966, p. 15.

2. The discussion that follows is drawn from Rajecki, 1982, pp. 4–7.

3. Gregory Bateson in his *Steps to an Ecology of Mind* provides an insightful analysis of instinct. Stuart Ewen's book *Captains of Consciousness* provides numerous references to instinct as applied by advertisers and advertising researchers to consumers.

4. Zimbardo and Ebbesen, 1969, p. 7.

5. O'Donnell and Kable, 1982, pp. 41–43.

6. See Katz, 1960 and McGuire, 1969; see too Maslow, 1970, and Wagner, 1969, pp. 4–18.

7. For an informed discussion on the behavior-attitude perspective and useful examples drawn from cognitive dissonance theory and self-perception theory, see Bem, 1970, pp. 66–69. For a discussion of reciprocal causation, see Kelman, 1974.

8. LaPiere, 1934. See also Wicker, 1969.

9. Reported in Ajzen and Fishbein, 1980, pp. 23–24; see Campbell, 1963, pp. 159–62. Zanna, Olson, and Fazio, 1980, report data that suggests a possible avenue for further understanding and explanation of the controversy. They tested the hypothesis that only people whose previous behaviors have been relatively consistent and who tend to infer attitude from those behaviors will express attitudes that summarize past behaviors and will predict future behaviors.

10. This brief history relies on material presented in Sklar, 1975, pp. 134–35, and Jowett, 1976, pp. 220–32. For additional information, see Czitrom, 1982, pp. 43–59,

and 124–25. Lowery and DeFleur, 1983, pp. 31–57, provide a useful summary of the Payne Fund research, and Rowland, 1983, pp. 19–86, offers an insightful analysis of media effects research, the rise of social science, and the development of mass communication research.

11. Jowett, 1976, p. 231, note 48.

12. See Forman, 1935, pp. 121–40. The publication of the Payne research provoked widespread controversy and discussion in both the popular press and academic journals. Mortimer Adler offered a philosophical critique in his 1937 book, *Art and Prudence*; Raymond Moley provided a layperson's "translation" of Adler's work in his 1938 volume titled *Are We Movie Made?*

13. Thurstone, 1930. See also Thurstone, 1928; Thurstone and Chave, 1929. Short, 1932, also summarizes the procedures followed by Thurstone.

14. For a discussion of alternatives, see O'Donnell and Kable, 1982, pp. 43–48; Rajecki, 1982, pp. 10–28; and Zimbardo and Ebbesen, 1969, pp. 123–28.

15. Perry, 1923. For discussion of this study, see "The Attitude of High School Students Toward Motion Pictures," 1933; "What Students Think of Movies," 1929.

16. See Jowett, 1976, pp. 126–27, 151–54, and Sklar, 1975, p. 325. For discussion of the Better Film National Council's relationship with the National Board of Review, see Barrett, 1926.

17. See Williams, 1933; Patel, 1952; Panda and Kanungo, 1962; Bannerman and Lewis, 1977; Austin, 1982.

18. On the use of college students in communication research, see Applbaum, 1985.

19. The data are from U.S. Bureau of Census, 1973, p. 42 (U.S. population); Sterling and Haight, 1978, p. 352 (1930 attendance figures); DeFleur and Ball-Rokeach, 1982, p. 59 (1970 attendance figures).

20. George, 1965.

21. See DeFeo, 1932; DeRuette, 1934; Greene, 1926; Kruse, 1933; and Nagaki, 1931.

22. See DeProspo, 1957; Lovedahl, 1977; Weisgerber, 1960; and Wickline, 1964.

23. Slesinger, 1942, p. 81.

24. Bartholomew, 1913, p. 12.

25. Tudor, 1974, p. 75.

26. Blumer, 1936.

27. For discussion of these concepts, see DeFleur and Ball-Rokeach, 1975, pp. 133–61.

28. Shuttleworth, 1932, p. 217.

29. Blumer, 1936, p. 123.

30. United States Senate, 1956, p. 62.

31. Miller, 1967 and 1969.

32. See Buccalo, 1977; Goldberg, 1951; Hoffman, 1979; McCoy, 1962; Post, 1965; Ritze, 1967; Schwartz, 1970; Schweitzer, 1963; Utz, 1968; and Williams, 1968.

33. See Hovland, Lumsdaine, and Sheffield, 1949. For a summary of these studies, see Lowery and DeFleur, 1983, pp. 114–47. Capra discusses the *Why We Fight* series in his autobiography, 1971.

34. Peterson and Thurstone, 1933.

35. See Short, 1981, for a lengthy essay detailing Hollywood's fight against anti-Semitism.

36. Rosen, 1948.

37. Middleton, 1960.

38. Moore, 1971.

39. Shook, 1972.

40. McGinnies et al., 1958.

41. Domino, 1983.

42. Rosenthal, 1934.

43. Bruner and Fowler, 1941.

44. Ramseyer, 1938, January 1939, and September 1939.

45. Hadsell, 1954; Hadsell and May, 1958.

46. Peri, 1968.

47. Shuttleworth and May, 1933, pp. 22–24.

48. See Ball-Rokeach and DeFleur, 1976; Ball-Rokeach, 1985; Ball-Rokeach, Rokeach, and Grube, 1984; and Rubin and Windahl, 1986.

49. Wilner, 1951. See also Cooper and Dinerman, 1951, p. 248; Kendall and Wolf, 1949.

Chapter 7

1. Ayer, Bates, and Herman, 1970, p. 791.

2. Ramsaye, 1926, p. 256. Additional reports of this incident are presented in Jowett, 1976, p. 109, and Randall, 1968, p. 11. For a useful primer on movies and self-regulation, including its history and development, see Inglis, 1947.

3. The 1915 case was *Mutual Film Corp.* v. *Ohio.* The Supreme Court didn't rule on film censorship again until 1952, when it heard *Burstyn, Inc.* v. *Wilson.* The Court alluded to the First Amendment protection for motion pictures in the 1948 *Paramount* case, stating: "We have no doubt that moving pictures, like newspapers and radio, are included in the press whose freedom is guaranteed by the First Amendment" (*United States* v. *Paramount Pictures,* 334 U.S. 166). However, the focus of *Paramount* was a monopoly, not a First Amendment, issue. For an interesting discussion of obscenity and regulation of cable television that touches on film issues, see Trauth and Huffman, 1986.

4. Inglis, 1947, pp. iv, vi. For a review of the different forms in which pressure had been exerted on the industry, see Charles Metzger, 1947. Among others he identifies legal, religious, social, professional, racial, international, and trade group efforts to control movies. Fisher, 1975, provides useful information on the National Board of Review; McCarthy, 1976, offers an analysis of movie censorship in Chicago during 1907–15. Additional information on film censorship may be found in Bottini, 1966; Schumach, 1964; and Vizzard, 1970.

5. On *The Outlaw* incident, see Haralovich, 1985, and Jowett, 1976, pp. 396–400.

6. On the SMA tag, see Randall, 1968, pp. 201–4. Randall's book provides the best single source of information on the regulation of movies through 1967. Jowett, 1976, offers useful updated information dovetailing with Randall's treatment. Leff, 1980, provides an excellent case study of *Virginia Woolf.* For further discussion of film classification, see Randall's 1970 report for the Commission on Obscenity and Pornography and Burroughs, 1971.

7. Valenti, no date, pp. 1, 3. The two Court decisions, decided on the same day (April 22, 1968) were *Interstate Circuit, Inc.* v. *Dallas* and *Ginsberg* v. *New York.* A thorough review of the social, legal, and industry events leading to the establishment of the rating system is presented in Ayer et al., 1970. Additional details of interest from constitutional and antitrust perspectives may be found in Friedman, 1973, and Gregory Howe, 1971, respectively. As this chapter was being written, the confrontation between the Parents' Music Resource Center (popularly labeled the "Washington wives" group) and the Recording Industry Association of America continued. One proposed solution to the perceived problem of "lewd lyrics" was RIAA adoption of a classification scheme for records, tapes, and discs similar to that of the MPAA's film rating system.

8. Neville Miller, quoted in Jassem, 1986. For additional information on the implementation of the rating system as a means to forestall externally imposed control, see Hodgson, 1981; Mayer, 1977; and Warga, 1968. For a sociological analysis of media self-regulation, see Best, 1981.

9. Valenti, no date, p. 5, emphasis in original.

10. On the drug use criterion, see McMasters, 1986, and Tusher, January 1986; for a response concerned with the censorshiplike qualities of this criterion, see Lond, June 1986.

11. See Tusher, July 1984.

12. See Wood, 1980. For additional discussion of producers' and distributors' concerns regarding the X rating, see "'Timing' Producer," 1980, and Champlin, October 1980.

13. See Austin, Summer 1982 (especially note 17), from which much of this chapter is drawn; see also Farber, 1972, pp. 21–37.

14. On British film classification, see Phelps, 1975, pp. 26–51; Ferman, 1979 (the BBFC secretary); and Richards, 1983. On Australian film classification, see Strickland, 1977. See also Hyams, 1964.

15. Brehm, 1966, p. 11.

16. Pennebaker, 1979. For additional research on reactance theory, see Brehm, 1972, and, as it relates to consumer behavior, Clee and Wicklund, 1980. See also Driscoll, Davis, and Lipetz, 1972.

17. Herman and Leyens, 1977, pp. 53, 51. For related research on U.S. television advisories, see Wurtzel and Surlin, 1978, and Slater and Thompson, 1984.

18. The Opinion Research Corporation conducts an annual poll for the MPAA, typically titled "An Appraisal of the Motion Picture Industry's Voluntary Rating System." See Commission on Obscenity, 1970, p. 40; and Robertus and Simon, 1970, p. 568.

19. Spainhour, 1980.

20. See Ronan, 1979.

21. Quoted in "The Family Movie," 1977, p. 307.

22. Quoted in Brandsdorfer and Walker, 1980, p. 29. See also "Rating the Rating System," 1977; Canby, 1972, p. 1; Heffner, 1980, p. 40.

23. Ferman, 1979, p. 13.

24. See Tusher, 1980; "MPAA, NATO," 1981, and "Mull Expansion," 1982. In 1982, I wrote to Valenti concerning the results of the Kansas-Missouri tests. The MPAA's director of research, Robert A. Franklin, responded: "The details of the test and the methodology employed are considered confidential and cannot be released at this time." To my knowledge, the results have not yet been made public. Like much of the film industry (as well as other industries), the MPAA is loath to reveal more than is necessary to outsiders. On this point see "Valenti Brings in News Leak Experts," 1975.

25. See Tusher, February 1984; Broeske, 1986.

26. See Robertus and Simon, 1970, p. 569; Yeager, 1971; *Los Angeles Times,* 1972, p. 44; O'Dell, 1973; Respress, 1973.

27. Jeffries, 1978, p. 51.

28. "Modern Kids," 1980, p. 7. Despite such remarks as these, a few producers are convinced that, with proper marketing, G-rated films can be profitable. See "G for Gold," 1977, and Auerbach, 1981.

29. Letter from Linden to me, April 24, 1978. My letter to Linden concerned a research proposal to investigate the relationship between ratings and movie attendance. Linden concluded his letter, "Therefore, we do not wish to encourage your attempting this futile effort."

30. Valenti, October 1977.

31. See United States, 1978, p. 56; Austin, 1980; and Austin, Nicolich, and Simonet, 1980 (for a complete discussion of the study; an abbreviated version was published in the Winter 1981–82 issue of *Film Quarterly*).

32. Respress, 1973, pp. 196 and 191. A qualification to the results reported is that 18 and 19 year-olds were not screened out.

33. Austin, September 1980; Austin, 1982–83; Austin, 1981; Austin, Fall 1984.

34. Commission on Obscenity, 1970, p. 41.

35. "WBBM in Live-Lens Survey," 1979. CARA chairman Richard Heffner's response to the WBBM report was that their findings were a "reflection of the community" in which the investigation was conducted and that these findings were probably not typical of all communities (telephone interview, January 15, 1980). See also Elias, 1970; Fuchs and Lyle, 1972; p. 253.

Chapter 8

1. Syd Silverman, 1983, p. 13. Much of the material for this chapter is drawn from Austin, 1986 and 1987.

2. Littlejohn (1983, pp. 29–43) provides an instructive introduction to General System Theory and references to additional sources of information. Edgerton, 1987, provides a useful analysis of symbiosis.

3. Sterling and Kittross, 1978, p. 29–32, 59, 66.

4. Ulloth, Klinge, and Ellis, 1983, p. 205; see also MacGowan, 1965, chapter 19, and Greenwald, 1952. A parody of a De Forest Phonofilm lecture appears in the 1952 film *Singin' in the Rain,* in which a Will Hays–like character carefully and clearly enunciates each word so viewers could determine that no trickery was involved.

5. Swindell, 1977, p. 25.

6. Walker, 1978, p. 20. See also Sterling and Kittross, 1978, p. 107. Not all, of course, welcomed sound films as an aesthetic improvement; see, especially, Arnheim, 1957, pp. 199–230.

7. Wenden, 1974, p. 170. See also Everson, 1978, p. 290; Jowett, 1976, pp. 191–92, 280.

8. "Fortune Survey: The Movies," 1939.

9. Hampton, 1931, p. 369.

10. Reported in Walker, 1978, p. 4.

11. Beuick, 1927, p. 615. See also Handel, July 1946.

12. Jewell, 1984. Edgerton, 1980–81, provides a thorough analysis of the symbiotic relationship between radio and motion pictures.

13. Harry Warner, 1946, p. 16; Goldwyn quoted in "Study Blames TV for Theatre Drop," 1958.

14. A host of reasons justifying the complacent response are reported by Stuart, 1976, pp. 48–53, and Murray, 1977, pp. 47–50. For an analysis of integration between the movie and TV industries through 1956, see Larson, 1979.

15. For an overview of the strategies used to fight TV, see Murray, 1977, and Stuart, 1976, pp. 48–101. Wide-screen processes are discussed in detail in articles contained in the *Velvet Light Trap,* no. 21, Summer 1985, by Belton, Hincha, Katz, Pratt, Chisholm, and Hartsough. Also of particular interest and value are Gomery's 1985 article on theater television and Leff's 1981 article on Electronovision. For research on color motion picture photography, see Kindem, 1979 and Spring 1981.

16. "Study Blames TV," 1958.

17. Translation: multipoint distribution service, low-power television, videocassette recorder, High Definition Television, direct broadcast satellite, subscription television, satellite master antenna television.

18. Littunen et al., 1980, p. 283. See also Monaco, August–September 1981, pp. 50, 52.

19. Quoted in Kearney, 1986, p. 55.

20. McCombs, 1972, p. 60. See also Maisel, 1973.

21. McQuail, 1983, pp. 223–24.

22. DeFleur and Ball-Rokeach, 1982, p. 65.

23. Olshavsky, 1980, p. 425.

24. See Stuart, 1976, pp. 82–91 (who also discusses Telemeter), and Gross, 1983, p. 70.

25. Goldwyn, 1949.

26. See Ostroff, 1983.

27. See Landro, 1983.

28. See Guback and Dombkowski, 1976, and Litman, 1982.

29. On the issue of antitrust, see White, 1985.

30. Zacks, 1986, and Gitlin, 1983, p. 329.

31. Segers, 1986; Roth, 1986.

32. Harmetz, 1988, p. 1 (Arts and Leisure).

33. See O'Connor, 1983, p. 20.

34. See "Movie Audience Marquee Values," 1981, p. 6; Krugman and Eckrich, 1982, p. 29; "Pay-TV," 1982, p. 8; Rothe, Harvey, and Michael, 1983, p. 21; and Webster, 1983, p. 121.

35. See Stanley Marcus, 1980; "Movie Audience Marquee Values," 1981; Krugman and Eckrich, 1982; and Rothe et al., 1983.

36. See Ducey, Krugman, and Eckrich, 1983, p. 160; Gale Metzger, 1983, p. 44; Mink, 1983, p. 64; Rothe et al., 1983, pp. 17–18; Krugman and Eckrich, 1982, p. 26; Roper Organization, 1981, p. 7; and S. Marcus, 1980, p. 43.

37. Stuart Kaplan, 1978; S. Marcus, 1980, p. 43; Rothe et al., 1983, p. 18.

38. Reported in Auerbach, 1983.

39. W. Williams and Shapiro, 1985.

40. Lachenbruch, 1983, p. 42.

41. Fantel, 1987.

42. See Levy, Autumn 1980, p. 23, and Summer 1980, p. 327; Dominick, 1980, p. 4; United States, 1982, p. 473; Newspaper Advertising Bureau, 1986.

43. *Entertainment Tonight,* 1/1/88.

44. Wax, 1984. See also Litman, 1982, p. 50.

45. Waterman, 1984, p. 5.

46. See Nielsen, 1984, p. 39; Caranicas, 1983, p. 43.

47. See Seidman, 1983, p. 396.

48. Reported in United States, 1982, p. 436.

49. Newspaper Advertising Bureau, 1986, p. 38.

50. Reported in Tusher, May 1986, p. 3.

51. Aldridge, 1981, traces exhibitors' reluctance to embrace technology to the introduction of sound.

52. See Nielsen, 1984.

53. See "Say Vid Exhibition," 1984.

54. Large-screen is discussed by Dowell and Heinrich, 1984; Stabiner, 1982; Stegman, 1982; on Showscan, see Hoban, 1984; Krohn and Lond, 1984.

55. Rothman, 1986.

56. Quoted in Auerbach, 1984, p. 11.

References

Abbott, Mary Allen. "A Study of the Motion Picture Preferences of the Horace Mann High Schools." *Teachers College Record* 28 (April 1927):819–35.

Adams, William B. "A Definition of Motion-Picture Research." *Quarterly of Film, Radio and Television* 7 (1952–53):408–21.

Adler, Kenneth P. "Art Films and Eggheads." *Studies in Public Communication* 2 (Summer 1959):7–15.

Adler, Mortimer J. *Art and Prudence.* New York: Longmans, Green, 1937.

Agostino, Donald E.; Herbert A. Terry; and Rolland C. Johnson. "Home Video Recorders: Rights and Ratings." *Journal of Communication* 30 (Autumn 1980):28–35.

Ajzen, Icek, and Martin Fishbein. *Understanding Attitudes and Predicting Social Behavior.* Englewood Cliffs, N.J.: Prentice-Hall, 1980.

Albert, Robert S. "The Role of the Critic in Mass Communications: I. A Theoretical Analysis." *Journal of Social Psychology* 48 (November 1958):265–74.

Albert, Robert S., and Peter Whitelam. "The Role of the Critic in Mass Communications: II. The Critic Speaks." *Journal of Social Psychology* 60 (1963):153–56.

Aldridge, Henry B. "New York Theatres and Film Exhibition in America." Paper presented at the Society for Cinema Studies conference, April 1981, New York City.

Allen, Irving Lewis. "Talking About Media Experiences: Everyday Life as Popular Culture." *Journal of Popular Culture* 16 (Winter 1982):106–15.

Allen, Robert C. "Contra the Chaser Theory." *Wide Angle* 3 (Spring 1979):4–11.

———. *Vaudeville and Film 1895–1915: A Study of Media Interaction.* New York: Arno Press, 1980.

———. "Looking at 'Another Look at the "Chaser Theory." ' " *Studies in Visual Communication* 10 (Fall 1984):45–50.

Allen, Robert C., and Douglas Gomery. *Film History: Theory and Practice.* New York: Knopf, 1985.

Allport, Gordon W. "Attitudes." In *A Handbook of Social Psychology,* vol. 2., edited by C. A. Murchison. New York: Russell & Russell, 1935.

———. "Attitudes in the History of Social Psychology." In *Attitudes,* edited by Marie Jahoda and Neil Warren, pp. 15–21. Baltimore: Penguin, 1966.

Allport, Gordon W., and Leo J. Postman. *The Psychology of Rumor.* New York: Holt, Rinehart and Winston, 1947.

"American Films and Foreign Audiences." *Film Comment* 3 (Summer 1965):50.

"Analysis Self-Xs Pic; Ducks MPAA." *Variety,* Aug. 13, 1980, p. 4.

Anast, Philip. "Differential Movie Appeals as Correlates of Attendance." *Journalism Quarterly* 44 (Spring 1967):86–90.

Ansen, David, with Peter McAlevey. "The Producer Is King Again." *Newsweek,* May 20, 1985, pp. 84–89.

Applbaum, Ronald L. "Subject Selection in Speech Communication Research: A Reexamination." *Communication Quarterly* 33 (Fall 1985):227–35.

Arndt, Johan, and Frederick E. May. "The Hypothesis of a Dominance Hierarchy of Information Sources." *Journal of the Academy of Marketing Science* 9 (Fall 1981):337–50.

Arnheim, Rudolf. *Film as Art.* Berkeley: University of California Press, 1957.

Atkinson, John W. *An Introduction to Motivation.* Princeton, N.J.: Van Nostrand, 1964.

Atlas, James. "Beyond Demographics." *Atlantic Monthly,* October 1984, pp. 49–58.

"The Attitude of High School Students Toward Motion Pictures." *Survey* 51 (Dec. 15, 1933):338.

Auerbach, Alexander. "New Firm Distributes Only Family Fare." *Boxoffice,* September 1981, p. 16.

———. "Despite the Christmas Season Chill, Circuit Heads Remain Optimistic." *Boxoffice,* April 1982, pp. 22–25.

———. "Pay Cable Helps Theatre Boxoffice, Market Study Shows." *Boxoffice,* July 1983, pp. 20–21.

———. "Supershow '83 Bullish on Future of Exhibition." *Boxoffice,* January 1984, pp. 10–12.

Augustin, Vernon E. "Motion Picture Preferences." *Journal of Delinquency* 7 (1927):206–9.

Austin, Bruce A. "The Influence of the MPAA's Film-Rating System on Motion Picture Attendance: A Pilot Study." *Journal of Psychology* 106 (September 1980):91–99.

———. "Rating the Movies." *Journal of Popular Film and Television* 7 (no. 4, 1980):384–99.

———. "MPAA Film Rating Influence on Stated Likelihood of High School Student Film Attendance: A Test of Reactance Theory." Ph.D. dissertation, Temple University, 1981.

———. "Film Attendance: Why College Students Chose to See Their Most Recent Film." *Journal of Popular Film and Television* 9 (Spring 1981):43–49.

———. "Portrait of a Cult Film Audience: *The Rocky Horror Picture Show.*" *Journal of Communication* 31 (Spring 1981):43–54.

———. "The Salience of Selected Variables on Choice for Movie Attendance Among High School Students." Paper presented at the Western Speech Communication Association conference, February 1982, Denver.

———. "A Factor Analytic Study of Attitudes Toward Motion Pictures." *Journal of Social Psychology* 117 (August 1982):211–17.

———. "G-PG-R-X: The Purpose, Promise and Performance of the Movie Rating System." *Journal of Arts Management and Law* 12 (Summer 1982):51–74.

———. "People's Attitudes Toward Motion Pictures." In *Film/Culture: Explorations of Cinema in Its Social Context,* edited by Sari Thomas, pp. 222–36. Metuchen, N.J.: Scarecrow Press, 1982.

———. "MPAA Film Ratings and Film Attendance: A Test of Reactance Theory." *Mass Comm Review* 10 (Winter & Spring 1982–83):29–34.

———. "Critics' and Consumers' Evaluation of Motion Pictures: A Longitudinal Test of the Taste Culture and Elitist Hypotheses." *Journal of Popular Film and Television* 10 (Winter 1983):156–67.

———. *The Film Audience: An International Bibliography of Research with Annotations and an Essay.* Metuchen, N.J.: Scarecrow Press, 1983.

————. "But Why *This* Movie?" *Boxoffice*, February 1984, pp. 16–18.

————. "Attitudes Toward Movies: A Literature Review and Case Study." *Media Information Australia*, no. 32 (May 1984), pp. 43–50.

————. "Motivations for Movie Attendance." *Boxoffice*, October 1984, pp. 13–16.

————. "The Effect of Movie Ratings on Movie Attendance." *Kentucky Journal of Communication Arts* 10 (Fall 1984):27–32.

————. "Portrait of an Art Film Audience." *Journal of Communication* 34 (Winter 1984):74–87.

————. "The Development and Decline of the Drive-in Movie Theater." In *Current Research in Film: Audiences, Economics, and Law,* vol. 1, edited by Bruce A. Austin, pp. 59–91. Norwood, N.J.: Ablex, 1985.

————. "Motivations for Movie Attendance." *Communication Quarterly* 34 (Spring 1986):115–26.

————. "The Film Industry, Its Audience, and New Communications Technologies." In *Current Research in Film: Audiences, Economics, and Law,* vol. 2, edited by Bruce A. Austin, pp. 80–116. Norwood, N.J.: Ablex, 1986.

————. "Film and the New Media." In *Film and the Arts in Symbiosis: A Resource Guide,* edited by Gary Edgerton. Westport, Conn.: Greenwood Press, 1988.

Austin, Bruce A., and Thomas F. Gordon. "Movies Genres: Toward a Conceptualized Model and Standardized Definitions." In *Current Research in Film: Audiences, Economics, and Law,* vol. 3, edited by Bruce A. Austin, pp. 12–33. Norwood, N.J.: Ablex, 1987.

Austin, Bruce A.; Mark J. Nicolich; and Thomas Simonet. "Movie Ratings and Revenues: Eleven Years of Success Ratios." Paper presented at the University Film Association conference, August 1980, Austin, Tex. (available in ERIC ED 191 102).

————. "MPAA Ratings and the Box Office: Some Tantalizing Statistics." *Film Quarterly* 35 (Winter 1981–82):28–30.

Ayer, Douglas; Roy E. Bates; and Peter J. Herman. "Self-Censorship in the Movie Industry: An Historical Perspective on Law and Social Change." *Wisconsin Law Review* (no. 3, 1970):791–838.

Babbie, Earl R. *The Practice of Social Research.* 2nd ed. Belmont, Calif.: Wadsworth, 1979.

Babrow, Austin S. "The Problematic Status of the Concept of 'Gratification' in Mass Communication Research." Paper presented at the Speech Communication Association conference, November 1985, Denver.

Babrow, Austin S., and David L. Swanson. "Disentangling the Antecedents of Media Exposure: An Extension of Expectancy-Value Analysis of Uses and Gratifications." Paper presented at the Speech Communication Association conference, November 1984, Chicago.

Balio, Tino. "Retrenchment, Reappraisal, and Reorganization: 1948 ————." In *The American Film Industry,* edited by Tino Balio, pp. 315–31. Madison: University of Wisconsin Press, 1976.

Ball-Rokeach, S. J. "The Origins of Individual Media-System Dependency: A Sociological Framework." *Communication Research* 12 (October 1985):485–510.

Ball-Rokeach, S. J., and M. L. DeFleur. "A Dependency Model of Mass-Media Effects." *Communication Research* 3 (January 1976):3–21.

Ball-Rokeach, Sandra J.; Milton Rokeach; and Joel W. Grube. *The Great American Values Test: Influencing Behavior and Belief Through Television.* New York: Free Press, 1984.

Bannerman, Julia, and Jerry M. Lewis. "College Students' Attitudes Toward Movies." *Journal of Popular Film* 6 (no. 2, 1977):126–39.

Barnouw, Erik. *The Golden Web: A History of Broadcasting in the United States, Volume II, 1933 to 1953.* New York: Oxford University Press, 1968.

Barrett, Wilton A. "The Work of the National Board of Review." *Annals of the American Academy of Political and Social Science* 128 (November 1926):175–86.

Barson, Michael. "Now Playing at a Bookstore Near You." *American Film,* April 1985, pp. 50–53, 73.

Bartholomew, Robert O. *Report of Censorship of Motion Pictures and of Investigation of Motion Picture Theatres of Cleveland.* Council of City of Cleveland, April 7, 1913.

Bateson, Gregory. *Steps to an Ecology of Mind.* New York: Ballantine, 1975.

Bauer, Raymond A. "The Obstinate Audience." *American Psychologist* 19 (May 1964):319–28.

———. "The Audience." In *Handbook of Communication,* edited by Ithiel de Sola Pool and Wilbur Schramm, pp. 141–52. Chicago: Rand McNally, 1973.

Bayus, Barry L. "Word of Mouth: The Indirect Effects of Marketing Efforts." *Journal of Advertising Research* 25 (June–July 1985):31–39.

Beard, Jacob G., and Mounir G. Ragheb. "Measuring Leisure Motivation." *Journal of Leisure Research* 15 (no. 3, third quarter, 1983):219–28.

Beaupre, Lee, and Anne Thompson. "Eighth Annual Grosses Gloss." *Film Comment,* April 1983, pp. 62–73.

Becker, Lee B., and Jeffrey W. Fruit. "Understanding Media Selection from a Uses and Motives Perspective." Paper presented at the International Communication Association conference, May 1982, Boston.

Behrens, Steve. "Shortcut to Home." *Channels,* May–June 1984, p. 30.

Belson, William A. "The Effect of Television on Cinema Going." *Audio-Visual Communication Review* 6 (1958):131–39.

Belton, John. "CinemaScope: The Economics of Technology." *Velvet Light Trap,* no. 21 (Summer 1985), pp. 35–43.

Bem, Daryl J. *Beliefs, Attitudes, and Human Affairs.* Belmont, Calif.: Brooks/Cole, 1970.

Berelson, Bernard. "What 'Missing the Newspaper' Means." In *Communications Research, 1948–1949,* edited by Paul F. Lazarsfeld and Frank N. Stanton, pp. 111–29. New York: Harper & Brothers, 1949.

———. "The State of Communication Research." *Public Opinion Quarterly* 23 (Spring 1959):1–6.

Berendt, John. "Critic Power." *Mainliner* (United Airlines' magazine), March 1977, pp. 29–31.

Berry, Chris. *"Making Love:* Attraction, Transaction, Rejection." Unpublished manuscript, Beijing, China, 1985.

Best, Joel. "The Social Control of Media Context." *Journal of Popular Culture* 14 (Spring 1981):611–17.

Bettman, James R. *An Information Processing Theory of Consumer Choice.* Reading, Mass.: Addison-Wesley, 1979.

Beuick, Marshall D. "The Limited Social Effect of Radio Broadcasting." *American Journal of Sociology* 32 (1927):615–22.

Bleich, Dina M. "Film and Attitudes." *High Points* 30 (October 1948):18–31.

Block, Martin. "Time Allocation in Mass Communication Research." In *Progress in Communication Sciences,* edited by Melvin J. Voigt and Gerhard J. Hanneman, pp. 29–49. Norwood, N.J.: Ablex, 1979.

Blum, Stanford. "Merchandising." In *The Movie Business Book,* edited by Jason E. Squire, pp. 378–84. Englewood Cliffs, N.J.: Prentice-Hall, 1983.

Blumer, Herbert. *Movies and Conduct.* New York: Macmillan, 1933.

———. "Moulding of Mass Behavior Through the Motion Picture." *Publications of the American Sociological Society* 29 (1936):115–27.

Blumer, Herbert, and Philip M. Hauser. *Movies, Delinquency and Crime.* New York: Macmillan, 1933.

Blumler, Jay G. "The Role of Theory in Uses and Gratification Studies." *Communication Research* 6 (January 1979):9–36.

Blumler, Jay G., and Elihu Katz, eds. *The Uses of Mass Communications: Current Perspectives on Gratifications Research.* Beverly Hills: Sage, 1974.

Bogart, Leo. *Strategy in Advertising: Matching Media and Messages to Markets and Motivations.* 2nd ed. Chicago: Crain Books, 1984.

Bold, Rudolph. "Rocky Horror: The Newest Cult." *Christian Century,* Sept. 12, 1979, pp. 860–61.

Boorstin, Daniel J. *The Image: A Guide to Pseudo-Events in America.* New York: Harper Colophon Books, 1961.

Bose, A. B. "Mass Communication: The Cinema in India." *Indian Journal of Social Research* 4 (1963):80–88.

Bottini, Ronald L. "Self-Regulation and Motion Picture Content." Master's thesis, University of Missouri, 1966.

Brandsdorfer, Ron, and Alison Walker. "Yes, But Can I Take My Kids: The Vagueness and Vagaries of the Movie Rating Systems." *Comment on the Media,* Spring 1980, pp. 28–29.

Breed, Warren. "Social Control in the Newsroom: A Functional Analysis." *Social Forces* 32 (May 1955):326–35.

Brehm, Jack W. *A Theory of Psychological Reactance.* New York: Academic Press, 1966.

———. *Responses to Loss of Freedom: A Theory of Psychological Reactance.* Morristown, N.J.: General Learning Corp., 1972.

Breitrose, Henry. "The Nontheatrical Film, 1960." *Film Quarterly* 14 (Spring 1961):40–42.

Briggs, Asa. *Mass Entertainment: The Origins of a Modern Industry.* Adelaide, Australia: Griffin Press, 1960.

———. *The History of Broadcasting in the United Kingdom, Volume I: The Birth of Broadcasting.* London: Oxford University Press, 1961.

Britt, Steuart Henderson. "The Strategy of Consumer Motivation." *Journal of Marketing* 14 (April 1950):666–74.

———. "What Is the Nature of the Drive-in Theater Audience?" *Media/scope* 4 (June 1960):100–102, 104.

Brock, R. Barrington. "The Effect of Motion Pictures on Body Temperature." *Science,* Sept. 7, 1945, p. 259.

Brodbeck, Arthur J. "An Exception to the Law of 'Adult Discount': The Need to Take Film Content into Account." *Psychological Reports* 8 (1961):59–61.

Broeske, Pat H. "One Toke Over the Line." *Rolling Stone,* March 27, 1986, pp. 41–42.

Brosnan, John. *Movie Magic: The Story of Special Effects in the Cinema.* New York: Plume Books, 1976.

Brown, Trevor. "Reviewers on Reviewing." *Journalism Quarterly* 55 (Spring 1978):32–38.

Bruner, Jerome S., and George Fowler. "The Strategy of Terror: Audience Response to *Blitzkrieg im Westen.*" *Journal of Abnormal and Social Psychology* 36 (October 1941):561–74.

Buccalo, William Raymond. "Mise-en-Scène Versus Montage: Viewer Response to Two Styles of Visual Communication." Ph.D. dissertation, Ohio State University, 1977.

Burroughs, Julian C., Jr. "X plus 2: The MPAA Classification System During Its First Two Years." *Journal of the University Film Association* 23 (no. 2, 1971):44–53.

Joseph Burstyn, Inc. v. *Wilson* 343 U.S. 495, 72 S. Ct. 777, 96 L. Ed. 1098 (1952).

Burton, Wilbur. "Chinese Reactions to the Cinema." *Asia* 34 (October 1934):594–600.

Burzynski, Michael H., and Dewey J. Bayer. "The Effect of Positive and Negative Prior Information on Motion Picture Appreciation." *Journal of Social Psychology* 101 (April 1977):215–18.

Byrge, Duane. "Movie Posters Are Vital in Promotion." *Hollywood Reporter,* Feb. 12, 1986, p. 16.

Caldecott, Thomas Porter. "The Function and Effectiveness of Local Newspaper Movie Reviewers in Three Northern California Cities." Master's thesis, University of Nevada, 1982.

California State Recreational Inquiry Committee. *Report of the State Recreational Inquiry Committee.* Sacramento: California State Printing Office, 1914.

Callenbach, Ernest. "U.S. Film Journalism—A Survey." *Hollywood Quarterly* 5 (Summer 1951):350–62.

"Camden's Drive-in Theater." *Literary Digest,* July 22, 1933, p. 19.

Campbell, Donald T. "Social Attitudes and Other Acquired Behavioral Dispositions." In *Psychology: A Study of Science,* vol. 6, edited by Sigmund Koch, pp. 94–172. New York: McGraw-Hill, 1963.

Campbell, Donald T., and Julian C. Stanley. *Experimental and Quasi-Experimental Designs for Research.* Chicago: Rand McNally, 1963.

Canby, Vincent. "The Ratings Are Wrong." *New York Times,* June 4, 1972, sec. 2 (Arts and Leisure), p. 1.

Capra, Frank. *The Name Above the Title: An Autobiography.* New York: Macmillan, 1971.

Caranicas, Peter. "Hollywood Wakes Up and Smells the Coffee." *Channels,* July–August 1983, pp. 43–45.

Carey, James W. "Changing Communications Technology and the Nature of the Audience." *Journal of Advertising* 9 (no. 2, 1980):3–9, 43.

Carlson, Harry C. "Movies and the Teenager." *Journal of the Screen Producers Guild,* March 1963, pp. 23–26, 30.

Cassady, Ralph, Jr. "The Impact of the Paramount Decision on Motion Picture Distribution and Price Making." *Southern California Law Review* 31 (February 1958):150–80.

Chalfen, Richard. "Home Movies as Cultural Documents." In *Film/Culture: Explorations of Cinema in Its Social Context,* edited by Sari Thomas, pp. 126–38. Metuchen, N.J.: Scarecrow Press, 1982.

Chamberlin, Philip. "The Art Film and Its Audience: I. Allies, Not Enemies: Commercial and Nontheatrical Experience on the West Coast." *Film Quarterly* 14 (Winter 1960):36–39.

Chambers, Robert W. "Need for Statistical Research." *Annals of the American Academy of Political and Social Science* 254 (November 1947):169–72.

Champlin, Charles. "Dialogue on Film: Charles Champlin." *American Film,* April 1980, pp. 39–46.

———. "Fifty Years of the Production Code: What Will H. Hays Begat." *American Film,* October 1980, pp. 42–47, 86–88.

Child, Mac A. " 'PG' and 'R' Misunderstandings" (letter to the editor). *Variety,* Nov. 12, 1980, p. 6.

Chisholm, Brad. "Widescreen Technologies." *Velvet Light Trap,* no. 21 (Summer 1985), pp. 67–74.

Choi, Yangsoo. "Expected Utility Model: A Paradigm of Audiences' Media and Message Selection." Paper presented at the International Communication Association conference, May 1985, Honolulu.

Cirlin, Bernard D., and Jack N. Peterman. "Pre-Testing a Motion Picture: A Case History." *Journal of Social Issues* 3 (Summer 1947):39–41.

Clark, John Bruce. "An Analysis of the Marketing of 153 Sponsored Films." Ph.D. dissertation, Texas Tech University, 1972.

Clee, Mona A., and Robert A. Wicklund. "Consumer Behavior and Psychological Reactance." *Journal of Consumer Research* 6 (March 1980):389–405.

Coffin, Thomas E. "Television's Effect on Leisure-Time Activities." *Journal of Applied Psychology* 32 (October 1948):550–58.

Collier, John. "Cheap Amusements." *Charities and the Commons,* April 11, 1908, pp. 73–76.

———. "The Motion Picture." *Proceedings of the Child Conference for Research and Welfare.* New York: G. E. Stechert, 1910.

"Columbia Working to Manage Word of Mouth on Pictures." *Hollywood Reporter,* May 15, 1978, p. 12.

Commission on Obscenity and Pornography. *Report of the Commission on Obscenity and Pornography.* New York: Bantam Books, 1970.

The Community and the Motion Picture. Report of the National Conference on Motion Pictures, Sept. 24–27, 1929, New York City. New York: Motion Picture Producers and Distributors of America, 1929 (reprinted by Jerome S. Ozer, 1971).

Compaine, Benjamin M. "Newspapers." In *Anatomy of the Communications Industry: Who Owns the Media?,* edited by Benjamin M. Compaine, pp. 27–93. White Plains, N.Y.: Knowledge Industry Publications, 1982.

"Computer-Testing to Pick Up Lost Elements of Film Audience." *Variety,* March 26, 1975, pp. 5, 33.

Comstock, George; Steven Chaffee; Natan Katzman; Maxwell McCombs; and Donald Roberts. *Television and Human Behavior.* New York: Columbia University Press, 1978.

Conant, Michael. *Antitrust in the Motion Picture Industry.* Berkeley: University of California Press, 1960.

Cooper, Eunice, and Helen Dinerman. "Analysis of the Film 'Don't Be a Sucker': A Study in Communication." *Public Opinion Quarterly* 15 (Summer 1951):243–64.

Cooper, Joseph B., and James L. McGaugh. "Attitude and Related Concepts." In *Attitudes,* edited by Marie Jahoda and Neil Warren, pp. 26–31. Baltimore, Penguin, 1966.

Cort, Robert W. "The Anatomy of Motion Picture Marketing." In *The Marketing of Motion Pictures,* edited by Roger A. Strang, pp. 4–17. Los Angeles: Graduate School of Business, University of Southern California, 1979.

Council of Motion Picture Organizations. *Special COMPO Report, November 1954.* Bringham Young University, Department of Archives and Manuscripts, National Association of Theatre Owners file, Box 9, Folder 9.

Craig, Hardin, ed. *The Complete Works of Shakespeare.* Glenview, Ill.: Scott, Foresman, 1961.

Crandall, Rick. "Motivations for Leisure." *Journal of Leisure Research* 12 (first quarter, 1980):45–53.

Crandall, Rick; S. M. Altengarten; S. M. Carson; M. M. Nolan; and J. T. Dixon. "A General Bibliography of Leisure Publications." *Journal of Leisure Research* 9 (first quarter, 1977):15–54.

Crane, Diana. *Invisible Colleges: Diffusion of Knowledge in Scientific Communities.* Chicago: University of Chicago Press, 1972.

Creedon, Carol. "The Film as a Research Tool." *Hollywood Quarterly* 2 (1946–47):107–11.

Csikszentmihalyi, Mihaly, and Robert Kubey. "Television and the Rest of Life: A Systematic Comparison of Subjective Experience." *Public Opinion Quarterly* 45 (Fall 1981):317–28.

Cullman, Marguerite W. "Double Feature—Movies and Moonlight." *New York Times Magazine,* Oct. 1, 1950, pp. 22, 68–69, 72.

Curran, James, and Jeremy Tunstall. "Mass Media and Leisure." In *Leisure and Society in Britain,* edited by Michael A. Smith, Stanley Parker, and Cyril S. Smith, pp. 199–213. London: Allen Lane, 1973.

Czitrom, Daniel J. *Media and the American Mind: From Morse to McLuhan.* Chapel Hill: University of North Carolina Press, 1982.

———. "The Redemption of Leisure: The National Board of Censorship and the Rise of Motion Pictures in New York City, 1900–1920." *Studies in Visual Communication* 10 (Fall 1984):2–6.

Daly, David Anthony. *A Comparison of Exhibition and Distribution Patterns in Three Recent Feature Motion Pictures.* New York: Arno, 1980.

Davis, Michael M., Jr. *The Exploitation of Pleasure: A Study of Commercial Recreations in New York City.* New York: Department of Child Hygiene of the Russell Sage Foundation, 1911.

DeBauche, Leslie Midkiff. "Advertising and the Movies 1908–1915." Paper presented at the Ohio University Film Conference, April 1982, Athens, Ohio.

DeCharms, Richard, and Marion S. Muir. "Motivation: Social Approaches." In *Annual Review of Psychology,* vol. 29, edited by Mark R. Rosenzweig and Lyman W. Porter, pp. 91–113. Palo Alto, Calif.: Annual Reviews, 1978.

DeFeo, George. "Le Monde Scolaire et le Film d'Enseignement." *International Review of Educational Cinematography* 4 (June–July–August 1932):504–18, 608–17, 696–702.

DeFleur, Melvin L., and Sandra Ball-Rokeach. *Theories of Mass Communication.* 4th ed. New York: Longman, Green, 1982.

DeGrazia, Sebastian. *Of Time, Work and Leisure.* New York: Doubleday, 1962.

DeLaurot, Edouard L. "On Critics and Criteria." *Film Culture* 1 (March–April 1955):4–11.

DeMaday, Andre. "An Enquiry Respecting the Cinematograph Made in the Schools of Geneva, Lausanne and Neuchatel." *International Review of Educational Cinematography* 1 (November 1929):531–52.

———. "An Enquiry Respecting the Cinematograph Made in the Schools of Neuchatel, Lausanne and Geneva." *International Review of Educational Cinematography* 1 (December 1929):638–67.

DeProspo, Nicholas D. "Developing Scientific Attitudes by Responding Actively to Motion Pictures: A Study to Determine if Responding Actively to Selected Motion Pictures by Identifying the Problem-Solving Skills They Portray Reinforces or Develops a Scientific Attitude in College Freshmen." Ph.D. dissertation, New York University, 1957.

DeRuette, Victor. "The Cinema and Child Psychology." *International Review of Educational Cinematography* 6 (January 1934):38–49.

Deshaies, Gabriel. "Les Fonctions Psychologiques de Cinéma." *Annales Medico-Psychologiques* 1 (May 1951):553–73.

"Dialogue on Film: Frank Capra." *American Film,* October 1978, pp. 39–50.

Diamond, S. J. "At Art Movie Theaters, Real Art Is in the Selling." *Los Angeles Times,* April 24, 1977, sec. 6, pp. 1–2, 9.

DiMaggio, Paul, and Michael Useem. "Cultural Democracy in a Period of Cultural Expansion: The Social Composition of the Arts Audiences in the United States." *Social Problems* 26 (December 1978):179–97.

Dimmick, John W.; Thomas A. McCain; and W. Theodore Bolton. "Media Use and the Life Span: Notes on Theory and Method." *American Behavioral Scientist* 23 (September–October 1979):7–31.

Doherty, Thomas. "Teenagers and Teenpics, 1955–1957: A Study of Exploitation Filmmaking." In *Current Research in Film: Audiences, Economics, and Law,* vol. 2, edited by Bruce A. Austin, pp. 47–61. Norwood, N.J.: Ablex, 1986.

"The Do-It-Yourself Market" (prepared by U.S. Department of Commerce). In *Mass Leisure,* edited by Eric Larrabee and Rolf Meyersohn, pp. 274–81. Glencoe, Ill.: Free Press, 1958.

Dominick, Joseph R. "New Technologies: Implications for Research." *Feedback* 22 (November 1980):3–6.

———. "Film Economics and Film Content: 1964–1983." In *Current Research in Film: Audiences, Economics, and Law,* vol. 3, edited by Bruce A. Austin, pp. 136–53. Norwood, N.J.: Ablex, 1987.

Domino, George. "Impact of the Film 'One Flew Over the Cuckoo's Nest' on Attitudes Towards Mental Illness." *Psychological Reports* 53 (August 1983):179–82.

Dowell, Pat, and Ray Heinrich. "Bigger Than Life." *American Film,* May 1984, pp. 49–53.

Downs, Anthony. "Drive-ins Have Arrived." *Journal of Property Management* 18 (March 1953):149–62.

Driscoll, R.; K. E. Davis; and M. E. Lipetz. "Parental Interference and Romantic Love: The Romeo and Juliet Effect." *Journal of Personality and Social Psychology* 24 (1972):1–10.

"Drive-in Film Business Burns Up the Prairies." *Life,* Sept. 24, 1951, pp. 104–6, 108.

Dronberger, Ilse. "Student Attitudes Toward the Foreign Film." *Journal of University Producers Association* 17 (1965):6–9, 19–22.

Ducey, Richard V.; Dean M. Krugman; and Donald Eckrich. "Predicting Market Segments in the Cable Industry: The Basic and Pay Subscribers." *Journal of Broadcasting* 27 (Spring 1983):155–61.

Dulles, Foster Rhea. *A History of Recreation: America Learns to Play.* 2nd ed. New York: Appleton-Century-Crofts, 1965.

Duncan, David J. "Leisure Types: Factor Analysis of Leisure Profiles." *Journal of Leisure Research* 10 (second quarter, 1978): 113–25.

Durant, Henry. *The Problem of Leisure.* London: George Routledge, 1938.

DuVall, Stephen. "Marketing: Universal's Team on Gameplan '82." *American Premiere,* December 1982–January 1983, pp. 23–29.

Earnest, Olen J. *"Star Wars:* A Case Study of Motion Picture Marketing." In *Current Research in Film: Audiences, Economics, and Law,* vol. 1, edited by Bruce A. Austin, pp. 1–18. Norwood, N.J.: Ablex, 1985.

Eastman, Susan Tyler; David E. Bradbury; and Robert S. Nemes. "The Influence of Previews on Movie Viewers' Expectations." In *Current Research in Film: Audiences, Economics, and Law,* vol. 1, edited by Bruce A. Austin, pp. 51–57. Norwood, N.J.: Ablex, 1985.

Edgerton, Gary. "Radio and Motion Pictures: A Case Study of Media Symbiosis." *Mass Comm Review* 8 (Winter 1980–81):21–29.

———. *American Film Exhibition and an Analysis of the Motion Picture Industry's Market Structure, 1963–1980.* New York: Garland Publishing, 1983 (reprint of a Ph.D. dissertation, University of Massachusetts, 1981).

Edgerton, Gary, ed. *Film and the Arts in Symbiosis: A Resource Guide.* Westport, Conn.: Greenwood Press, 1988.

Editors of *Fortune. The Changing American Market.* Garden City, N.Y.: Hanover House, 1955.

Edwards, Richard Henry. *Popular Amusements.* New York: Association Press, 1915.

Einsiedel, Edna F.; Kandice Salomone; and Fred Schneider. "A Field Experiment on Immediate and Delayed Effects of Aggressive-Erotic, Mild- and Hard-Core Erotic Films on Attitudes Toward Sexual Violence." Paper presented at the International Communication Association conference, May 1982, Boston.

"Electric Movie 'Reviewers' Record Reaction to Film." *Popular Mechanics,* May 1947, p. 149.

Elias, James. "Exposure of Adolescents to Erotic Materials." In *Technical Reports of the Commission on Obscenity and Pornography,* vol. 9, pp. 273–312. Washington, D.C.: U.S. Government Printing Office, 1970.

Elliott, William R., and Cynthia P. Quattlebaum. "Similarities in Patterns of Media Use: A Cluster Analysis of Media Gratifications." *Western Journal of Speech Communication* 43 (Winter 1979):61–72.

Elliott, William R., and William J. Schenck-Hamlin. "Film, Politics and the Press: The Influence of 'All the President's Men.'" *Journalism Quarterly* 56 (Autumn 1979):546–53.

England, Leonard. "The Critics and the Box-Office." *Sight and Sound,* June 1951, pp. 43–44.

English, John W. *Criticizing the Critics.* New York: Hastings House, 1979.

Esser, Carl. "Adult Films Threatened by Video Takeover." *Boxoffice,* May 1985, pp. 22–24.

Everson, William K. *American Silent Film.* New York: Oxford University Press, 1978.

———. "Top Secret." *Films in Review* 35 (June–July 1984):342–46.

Ewen, Stuart. *Captains of Consciousness: Advertising and the Social Roots of the Consumer Culture.* New York: McGraw-Hill, 1976.

"Eye Strain in Motion Picture Theaters." *American Journal of Public Health* 11 (October 1921):936–37.

Faber, Ronald J.; Andrew P. Hardy; and Thomas C. O'Guinn. "Popular Films and Art Films: Audience Self-Selection and Market Segmentation." In *Current Research in Film: Audiences, Economics, and Law,* vol. 4., edited by Bruce A. Austin. Norwood, N.J.: Ablex, in press.

Faber, Ronald J., and Thomas C. O'Guinn. "Effects of Media Advertising and Other Sources on Movie Selection." *Journalism Quarterly* 61 (Summer 1984):371–77.

Fadiman, William. *Hollywood Now.* New York: Liveright, 1972.

Falewicz, Jan. "Effect of Criticism on Urban Film Taste." *Polish Sociological Bulletin* 9 (1964):90–95.

"The Family Movie Could Be an Energy Saver." In *Mass Media Issues: Articles and Commentaries,* edited by Leonard L. Sellers and William L. Rivers, pp. 305–8. Englewood Cliffs, N.J.: Prentice-Hall, 1977.

Fantel, Hans. "The Year the VCR Became Ubiquitous." *New York Times,* Dec. 27, 1987, p. H-26.

Farber, Stephen. *The Movie Rating Game.* Washington, D.C.: Public Affairs Press, 1972.

———. "Which Movies Make Money." *New York Times,* Aug. 17, 1975, sec. 2, pp. 11, 16.

———. "Not Coming to a Theater Near You." *TWA Ambassador,* April 1981, pp. 27–32.

Fearing, Franklin. "Influence of the Movies on Attitudes and Behavior." *Annals of the American Academy of Political and Social Science* 254 (November 1947):70–79.

Federal Council of the Churches of Christ in America, Department of Research and Education. *The Public Relations of the Motion Picture Industry.* New York: FCCCA, 1931.

Ferman, James. "Film Censorship Today." Paper presented at the Association of Independent Cinemas All-Industry Seminar, 1979, Great Britain.

Festinger, Leon. *A Theory of Cognitive Dissonance.* Stanford, Calif.: Stanford University Press, 1957.

Fielding, Raymond. *A Technological History of Motion Pictures and Television.* Berkeley: University of California Press, 1967.

———. "The Technological Antecedents to the Coming of Sound: An Introduction." In *Sound and the Cinema: The Coming of Sound to American Film,* edited by Evan William Cameron, pp. 2–23. Pleasantville, N.Y.: Redgrave, 1980.

"Film Subject Matter Looms Large in Stay-Away; Ticket Prices Are Related to Age; Income Strata." *Variety,* Nov. 18, 1981, pp. 5, 32.

Fischer, Heinz-Dietrich, and Stefan Reinhard Melnick, eds. *Entertainment: A Cross-Cultural Examination.* New York: Hastings House, 1979.

Fishbein, Martin, and Icek Ajzen. *Belief, Attitude, Intention and Behavior: An Introduction to Theory and Research.* Reading, Mass.: Addison-Wesley, 1975.

Fisher, Robert. "Film Censorship and Progressive Reform: The National Board of Censorship of Motion Pictures, 1909–1922." *Journal of Popular Film* 4 (no. 2, 1975):143–56.

Fiske, Marjorie, and Leo Handel. "New Techniques for Studying the Effectiveness of Films." *Journal of Marketing* 11 (April 1947):390–93.

Flaherty, W. "Drive-in Theatres." *British Kinematography* 23 (September 1953):66–72.

Ford, Richard. "What One Public Says It Likes." *Sight and Sound,* Summer 1937, p. 70.

———. *Children in the Cinema.* London: George Allen and Unwin, 1939.

Forman, Henry James. *Our Movie Made Children.* New York: Macmillan, 1935.

"Fortune Survey: The Movies." *Fortune,* November 1939, p. 176.

"The Fortune Survey. The People's Taste in Movies, Books, and Radio." *Fortune,* March 1949, pp. 39–40, 43–44.

Francis, Barbara. "Movie Trailers: The Lure of the Filmstrip Tease." *Los Angeles Times,* Oct. 7, 1979, Calendar sec., p. 7.

Freidson, Eliot. "Adult Discount: An Aspect of Children's Changing Taste.' *Child Development* 24 (March 1953):39–49.

Friedman, Jane M. "The Motion Picture Rating System of 1968: A Constitutional Analysis of Self-Regulation by the Film Industry." *Columbia Law Review* 73 (February 1973):185–240.

Fry, C. Luther, with Mary Frost Jessup. "Changes in Religious Organizations." In *Recent Social Trends in the United States: Report of the President's Research Committee on Social Trends,* pp. 1009–60. New York: McGraw-Hill, 1934.

Fuchs, Douglas A., and Jack Lyle. "Mass Media Portrayal—Sex and Violence." In *Current Perspectives in Mass Communication Research,* edited by F. Gerald Kline and Phillip J. Tichenor, pp. 235–64. Beverly Hills: Sage, 1972.

Fulk, Joseph R. "The Effect on Education and Morals of the Moving-Picture Shows." *Proceedings of the National Education Association Annual Meeting* (1912):456–61.

"G for Gold." *Time,* Jan. 3, 1977, p. 74.

Gaer, Felice D. "The Soviet Film Audience: A Confidential View." *Problems of Communism* 23 (January 1974):56–70.

Galloway, John J., and Louise F. Meek. "Audience Uses and Gratifications: An Expectancy Model." *Communication Research* 8 (October 1981):435–49.

"Gallup Gadget." *Business Week,* Feb. 3, 1945, p. 80.

"Gallup Gadget Charts Movie Appeal." *Science Digest,* April 1945, p. 6.

"Gallup Looks at the Movies: Movie Audience, Marquee Values Traced Since 40s." *Gallup Report,* no. 195 (December 1981), pp. 3–26.

Garner, Jack. "Sneak Preview Gambles." Rochester, N.Y., *Democrat and Chronicle,* Feb. 1, 1983, pp. B-1, 6.

Garramone, Gina M. "Motivational Models: Replication Across Media for Political Campaign Content." *Journalism Quarterly* 61 (Autumn 1984):537–41, 691.

Garrison, Lee Cedric, Jr. "Decision Processes in Motion Picture Production: A Study of Uncertainty." Ph.D. dissertation, Stanford University, 1971.

————. "The Needs of Motion Picture Audiences." *California Management Review* 15 (Winter 1972):144–52.

Gatignon, Hubert, and Thomas S. Robertson. "A Propositional Inventory for New Diffusion Research." *Journal of Consumer Research* 11 (March 1985):849–67.

Gelmis, Joseph, ed. *The Film Director as Superstar.* New York: Anchor Press, 1970.

George, Francis Blaine. "A Study of the Attitudes of Selected Officers of the California Congress of Parents and Teachers Toward the Relationship of Motion Pictures and Television to Children." Ed.D. dissertation, University of Southern California, 1965.

Gertner, Richard, ed. *Motion Picture Almanac 1980.* New York: Quigley, 1980.

————. *Motion Picture Almanac 1985.* New York: Quigley, 1985.

————. *1986 International Motion Picture Almanac.* New York: Quigley, 1986.

Gillette, Don Carle. "New Film-Reviewing System Needed." *Journal of the Producers Guild of America,* September 1972, pp. 31–33.

Ginsberg, Sidney. "Kids and X Tag Are Both Outdated" (letter to the editor). *Variety,* Oct. 1, 1980, p. 4.

Ginsberg, Steven. "Drive-ins Rate Firstrun; Hardtop Sites Re-Valued." *Variety,* April 26, 1978, p. 23.

Gitlin, Todd. "Media Sociology: The Dominant Paradigm." *Theory and Society* 6 (1978):205–53.

————. *Inside Prime Time.* New York: Pantheon Books, 1983.

Gluckson, Jim. " 'Casting' Products in Films." *Boxoffice,* December 1985, pp. 34–36.

Gold, Richard. "February Youth Pics Not Pulling Biz, Sneak Previews Could Be Bane." *Variety,* Feb. 27, 1985, pp. 3, 35.

————. "Cool Summer for Film Merchandising." *Variety,* June 13, 1985, pp. 7, 22.

Goldberg, Herman D. "The Role of 'Cutting' in the Perception of the Motion Picture." *Journal of Applied Psychology* 35 (February 1951):70–71.

Goldwyn, Samuel. "Hollywood in the Television Age." *New York Times Magazine,* Feb. 13, 1949, pp. 15, 44, 47.

Gomery, Douglas. "The American Film Industry in the 1970s: Stasis in the 'New Hollywood.' " *Wide Angle* 5 (no. 4, 1983):52–59.

————. "The Coming of Television and the 'Lost' Motion Picture Audience." *Journal of Film and Video* 37 (Summer 1985):5–11.

————. "Theatre Television: The Missing Link of Technological Change in the U.S. Motion Picture Industry." *Velvet Light Trap,* no. 21 (Summer 1985), pp. 54–61.

Graham, Jefferson. "Movie Moguls Go for Safety of Sequels." *USA Today,* March 29, 1985, pp. D-1, 2.

Grant, Lee. "The Private Diary of a Movie." *Los Angeles Times,* July 24, 1983, Calendar sec., pp. 1, 4–8.

Green, J. Ronald. "Film and Not-for-Profit Media Institutions." In *Film/Culture: Explorations of Cinema in Its Social Context,* edited by Sari Thomas, pp. 37–59. Metuchen, N.J.: Scarecrow Press, 1982.

Greenberg, Bradley S. "Gratifications of Television Viewing and Their Correlates for British Children." In *The Uses of Mass Communication: Current Perspectives on*

Gratifications Research, edited by Jay G. Blumler and Elihu Katz, pp. 71–92. Beverly Hills: Sage, 1974.

Greene, Nelson L. "Motion Pictures in the Classroom." *Annals of the American Academy of Political and Social Science* 217 (November 1926):122–30.

Greenwald, William I. "The Impact of Sound upon the Film Industry: A Case Study of Innovation." *Explorations in Entrepreneurial History* 4 (May 15, 1952):178–92.

Gross, Lynne Schafer. *The New Television Technologies.* Dubuque, Iowa: Wm. C. Brown, 1983.

Guback, Thomas H. "Hollywood's International Market." In *The American Film Industry,* edited by Tino Balio, pp. 387–409. Madison: University of Wisconsin Press, 1976.

———. "Are We Looking at the Right Things in Film?" Paper presented at the Society for Cinema Studies conference, 1978, Philadelphia.

———. "Theatrical Film." In *Who Owns the Media,* edited by Benjamin M. Compaine, pp. 179–241. White Plains, N.Y.: Knowledge Industries Publications, 1979.

Guback, Thomas H., and Dennis J. Dombkowski. "Television and Hollywood: Economic Relations in the 1970s." *Journal of Broadcasting* 20 (Fall 1976):511–27.

Gutman, Jonathan. "The Impact of Advertising at the Time of Consumption." *Journal of Advertising Research* 22 (August–September 1982):35–40.

Hadsell, Reign S. "Effects of Films and Reading and Test Materials on Attitudes Toward Due Process of Law." Ph.D. dissertation, Yale University, 1954.

Hadsell, Reign S., and Mark A. May. "Change in Attitude Toward Due Process of Law." In *Learning from Films,* edited by Mark A. May and Arthur A. Lumsdaine. New Haven, Conn.: Yale University Press, 1958.

Haley, Jay. "The Appeal of the Moving Picture." *Quarterly of Film, Radio and Television* 6 (1952):361–74.

Hampton, Benjamin B. *A History of the Movies.* 1931. Reprint. New York: Dover, 1970.

Handel, Leo. "Radio, Movies, Publications Increase Each Other's Audience." *Printers' Ink,* July 19, 1946, pp. 42–43.

———. "This Thing Called Audience Research." *Hollywood Reporter,* 1946 Anniversary Edition.

———. "A Study to Determine the Drawing Power of Male and Female Stars upon Movie-Goers of Their Own Sex." *International Journal of Opinion and Attitude Research* 2 (Summer 1948):215–20.

———. *Hollywood Looks at Its Audience.* Urbana: University of Illinois Press, 1950.

———. "Hollywood Market Research." *Quarterly of Film, Radio and Television* 7 (Spring 1953):304–10.

Hansen, Flemming. "Psychological Theories of Consumer Choice." In *Selected Aspects of Consumer Behavior: A Summary from the Perspective of Different Disciplines,* pp. 33–69. (Report prepared for the National Science Foundation under Grant No. 38971.) Washington, D.C.: U.S. Government Printing Office, no date.

Haralovich, Mary Beth. "Film Advertising, the Film Industry and the Pin-up: The Industry's Accommodations to Social Forces in the 1940s." In *Current Research in Film: Audiences, Economics, and Law,* vol. 1, edited by Bruce A. Austin, pp. 127–64. Norwood, N.J.: Ablex, 1985.

Harmetz, Aljean. *Rolling Breaks and Other Movie Business.* New York: Knopf, 1983.

————. *New York Times,* January 10, 1988.

Hartsough, Denise. "An Annotated Widescreen Bibliography." *Velvet Light Trap,* no. 21 (Summer 1985), pp. 75–79.

Havighurst, Robert J., and Kenneth Feigenbaum. "Leisure and Life-Style." *American Journal of Sociology* 64 (January 1959): 396–404.

Haynes, Rowland. "Recreation Survey, Milwaukee, Wisconsin." *Playground* 6 (May 1912):38–66.

Heckhausen, Heinz. "Achievement Motivation and Its Constructs: A Cognitive Model." *Motivation and Emotion* 1 (December 1977):283–329.

Heffner, Richard D. "What G, PG, R and X Really Mean." *TV Guide,* Oct. 4, 1980, pp. 38–46.

Henderson, James M., and Richard E. Quandt. *Microeconomic Theory: A Mathematical Approach.* New York: McGraw-Hill, 1958.

Hendricks, Gordon. "The History of the Kinetoscope." In *The American Film Industry,* edited by Tino Balio, pp. 33–45. Madison: University of Wisconsin Press, 1976.

Henkin, Bill. *The Rocky Horror Picture Show Book.* New York: Hawthorn Books, 1979.

Herman, Ginette, and Jacques-Philippe Leyens. "Rating Films on TV." *Journal of Communication* 27 (Autumn 1977):48–53.

Herzog, Herta. "What Do We Really Know About Daytime Serial Listeners?" In *Radio Research, 1942–1943,* edited by Paul F. Lazarsfeld and Frank N. Stanton, pp. 3–33. New York: Duell, Sloan, and Pearce, 1944.

Hibben, Paxton. "The Movies in Russia." *Nation,* Nov. 11, 1925, pp. 539–40.

Hickey, Florence E. "Children's Interests in Moving Pictures, Radio Programs, and Voluntary Book Reading." Master's thesis, Boston University, 1948.

Hillwig, Jack Leonard. "Film Criticism: Its Relationship to Economically Successful Films and an Application of Rhetoric to Improving the Critic's Methods." Ph.D. dissertation, Ohio State University, 1980.

Hincha, Richard. "Selling CinemaScope: 1953–1956." *Velvet Light Trap,* no. 21 (Summer 1985), pp. 44–53.

Hoban, Phoebe. "Fast Films." *Omni,* February 1984, p. 100.

Hoberman, J., and Jonathan Rosenbaum. *Midnight Movies.* New York: Harper Colophon Books, 1983.

Hodgson, Moira. "Movie Ratings—Do They Serve Hollywood or the Public?" *New York Times,* May 24, 1981, sec. 2, pp. 1, 13.

Hoffman, Bernd-Wolfgang. "An Experimental Study of Learning and Attitude Change Through Film and the Effects of Music-Montage Interludes in a Film." Master's thesis, University of Wisconsin, 1979.

Holbrook, Morris B., and Elizabeth C. Hirschman. "The Experiential Aspects of Consumption: Consumer Fantasies, Feelings, and Fun." *Journal of Consumer Research* 9 (September 1982):132–40.

Holbrook, Morris B., and Donald R. Lehmann. "Allocating Discretionary Time: Complementarity Among Activities." *Journal of Consumer Research* 7 (March 1981):395–406.

Hollinger, Hy. "Hollywood's View of Research Depends on Just Who's Being Asked, What Methods Are Used." *Variety,* Jan. 12, 1983, pp. 10, 36, 38, 52.

Hollonquist, Tore, and Edward A. Suchman. "Listening to the Listener: Experiences with the Lazarsfeld-Stanton Program Analyzer." In *Radio Research 1942–1943,* edited by Paul F. Lazarsfeld and Frank N. Stanton, pp. 265–334. New York: Essential Books, 1944.

"Hollywood Learns How to Live with TV." *Business Week,* Aug. 9, 1952, pp. 46–48.

"Hours and Earnings by Industry Division, Selected Years, 1950–82." *Monthly Labor Review* 106 (December 1983):73.

Hovland, Carl I.; Arthur A. Lumsdaine; and Fred D. Sheffield. *Experiments in Mass Communications.* Princeton, N.J.: Princeton University Press, 1949.

"How Children Are Entertained." *Journal of Education,* Feb. 25, 1915, pp. 207, 212.

Howard, John A., and Jagdish N. Sheth. *The Theory of Buyer Behavior.* New York: John Wiley, 1969.

Howe, Frederic C. "Leisure." *Survey* 31 (Jan. 5, 1914):415–16.

———. "What to Do with the Motion-Picture Show: Shall It Be Censored?" *Outlook,* June 20, 1914, pp. 412–16.

Howe, Gregory J. "An Antitrust Challenge to the GGPRX Movie Rating System." *Harvard Civil Rights–Civil Liberties Law Review* 6 (May 1971):545–57.

Huettig, Mae D. *Economic Control of the Motion Picture Industry: A Study in Industrial Organization.* Philadelphia: University of Pennsylvania Press, 1944.

Hughes, Bertha B. "Results of a Motion-Picture Survey." *Educational Screen* 2 (September 1923):324–29.

Hulett, J. E. "Estimating the Net Effect of a Commercial Motion Picture upon the Trend of Local Public Opinion." *American Sociological Review* 14 (April 1949):263–75.

———. "Comments on Mr. Zeisel's Note." *American Sociological Review* 14 (August 1949):551–52.

Hungerford, Chris. "A Survey of Los Angeles Theater Attendance of Two Motion Pictures Which Were Advertised on Television." Master's thesis, University of Southern California, 1955.

Hurlin, Ralph G., and Meredith B. Givens. "Shifting Occupational Patterns." In *Recent Social Trends in the United States: Report of the President's Research Committee on Social Trends,* pp. 268–324. New York: McGraw-Hill, 1934.

Hyams, Joe. "What Should We Do About the Crisis in Movie Morals? The Answer: 'Graded' Films." In *Film and Society,* edited by Richard Dyer MacCann, pp. 119–20. New York: Scribner, 1964.

"Imagemakers." *American Film,* June 1985, pp. 22–30, 97–103.

Inglis, Ruth A. *Freedom of the Movies: A Report on Self-Regulation from the Commission on Freedom of the Press.* Chicago: University of Chicago Press, 1947.

Isenberg, Michael T. *War on Film: The American Cinema and World War I, 1914–1941.* Rutherford, N.J.: Fairleigh Dickinson University Press, 1981.

"It's Film's Plot, Not Star, That Attracts Moviegoers." *Science Digest,* May 1958, p. 21.

Jacobs, Lewis. *The Rise of the American Film: A Critical History.* New York: Teachers College Press, 1939.

Jacoby, Jacob. "Consumer and Industrial Psychology: Prospects for Construct Validation and Mutual Contribution." In *Handbook of Industrial and Organizational Psychology,* edited by Marvin D. Dunnette. Chicago: Rand McNally, 1976.

Jacoby, Jacob, and Jerry C. Olson. "An Extended Expectancy Model of Consumer Comparison Processess." In *Advances in Consumer Research,* vol. 1, edited by Scott Ward and Peter Wright, pp. 319–33. Urbana, Ill.: Association for Consumer Research, 1974.

"Japanese Auds Prefer Sci-Fi, Action, Drama." *Variety,* May 4, 1983, p. 346.

Jarvie, I. C. "Film and the Communication of Values." *Archives Européennes de Sociologie* 10 (1969):205–19.

———. *Movies and Society.* New York: Basic Books, 1970.

Jassem, Harvey C. "Media Rating Systems: Do They Protect Anyone? Lessons from Other Media." Paper presented at the Eastern Communication Association conference, May 1986, Atlantic City, N.J.

Jeffres, Leo W. "Cable TV and Viewer Selectivity." *Journal of Broadcasting* 22 (Spring 1978):167–77.

Jeffries, Georgia. "The Problem with G." *American Film,* June 1978, pp. 50–57.

Jewell, Richard B. "Hollywood and Radio: Competition and Partnership in the 1930s." *Historical Journal of Film, Radio and Television* 4 (October 1984):125–41.

Jobes, Gertrude. *Motion Picture Empire.* Hamden, Conn.: Archon Books, 1966.

Jones, Dorothy B. "Quantitative Analysis of Motion Picture Content." *Public Opinion Quarterly* 6 (Fall 1942):411–28.

Jones, Harold Ellis, and Herbert S. Conrad. "Rural Preferences in Motion Pictures." *Journal of Social Psychology* 1 (1930):419–23.

Jowett, Garth. *Film: The Democratic Art.* Boston: Little, Brown, 1976.

———. "Giving Them What They Want: Movie Audience Research Before 1950." In *Current Research in Film: Audiences, Economics, and Law,* vol. 1, edited by Bruce A. Austin, pp. 19–35. Norwood, N.J.: Ablex, 1985.

Jowett, Garth, and James M. Linton. *Movies as Mass Communication.* Beverly Hills: Sage, 1980.

Kael, Pauline. "Fantasies of the Art-House Audience." *Sight and Sound,* Winter 1961–62, pp. 5–9.

Kahn, Richard. "The Tools of Marketing and Their Implications." In *The Marketing of Motion Pictures,* edited by Roger A. Strang, pp. 23–36. Los Angeles: Graduate School of Business, University of Southern California, 1979.

———. "Motion Picture Marketing." In *The Movie Business Book,* edited by Jason E. Squire, pp. 263–72. Englewood Cliffs, N.J.: Prentice-Hall, 1983.

Kahn, Robert D. "More Messages from the Medium." *Technology Review* 86 (January 1983):49–51.

Kaminsky, Stuart M. *American Film Genres.* New York: Dell, 1974.

Kando, Thomas M. *Leisure and Popular Culture in Transition.* 2nd ed. St. Louis: C. V. Mosby, 1980.

Kantor, Bernard R. "Infrared Motion-Picture Technique in Observing Audience Reactions." *Journal of the Society of Motion Picture and Television Engineers* 64 (November 1955):626–28.

Kaplan, Max. *Leisure in America: A Social Inquiry.* New York: John Wiley, 1960.

Kaplan, Stuart J. "The Impact of Cable Television Services on the Use of Competing Media." *Journal of Broadcasting* 22 (Spring 1978):155–65.

Karp, Alan. "It Came from the Refrigerator: Larry Cohen Talks About 'The Stuff.'" *Boxoffice,* July 1985, pp. 14–15.

Katz, Daniel. "The Functional Approach to the Study of Attitudes." *Public Opinion Quarterly* 24 (Summer 1960):163–204.

Katz, David. "A Widescreen Chronology." *Velvet Light Trap,* no. 21 (Summer 1985), pp. 62–64.

Katz, Elihu. "Mass Communication Research and the Study of Popular Culture: An Editorial Note on a Possible Future for This Journal." *Studies in Public Communication* 2 (1959):1–6.

Katz, Elihu; Jay G. Blumler; and Michael Gurevitch. "Utilization of Mass Communication by the Individual." In *The Uses of Mass Communications: Current Perspectives on Gratifications Research,* edited by Jay G. Blumler and Elihu Katz, pp. 19–32. Beverly Hills: Sage, 1974.

Katz, Elihu, and David Foulkes. "On the Use of the Mass Media as 'Escape': Clarification of a Concept." *Public Opinion Quarterly* 26 (Fall 1962):377–88.

Katz, Elihu, and Paul F. Lazarsfeld. *Personal Influence.* Glencoe, Ill.: Free Press, 1955.

Katz, Elihu; Martin L. Levin; and Herbert Hamilton. "Traditions of Research on the Diffusion of Innovation." *American Sociological Review* 28 (April 1963):237–52.

Kaufman, Kenneth Alan. "Why Do People Go to the Movies? A Study of Motion Picture Attendance as a Socially Comfortable Activity." Master's thesis, University of Pennsylvania, 1973.

Kearney, Jill. "All About Sneaks." *American Film,* March 1985, pp. 45–49.

———. "What's Wrong with Today's Films?" *American Film,* May 1986, pp. 53–56.

Keliher, Alice V. "Children and Movies: A Critical Summary of the Scientific Literature." *Films* 1 (Summer 1940):40–48.

Kelly, John R. *Leisure.* Englewood Cliffs, N.J.: Prentice-Hall, 1982.

Kelman, Herbert C. "Attitudes Are Alive and Well and Gainfully Employed in the Sphere of Action." *American Psychologist* 29 (1974):310–24.

Kendall, Patricia L., and Katherine M. Wolf. "The Analysis of Deviant Cases in Communication Research." In *Communication Research 1948–1949,* edited by Paul F. Lazarsfeld and Frank N. Stanton, pp. 152–79. New York: Harper, 1949.

Kendler, Howard H. "Motivation and Behavior." In *Nebraska Symposium on Motivation, 1965,* vol. 13, edited by David Levine, pp. 1–23. Lincoln: University of Nebraska Press, 1965.

Key, Wilson Bryan. *Subliminal Seduction.* New York: Signet Books, 1973.

———. *Media Sexploitation.* Englewood Cliffs, N.J.: Prentice-Hall, 1976.

Kilday, Gregg. "Ninth Annual Grosses Gloss." *Film Comment,* March–April 1984, pp. 62–66.

Kindem, Gorham. "Hollywood's Conversion to Color: The Technological, Economic, and Aesthetic Factors." *Journal of the University Film Association* 31 (Spring 1979):29–36.

———. "Statistical Analysis of Non-Theatrical Feature Film Exhibition: A Predictive Model for University Film Attendance." *Journal of the University Film Association* 32 (Fall 1980):55–59.

———. "Hollywood's Movie Star System and the Film Industry in the 1940s." Paper presented at the International Conference on Culture and Communication, April 1981, Philadelphia.

———. "The Demise of Kinemacolor: Technological, Legal, Economic, and Aesthetic Problems in Early Color History." *Cinema Journal* 20 (Spring 1981):3–14.

————. "Hollywood's Movie Star System: A Historical Overview." In *The American Movie Industry: The Business of Motion Pictures,* edited by Gorham Kindem, pp. 79–93. Carbondale: Southern Illinois University Press, 1982.

Kleitman, N. "The Effect of Motion Pictures on Body Temperature." *Science,* May 18, 1945, pp. 507–8.

Klenow, Daniel J., and Jeffrey L. Crane. "Selected Characteristics of the X-Rated Movie Audience: Toward a National Profile of the Recidivist." *Sociological Symposium* 20 (Fall 1977):78–83.

Knapp, Steven Duncan. "Predictors of Motion Picture Attendance." Master's thesis, University of Georgia, 1983.

Knapp, Steven, and Barry L. Sherman. "Motion Picture Attendance: A Market Segmentation Approach." In *Current Research in Film: Audiences, Economics, and Law,* vol. 2, edited by Bruce A. Austin, pp. 35–46. Norwood, N.J.: Ablex, 1986.

Knight, Howard R. *Play and Recreation in a Town of 6000.* New York: Department of Recreation, Russell Sage Foundation, 1915.

Koch, Stephen. "The Cruel, Cruel Critics." *Saturday Review,* Dec. 26, 1970, pp. 12–14, 51.

Kozielecki, Jozef. *Psychological Decision Theory.* Warsaw: Polish Scientific Publishers, 1981.

Kracauer, Siegfried. *From Caligari to Hitler: A Psychological History of German Film.* Princeton, N.J.: Princeton University Press, 1947.

Krohn, Bill, and Harley Lond. "Showscan: A New Type of Exhibition for a Revolutionary Film Process." *Boxoffice,* February 1984, pp. 10–11.

Krugman, Dean M., and Donald Eckrich. "Differences in Cable and Pay-Cable Audiences." *Journal of Advertising Research* 22 (August–September 1982):23–29.

Kruse, William F. "The Motion Picture and the American School." *International Review of Educational Cinematography* 4 (1933):645–54.

Kuhn, Thomas S. *The Structure of Scientific Revolutions.* 2nd ed., enlarged. Chicago: University of Chicago Press, 1970.

Lachenbruch, David. "Home Video: Home Is Where the Action Is." *Channels,* November–December 1983, pp. 42–43.

Landro, Laura. "Pay-TV Industry Facing Problems After Misjudging Market Demands." *Wall Street Journal,* June 29, 1983, p. 37.

Lanphier, Marion F. "A Experiment—The Child's Matinee." *Educational Screen* 1 (June 1922):183–98.

LaPiere, Richard T. "Attitudes Vs. Actions." *Social Forces* 13 (1934):230–37.

Larrabee, Eric, and Rolf Meyersohn, eds. *Mass Leisure.* Glencoe, Ill.: Free Press, 1958.

Larson, Allan David. "Integration and Attempted Integration Between the Motion Picture and Television Industries Through 1956." Ph.D. dissertation, Ohio University, 1979.

Lassner, Rudolf. "Sex and Age Determinants of Theatre and Movie Interests." *Journal of General Psychology* 31 (October 1944):241–71.

Lasswell, Harold D. "The Structure and Function of Communications in Society." In *The Communication of Ideas,* edited by Lyman Bryson, pp. 37–51. New York: Harper, 1948.

"Laughlin Boasting New Way with Coin on 4th 'Billy Jack.'" *Variety,* Nov. 13, 1985, pp. 7, 37.

Lazarsfeld, Paul F. "Audience Research in the Movie Field." *Annals of the American Academy of Political and Social Science* 254 (November 1947):160–68.

———. Foreword to *Hollywood Looks at Its Audience*, by Leo A. Handel. Urbana: University of Illinois Press, 1950.

Lazarsfeld, Paul F., and Frank N. Stanton. *Communications Research, 1948–1949*. New York: Harper, 1949.

League of Nations, Child Welfare Committee. *Reports on the Work of the Advisory Committee for the Protection and Welfare of Children and Young People*. London: George Allen and Unwin, 1938.

Lederer, Richard. "The Evolution of Movie Marketing." In *The Marketing of Motion Pictures*, edited by Roger A. Strang, pp. 45–56. Los Angeles: Graduate School of Business, University of Southern California, 1979.

Lees, David, and Stan Berkowitz. *The Movie Business*. New York: Vintage Books, 1981.

Leff, Leonard J. "A Test of American Film Censorship: *Who's Afraid of Virginia Woolf?*" *Cinema Journal* 14 (Spring 1980):41–55.

———. "Instant Movies: The Short Unhappy Life of William Sargent's Electronovision (1964–65)." *Journal of Popular Film and Television* 9 (Spring 1981):20–29.

"Leisure Time Activities." *Gallup Opinion Index*, September 1977, report #146, pp. 14–15.

Lentz, Philip. "Word of Mouth Can Make or Break a Movie." Philadelphia *Bulletin*, Jan. 7, 1979, pp. F-1, 5.

Levy, Mark R. "Program Playback Preferences in VCR Households." *Journal of Broadcasting* 24 (Summer 1980):327–36.

———. "Home Video Recorders: A User Survey." *Journal of Communication* 30 (Autumn 1980):23–27.

———. "Home Video Recorders and Time Shifting." *Journalism Quarterly* 58 (Fall 1981):401–5.

———. "The Lazarsfeld-Stanton Program Analyzer: An Historical Note." *Journal of Communication* 32 (Autumn 1982):30–38.

———. "The Time-Shifting Use of Home Video Recorders." *Journal of Broadcasting* 27 (Summer 1983):263–68.

Lewin, Kurt. *A Dynamic Theory of Personality*. New York: McGraw-Hill, 1935.

Lewis, Howard T. *The Motion Picture Industry*. New York: Van Nostrand, 1933.

Liebert, Robert M., and Neala S. Schwartzberg. "Effects of Mass Media." In *Annual Review of Psychology*, vol. 28, edited by Mark R. Rosenzweig and Lyman W. Porter, pp. 141–73. Palo Alto, Calif.: Annual Reviews, 1977.

Linck, David. "Brand Names Go Hollywood: Props That Sell." *Boxoffice*, April 1982, pp. 32–33.

Lindquist, Rae Andre. "The Evolution of an Image: Marketing Techniques of the American Motion Picture Industry, 1946–1969." Master's thesis, University of California, Los Angeles, 1969.

Lindsay, Vachel. *The Art of the Moving Picture*. New York: Macmillan, 1915.

Lipton, David A. "Advertising and Publicity." In *The Movie Business: American Film Industry Practice*, edited by A. William Bluem and Jason E. Squire, pp. 227–33. New York: Hastings House, 1972.

Litman, Barry R. "Decision-Making in the Film Industry: The Influence of the TV Market." *Journal of Communication* 32 (Summer 1982):33–52.

———. "Predicting Success of Theatrical Movies: An Empirical Study." *Journal of Popular Culture* 16 (Spring 1983):159–75.

Littlejohn, Stephen W. *Theories of Human Communication.* 2nd ed. Belmont, Calif.: Wadsworth, 1983.

Littunen, Yrjo, with Pertti Hemanus; Kaarle Nordenstreng; and Tapio Varis. "Cultural Problems of Direct Satellite Broadcasting." *International Social Science Journal,* no. 2 (1980), pp. 283–303.

Lond, Harley W. "Censorship." *Boxoffice,* June 1986, p. 6.

Los Angeles Times. A Look at Southern California Movie-Going. Los Angeles: *Los Angeles Times,* Marketing Research Dept., 1972.

Los Angeles Times. Movie Attendance in Los Angeles. Los Angeles: *Los Angeles Times,* 1976.

Lounsbury, Myron Osborn. *The Origins of American Film Criticism, 1909–1939.* New York: Arno Press, 1973 (reprint of Ph.D. dissertation, University of Pennsylvania, 1966).

Lovedahl, Gerald Grey. "An Assessment of the Effectiveness of a Film Presentation in Changing Audience Attitudes Toward and Knowledge of Industrial Arts." Ph.D. dissertation, Ohio State University, 1977.

Low, Rachel. "The Implications Behind the Social Survey." *Penguin Film Review* 2 (no. 7, 1948):107–12.

Lowery, Shearon, and Melvin L. DeFleur. *Milestones in Mass Communication Research: Media Effects.* New York: Longman, Green, 1983.

Lundberg, George A.; Mirra Komarovsky; and Mary Alice McInerny. *Leisure: A Suburban Study.* New York: Columbia University Press, 1934.

Luther, Rodney. "Marketing Aspects of Drive-in Theaters." *Journal of Marketing* 15 (July 1950):41–47.

———. "Drive-in Theaters: Rags to Riches in Five Years." *Hollywood Quarterly* 5 (Summer 1951):401–11.

———. "Television and the Future of Motion Picture Exhibition." *Hollywood Quarterly* 5 (1951):164–77.

Lydgate, William A. "Audience Pre-Testing Heads Off Flops, Forecasts Hits for Movie Producers." *Sales Management,* March 15, 1944, pp. 90, 94–98.

Lynd, Robert S., with Alice C. Hanson. "The People as Consumers." In *Recent Social Trends in the United States: Report of the President's Research Committee on Social Trends,* pp. 857–911. New York: McGraw-Hill, 1934.

Lynd, Robert S., and Helen Merrell Lynd. *Middletown.* New York: Harcourt, Brace and World, 1929.

———. *Middletown in Transition.* New York: Harcourt, Brace and World, 1937.

Mabie, E. C. "The Responses of Theatre Audiences, Experimental Studies." *Speech Monographs* 19 (November 1952):235–43.

MacCann, Richard Dyer. "Film Scholarship: Dead or Alive?" *Journal of the University Film Association* 28 (Winter 1976):3–10.

McCarthy, Kathleen D. "Nickel Vice and Virtue: Movie Censorship in Chicago, 1907–1915." *Journal of Popular Film* 5 (no. 1, 1976):37–55.

Maccoby, Eleanor E. "Why Do Children Watch TV?" *Public Opinion Quarterly* 18 (1954):239–44.

McCombs, Maxwell E. "Mass Media in the Marketplace." *Journalism Monographs,* no. 24 (August 1972).

McCombs, Maxwell E., and Chaim H. Eyal. "Spending on Mass Media." *Journal of Communication* 30 (Winter 1980):153–58.

McCoy, Edward P. "Influence of Color on Audiences' Rated Perception of Reality in Film." *Audiovisual Communication Review* 10 (January–February 1962):70–72.

McGilligan, Patrick. "Open Season on Critics." *American Film,* June 1979, pp. 6–7.

McGinnies, Elliott; Robert Lana; and Clagett Smith. "The Effects of Sound Films on Opinions About Mental Illness in Community Discussion Groups." *Journal of Applied Psychology* 42 (February 1958):40–46.

MacGowan, Kenneth. *Behind the Screen: The History and Technique of Motion Pictures.* New York: Dell, 1965.

McGuigan, Cathleen, with Peter McAlevey. "Rock Music Goes Hollywood." *Newsweek,* March 11, 1985, p. 78.

McGuire, William J. "The Nature of Attitudes and Attitude Change." In *The Handbook of Social Psychology,* 2nd ed., vol. 3, edited by G. Lindzey and E. Aronson. Reading, Mass.: Addison-Wesley, 1969.

———. "Persuasion, Resistance, and Attitude Change." In *Handbook of Communication,* edited by Ithiel de Sola Pool and Wilbur Schramm, pp. 216–52. Chicago: Rand McNally, 1973.

McKenzie, R. D. "The Rise of Metropolitan Communities." In *Recent Social Trends in the United States: Report of the President's Research Committee on Social Trends,* pp. 443–96. New York: McGraw-Hill, 1934.

McLeod, Jack M.; Carl R. Bybee; and Jean A. Durall. "Evaluating Media Performance by Gratifications Sought and Received." *Journalism Quarterly* 59 (Spring 1982):3–12, 59.

McMasters, Theresa. "MPAA Issues New Guidelines re Film Ratings." *Hollywood Reporter,* April 9, 1986, pp. 1, 7.

McQuail, Denis, ed. *Sociology of Mass Communications.* Baltimore: Penguin, 1972.

McQuail, Denis. *Mass Communication Theory.* Beverly Hills: Sage, 1983.

McQuail, Denis; Jay G. Blumler; and J. R. Brown. "The Television Audience: A Revised Perspective." In *Sociology of Mass Communications,* edited by Denis McQuail, pp. 135–65. Baltimore: Penguin, 1972.

Madsen, Axel. *The New Hollywood: American Movies in the 70s.* New York: Thomas Y. Crowell, 1975.

Madsen, K. B. *Theories of Motivation.* 4th ed. Copenhagen: Munksgaard, 1968.

Maisel, Richard. "The Decline of Mass Media." *Public Opinion Quarterly* 37 (Summer 1973):159–70.

Mano, D. Keith. "The Rocky Horror Cult." *National Review,* Nov. 24, 1978, pp. 1493–94, 1496.

Marcus, Robert D. "Moviegoing and American Culture." *Journal of Popular Culture* 3 (Spring 1970):755–66.

Marcus, Stanley. "The Viewers' Verdict So Far—On Cable TV." *Panorama* 1 (October 1980):42–45.

Margulies, Lee. "Will Movie Theaters Survive Video?" *Home Video* 3 (November 1982):50–53.

Marich, Bob. "TV Commercials in the Next Century? '2010' Offers Peek." *Advertising Age,* Dec. 3, 1984, pp. 4, 98.

"Market Research for Film Sell; Parables for Believers, Skeptics." *Variety,* May 12, 1976, pp. 162, 168, 172.

Maruyama, Magoroh. "The Second Cybernetics: Deviation-Amplifying Mutual Causal Processes." *American Scientist* 51 (1963):164–79.

Marx, Samuel. *Mayer and Thalberg: The Make-Believe Saints.* New York: Random House, 1975.

Maslow, Abraham H. *Motivation and Personality.* New York: Harper & Row, 1970.

Mason, Warren Edward, Jr. "The Effects of the Synergistic Relationship of the Mass Media and Tie-in Novels upon Adolescent Reading Interests." Ed.D. dissertation, Boston University, 1980.

Mast, Gerald. *A Short History of the Movies.* 2nd ed. Indianapolis: Bobbs-Merrill, 1976.

Matthews, Tom. "Trailers: They're Not Just for Advertising Anymore." *Boxoffice,* March 1986, pp. 22–28.

———. "Art Films: *Handle with Care.*" *Boxoffice,* May 1986, pp. 14–18.

Mauerhofer, Hugo. "Psychology of Film Experience." In *Film: A Montage of Theories,* edited by Richard Dyer MacCann, pp. 229–35. New York: E. P. Dutton, 1966.

Mauk, Marion. "An Artist in the Art of Pushing Little Films." *Los Angeles Times,* Nov. 15, 1981, Calendar sec., p. 37.

May, Lary. *Screening Out the Past: The Birth of Mass Culture and the Motion Picture Industry.* New York: Oxford University Press, 1980.

Mayer, Michael. "The Rating System." *Take One,* March 1977, p. 39.

———. *The Film Industries.* 2nd ed. New York: Hastings House, 1978.

Mead, Margaret. "The Patterns of Leisure in Contemporary American Culture." *Annals of the American Academy of Political and Social Science* 313 (September 1957):11–15.

Mendelsohn, Harold. *Mass Entertainment.* New Haven, Conn.: College and University Press, 1966.

Merton, Robert K., and Patricia L. Kendall. "The Focused Interview." *American Journal of Sociology* 51 (May 1946):541–57.

Messaris, Paul. "The Film Audience's Awareness of the Production Process." *Journal of the University Film Association* 33 (Fall 1981):53–56.

Metzger, Charles R. "Pressure Groups and the Motion Picture Industry." *Annals of the American Academy of Political and Social Science* 254 (November 1947):110–15.

Metzger, Gale D. "Cable Television Audiences." *Journal of Advertising Research* 23 (August–September 1983):41–47.

Middleton, Russell. "Ethnic Prejudice and Susceptibility to Persuasion." *American Sociological Review* 25 (October 1960):679–86.

Miller, George. "The Magic Number Seven, Plus or Minus Two: Some Limits on Our Capacity for Processing Information." In *The Psychology of Communication: Seven Essays,* edited by George Miller. New York: Basic Books, 1967.

Miller, Norman P., and Duane M. Robinson. *The Leisure Age: Its Challenge to Recreation.* Belmont, Calif.: Wadsworth, 1963.

Miller, William C. "An Experimental Study of the Relationship of Film Movement and Emotional Involvement Response, and Its Effect on Learning and Attitude Formation." Ph.D. dissertation, University of Southern California, 1967.

————. "Film Movement and Affective Response and the Effect on Learning and Attitude Formation." *AV Communication Review* 17 (Summer 1969):172–81.

Mills, Bart. "Hard Core, Soft Sell." *American Film,* April 1986, pp. 46–51.

Mink, Edward. "Why the Networks Will Survive Cable." *Atlantic Monthly,* December 1983, pp. 63–68.

Mitchell, Alice Miller. *Children and Movies.* Chicago: University of Chicago Press, 1929.

Mitchell, Arnold. *The Nine American Lifestyles.* New York: Warner Books, 1983.

"Modern Kids Shy from G: 'Marker' Happy with PG." *Variety,* April 9, 1980, pp. 7, 30.

Moley, Raymond. *Cleveland Recreation Survey: Commercial Recreation.* Cleveland: Cleveland Foundation Committee, 1920.

————. *Are We Movie Made?* New York: Macy-Masius, 1938.

Moller, K. E. Kristian, and Pirjo Karppinen. "Role of Motives and Attributes in Consumer Motion Picture Choice." *Journal of Economic Psychology* 4 (November 1983):239–62.

Monaco, James. *American Film Now.* New York: New American Library, 1979.

————. "The Brethren." *American Film,* March 1980, pp. 36–40.

————. "The Silver Screen Under Glass." *Channels,* August–September 1981, pp. 50–53.

————. *Who's Who in American Film Now.* New York: New York Zoetrope, 1981.

Moore, Douglas Cameron. "A Study of the Influence of the Film *The Birth of a Nation* on the Attitudes of Selected High School White Students Toward Negroes." Ph.D. dissertation, University of Illinois at Urbana-Champaign, 1971.

Morrisroe, Patricia. "Exclusive Interview: Sue Blane." *Rocky Horror Picture Show Official Magazine.* 1979.

————. "Making Movies the Computer Way." *Parade,* Feb. 3, 1980, p. 16.

" 'Mother's Day' Ducks X Tag from MPAA." *Variety,* Sept. 24, 1980, p. 5.

"Movie Audience Marquee Values Traced Since 1940." *Gallup Report,* December 1981, pp. 3–26.

"Movies and Movie Stars." *Fortune,* July 1937, pp. 103–4.

"The Moving Picture and the National Character." *American Review of Reviews,* September 1910, pp. 315–20.

"MPAA, NATO to Expand Testing of Info-Laden Ratings." *Variety,* Aug. 12, 1981, p. 3.

"Mull Expansion of Info-Laden Ratings." *Variety,* Jan. 6, 1982, p. 5.

Munsterberg, Hugo. *The Film: A Psychological Study, The Silent Photoplay in 1916* (originally published in 1916 under the title *The Photoplay: A Psychological Study*). New York: Dover, 1970.

Murphy, William Charles. "The Relationship Between Mental Age and the Types of Motion Pictures Liked by Children in Grades 4 to 9, Inclusive." Master's thesis, Ohio State University, 1935.

Murray, Lawrence L. "Complacency, Competition and Cooperation: The Film Industry Responds to the Challenge of Television." *Journal of Popular Film* 6 (no. 1, 1977):47–70.

Musser, Charles. "Another Look at the 'Chaser Theory.' " *Studies in Visual Communication* 10 (Fall 1984):24–44.

————. "Musser's Reply to Allen." *Studies in Visual Communication* 10 (Fall 1984):51–52.

Musun, Chris. *The Marketing of Motion Pictures: Both Sides of the Coin—Art and Business.* Los Angeles: Chris Musun Co., 1969 (reprint of a D.B.A. dissertation, University of Southern California, 1969).

Mutual Film Corp. v. *Ohio* 236 U.S. 230 (1915).

Nagaki, Teiichi. *Jido Eiga to Jido Geki.* Tokyo: Senshin-Sha, 1931.

National Broadcasting Company. "Prime Time Sunday" (transcript), broadcast July 8, 1979.

National Research Center of the Arts. *Americans and the Arts.* New York: National Committee for Cultural Resources, 1975.

"NATO Demo Promise: Pre-Knowledge of Audience Response." *Variety,* Oct. 30, 1968, p. 14.

New York (City) Committee on the Use of Leisure Time. *Report of the New York Committee on the Use of Leisure Time.* New York: Van Rees Press, 1934.

Newspaper Advertising Bureau. *Movie Going in the Metropolis.* New York: NAB, 1978.

———. *Movie Going in the United States and Canada.* New York: NAB, October 1981.

———. *Movie Going in the United States.* New York: NAB, February 1986.

Nielsen, Michael. "Hollywood's High Frontier: The Emergence of Electronic Cinema." *Journal of Film and Video* 36 (Spring 1984):31–42, 72.

North, C. J., and N. D. Golden. "The Latin American Audience Viewpoint on American Films." *Journal of the Society of Motion Picture Engineers* 17 (July 1931):18–25.

O'Brien, James McGeoghegan. "Experiencing the Popular Film: An Audience Gratifications Study." Ph.D. dissertation, Northwestern University, 1977.

O'Connor, J. Patrick. "Cable Viewers: How to Pick the Right Channel for You." *TV Guide,* Oct. 29, 1983, pp. 20–22.

O'Dell, Sylvia Lynn. "A Study of Parents' Attitudes Towards the Motion Picture Association of American Rating System." Master's thesis, Oklahoma State University, 1973.

O'Donnel, Victoria, and June Kable. *Persuasion: An Interactive-Dependency Approach.* New York: Random House, 1982.

Ogburn, William F., with Clark Tibbitts. "The Family and Its Functions." In *Recent Social Trends in the United States: Report of the President's Research Committee on Social Trends.* New York: McGraw-Hill, 1934.

O'Guinn, Thomas. "The Audience's Choice: Movie Selection and Word of Mouth." Paper presented at the International Communication Association conference, May 1981, Minneapolis.

———. "The Diffusion of Information Concerning New Motion Pictures." Ph.D. dissertation, University of Texas at Austin, 1982.

O'Guinn, Thomas C.; Ronald J. Faber; and Timothy P. Meyer. "Personal Influence and New Movie Selection: Identifying and Targeting Opinion Leaders." In *Proceedings of the Southern Marketing Association Annual Convention,* 1983, edited by Ronald Taylor, pp. 325–92.

Olasky, Marvin N. "The Failure of Movie Industry Public Relations, 1921–1934." *Journal of Popular Film and Television* 12 (Winter 1984–85):163–70.

Olshavsky, Richard W. "Time and Rate of Adoption of Innovations." *Journal of Consumer Research* 6 (March 1980):425–28.

Opinion Research Corporation. *The Public Appraises Movies: A Survey for Motion Picture Association of America* (1957). Brigham Young University, Department of Archives and Manuscripts, National Association of Theatre Owners file, Box 9, Folder 10.

Ostlund, Lyman E. "Perceived Innovation Attributes as Predictors of Innovativeness." *Journal of Consumer Research* 1 (September 1974):23–29.

Ostroff, David H. "A History of STV Inc. and the 1964 California Vote Against Pay Television." *Journal of Broadcasting* 27 (Fall 1983):371–86.

Otis, Laura. "Selective Exposure to the Film *Close Encounters.*" *Journal of Psychology* 101 (March 1979):293–95.

Owens, Dallas, and Roger Rollin. "A Model for Explaining Movie Popularity." Paper presented at the Popular Culture Association conference, April 1979, Pittsburgh.

Paletz, David, and Michael Noonan. "The Exhibitors." *Film Quarterly* 19 (Winter 1965–66):14–40.

Palmer, C. A. "Commercial Practices in Audience Analysis." *Journal of the University Film Association* 6 (Spring 1954):9–10.

Palmgreen, Philip, and J. D. Rayburn II. "Gratifications Sought and Media Exposure: An Expectancy Value Model." *Communication Research* 9 (October 1982):561–80.

———. "An Expectancy-Value Approach to Media Gratifications." In *Media Gratifications Research: Current Perspectives,* edited by Karl Erik Rosengren, Lawrence A. Wenner, and Philip Palmgreen, pp. 61–72. Beverly Hills: Sage, 1985.

Palmgreen, Philip; Lawrence A. Wenner; and J. D. Rayburn. "Relations Between Gratifications Sought and Obtained: A Study of Television News." *Communication Research* 7 (April 1980):161–92.

———. "Gratification Discrepancies and News Program Choice." *Communication Research* 8 (October 1981):451–78.

Palmgreen, Philip; Lawrence A. Wenner; and Karl Erik Rosengren. "Uses and Gratifications Research: The Last Ten Years." Paper presented at the International Communication Association conference, May 1984, San Francisco.

Panda, K. C.; J. K. Das; and R. N. Kanungo. "A Cross-Cultural Study of Film Preferences on an Indian Student Population." *Journal of Social Psychology* 57 (1962):93–104.

Panda, K. C., and R. N. Kanungo. "A Study of Indian Students' Attitude Towards the Motion Picture." *Journal of Social Psychology* 57 (June 1962):23–31.

"Papers Outscore TV in Movie Ad Test." *Editor & Publisher,* June 7, 1975, p. 40.

Parker, Stanley. *The Sociology of Leisure.* London: George Allen and Unwin, 1976.

Patel, A. S. "Attitudes of Adolescent Pupils Toward Cinema Films: A Study." *Journal of Education and Psychology* 9 (no. 4, 1952):225–30.

"Pay-TV: An *InterMedia* Study." *InterMedia* 10 (January 1982):1–16.

Peary, Danny. *Cult Movies.* New York: Delta, 1981.

Peck, Jeff. "The Child Audience for Theatrical Films in Australia." *Media Information Australia,* August 1980, pp. 43–46.

Pennebaker, James W. "Truckin' with Country-Western Psychology." *Psychology Today,* November 1979, pp. 18, 20.

"The People's Taste in Movies, Books, and Radio." *Fortune,* March 1949, pp. 39–44.

Peri, Joseph. "The Effects of Film Repetition, Programmed Discussion and Audience-Set on the Changing of Verbally Professed Attitudes Toward Due Process of Law." Ed.D. dissertation, University of California, Los Angeles, 1968.

Perkins, Daniel J. "The Sponsored Film: A New Dimension in American Film Research." *Historical Journal of Film, Radio and Television* 2 (October 1982):133–40.

Perry, Clarence Arthur. "Frequency of Attendance of High-School Students at the Movies." *School Review* 31 (October 1923):573–87.

Perry, Paul K. "Marketing and Attitude Research Applied to Motion Pictures." Paper presented at the International Gallup Conference, March 26, 1968, New Delhi, India.

Peterson, Ruth C., and L. L. Thurstone. *Motion Pictures and the Social Attitudes of Children.* New York: Macmillan, 1933.

Phelan, Rev. J. J. *Motion Pictures as a Phase of Commercialized Amusement in Toledo, Ohio.* Toledo: Little Book Press, 1919.

Phelps, Guy. *Film Censorship.* London: Victor Gollancz, 1975.

Political and Economic Planning. *The British Film Industry.* London: PEP, 1952.

Polon, Martin. "Future Technologies in Motion Pictures." In *The Movie Business Book,* edited by Jason E. Squire, pp. 388–403. Englewood Cliffs, N.J.: Prentice-Hall, 1983.

Post, Gene Leroy. "A Study of the Effect of a Subliminal Stimulus upon Attitudes Developed Toward a Character Portrayed in a Motion Picture Film." Ph.D. dissertation, Oklahoma State University, 1965.

Powdermaker, Hortense. *Hollywood: The Dream Factory.* Boston: Little, Brown, 1950.

Pratt, David. "Widescreen Box Office Performance to 1959." *Velvet Light Trap,* no. 21 (Summer 1985), pp. 64–65.

Pryluck, Calvin. " 'There's Nothing So Practical as a Good Theory.' " *AFI Education Newsletter* 5 (September–October 1981):1–2.

————. "Industralization of Entertainment in the United States." In *Current Research in Film: Audiences, Economics, and Law,* vol. 2, edited by Bruce A. Austin, pp. 117–35. Norwood, N.J.: Ablex, 1986.

Pryor, Thomas M. "Sneaks Aren't Sneaky, So What Do They Prove?" *Variety,* Jan. 12, 1983, pp. 6, 46.

Punj, Girish N., and David W. Stewart. "An Interaction Framework of Consumer Decision Making." *Journal of Consumer Research* 10 (September 1983):181–96.

Raines, I. I. "Preferences of a Small Town Motion Picture Audience." *Current Economic Comment,* May 1951, pp. 51–59.

Raitt, Charles B. *A Survey of Recreational Facilities in Rochester, NY.* Rochester: Council of Social Agencies, June 1929.

Rajecki, D. W. *Attitudes: Themes and Advances.* Sunderland, Mass.: Sinauer Associates, 1982.

Ramsaye, Terry. *A Million and One Nights: A History of the Motion Picture Through 1925.* New York: Simon and Schuster, 1926.

Ramseyer, Lloyd L. "A Study of the Influence of Documentary Films." Ph.D. dissertation, Ohio State University, 1938.

————. "Factors Influencing Attitudes and Attitude Change." *Educational Research Bulletin* 18 (January 1939):9–14, 30.

————. "Measuring the 'Intangible' Effects of Motion Pictures." *Educational Screen* 18 (September 1939):237–38, 261.

Randall, Richard S. *Censorship of the Movies: The Social and Political Control of a Mass Medium.* Madison: University of Wisconsin Press, 1968.

――――. "Classification by the Motion Picture Industry." In *Technical Reports of the Commission on Obscenity and Pornography,* vol. 5, p. 219–92. Washington, D.C.: U.S. Government Printing Office, 1970.

Raths, Louis E., and Frank N. Trager. "Public Opinion and *Crossfire.*" *Journal of Educational Sociology* 21 (February 1948):345–68.

"Rating the Rating System." *Time,* May 31, 1977, pp. 72–73.

Real, Michael R. "Understanding Oscar: The Academy Awards Telecast as International Media Event." In *Popular Culture and Media Events,* edited by Vincent Mosco and Janet Wasko, pp. 153–78. The Critical Communications Review, vol 3. Norwood, N.J.: Ablex, 1985.

"Replies to a Questionnaire." *Sight and Sound,* October–December 1953, pp. 99–104, 112.

Respress, James R. "The New Motion Picture Rating Code and Its Effect on Teenage Audiences." Master's thesis, Michigan State University, 1973.

Ressner, Jeffrey. "Film Soundtracks to Flood '86 Market." *Hollywood Reporter,* Dec. 12, 1985, pp. 4, 17.

――――. "Labels Usher In '86 Soundtracks." *Hollywood Reporter,* Jan. 27, 1986, pp. 1, 12.

Richard, Julie. "Movie Sequels . . . More to Come." *Boxoffice,* December 1985, pp. 38–40.

Richards, Jeffrey. "Controlling the Screen: The British Cinema in the 1930s." *History Today* 33 (March 1983):11–17.

Riesman, David. "The Suburban Dislocation." *Annals of the American Academy of Political and Social Science* 314 (November 1957):123–46.

Riesman, David, and Evelyn Riesman. "Movies and Audiences." *American Quarterly* 4 (1952):195–202.

Riley, Matilda White, and John W. Riley, Jr. "A Sociological Approach to Communications Research." *Public Opinion Quarterly* 15 (Fall 1951):445–60.

Ritze, Frederick Henry. "Responses of Pakistani College Students to a Selected American Film." Ed.D. dissertation, Columbia University, 1967.

Rivkin, Allen. "The Hollywood Letter." *Free World* 12 (October 1946):66–67.

Robbins, Jim. "Survey Says Public Likes Sci-Fi But Really Loves Comedy." *Variety,* Sept. 22, 1982, p. 22.

Roberts, Kenneth. *Leisure.* London: Longman Group, 1970.

Robertus, Patricia, and Rita James Simon. "The Movie Code: A View from Parents and Teenagers." *Journalism Quarterly* 47 (Autumn 1970):568–69, 629.

Robinson, Deanna Mae Campbell. "Film Analyticity: Variations in Viewer Orientation." Ph.D. dissertation, University of Oregon, 1974.

Robinson, John P. *How Americans Use Their Time: A Social-Psychological Analysis of Everyday Behavior.* New York: Praeger, 1977.

Rogers, Everett M. *Diffusion of Innovations.* 3rd ed. New York: Free Press, 1983.

Ronan, Margaret. "Increasing Unhappiness with Movie Ratings." *Senior Scholastic,* Nov. 29, 1979, pp. 12–13.

Rook, Dennis W. "The Ritual Dimension of Consumer Behavior." *Journal of Consumer Research* 12 (December 1985):251–64.

Roper Organization. *Evolving Public Attitudes Toward Television and Other Mass Media.* New York: Television Information Office, 1981.

Rose, Ernest Daniel. "Attitude as a Function of Discrepancy Resolution in Multiple Channel Communication." Ph.D. dissertation, Stanford University, 1964.

Rose, Nicholas. "Some Comments on Motion Picture Research." *Journal of the University Film Producers Association* 6 (Spring 1954):3–8.

Rosen, Irwin C. "The Effect of the Motion Picture 'Gentleman's Agreement' on Attitudes Toward Jews." *Journal of Psychology* 26 (October 1948):525–36.

Rosenfield, Jonas, Jr. "Introduction." In *The Marketing of Motion Pictures,* edited by Roger A. Strang, pp. 1–3. Los Angeles: Graduate School of Business, University of Southern California, 1979.

Rosengren, Karl Erik; Lawrence A. Wenner; and Philip Palmgreen, eds. *Media Gratifications Research: Current Perspectives.* Beverly Hills: Sage, 1985.

Rosenthal, Solomon P. "Change of Socio-Economic Attitudes Under Radical Motion Picture Propaganda." *Archives of Psychology* 166 (April 1934):5–46.

Rosenzweig, Roy. *Eight Hours for What We Will: Workers and Leisure in an Industrial City, 1870–1920.* Cambridge: Cambridge University Press, 1983.

Rosnow, Ralph L. "Psychology of Rumor Reconsidered." *Psychological Bulletin* 87 (1980):578–91.

Rosnow, Ralph L., and Allan J. Kimmel. "Lives of a Rumor." *Psychology Today,* June 1979, pp. 88–92.

Rosten, Leo C. "A 'Middletown' Study of Hollywood." *Public Opinion Quarterly* 5 (April 1939):314–20.

Roth, Morry. "Teens Leaving Theaters for Homevid." *Variety,* Feb. 26, 1986, pp. 3, 34.

Rothe, James T.; Michael G. Harvey; and George C. Michael. "The Impact of Cable Television on Subscriber and Non-Subscriber Behavior." *Journal of Advertising Research* 23 (August–September 1983):15–23.

Rothman, Cliff. "Disney Logo Helps Box Office." *Hollywood Reporter,* Nov. 27, 1985, pp. 1, 10.

———. "NATO to Hear $22 Mil Plan to Lure Audiences to Theaters." *Hollywood Reporter,* March 14, 1986, pp. 1, 32.

Rotkin, Nora J. "Product Visibility in Motion Pictures." *Marketing Communications,* July 1982, pp. 4–5.

Rowland, Willard D., Jr. *The Politics of TV Violence: Policy Uses of Communication Research.* Beverly Hills: Sage, 1983.

Rubin, Alan M. "Ritualized and Instrumental Uses of Television." Paper presented at the Speech Communication Association conference, Washington, D.C., November 1983.

Rubin, Alan M., and Sven Windahl. "The Uses and Dependency Model of Mass Communication." *Critical Studies in Mass Communication* 3 (June 1986):184–99.

Ryan, Bryce, and Neal Gross. "The Diffusion of Hybrid Seed Corn in Two Iowa Communities." *Rural Sociology* 7 (March 1943):15–24.

Ryan, Steve S. "An Adjective Rating Scale for Film Previews." Paper presented at the University Film Association conference, August 1977, College Park, Md. (available in ERIC ED 144 157).

Samuels, Stuart. *Midnight Movies.* New York: Collier Books, 1983.

Samuelson, Robert J. "The Joy of Statistics." *Newsweek,* Nov. 4, 1985, p. 55.

"Say Vid Exhibition 5 Years in Future." *Variety,* April 14, 1984, p. 7.

Sayre, Nora. "Cult Films." *Horizon,* September 1979, pp. 64–69.

Schatz, Thomas. *Hollywood Genres.* Philadelphia: Temple University Press, 1981.

Schramm, Wilbur. "How Communication Works." In *The Process and Effects of Mass Communication,* edited by Wilbur Schramm, pp. 3–26. Urbana: University of Illinois Press, 1954.

Schumach, Murray. *The Face on the Cutting Room Floor: The Story of Movie and Television Censorship.* New York: Da Capo Press, 1964.

Schwartz, Stanley. "Film Music and Attitude Change: The Effect of Manipulating a Musical Soundtrack upon Changes in Attitude Toward Militarism-Pacifism Held by Tenth-Grade Social Studies Students." Ph.D. dissertation, Syracuse University, 1970.

Schweitzer, Harold Clayton, Jr. "Comparison of Color and Black and White Films in the Modification of Attitudes." Ph.D. dissertation, Fordham University, 1963.

Scott, Edward M. "Personality and Movie Preference." *Psychological Reports* 3 (March 1957):17–18.

Seagoe, May V. "Children's Television Habits and Preferences." *Quarterly of Film, Radio and Television* 6 (1951–52):143–53.

Segers, Frank. "Gallup Check re Likes: Theatre, and/or, Homes." *Variety,* May 25, 1977, pp. 13, 38.

———. "Say VCR Effect on Tix Sales Peaking." *Variety,* Jan. 15, 1986, pp. 7, 36.

Seidman, Tony. "Homevid Aids Cinema B.O. for Two Pics." *Variety,* Oct. 26, 1983, pp. 1, 396.

"Selig Nixes Drive-in Doomcriers: L.A. Ozoner Biz Hit Peak in '82." *Variety,* June 22, 1983, p. 23.

Selltiz, Claire; Lawrence S. Wrightsman; and Stuart W. Cook. *Research Methods in Social Relations.* 3rd ed. New York: Holt, Rinehart and Winston, 1976.

Shaffer, Helen B. "Movie-TV Competition." *Editorial Reports,* Jan. 18, 1957, pp. 45–61.

Shah, Diane K.; with Jennifer Foote and Joseph B. Cumming, Jr. "Horror Show." *Newsweek,* July 17, 1978, p. 93.

Shaw, David. *Journalism Today.* New York: Harper's College Press, 1977.

Shook, Mollie Stell Wiggans. "Changing the Racial Attitudes of White Students Toward Blacks Using Commercially Produced Films." Ed.D. dissertation, Duke University, 1972.

Short, K. R. M. "Hollywood Fights Anti-Semitism, 1945–1947." In *Feature Films as History,* edited by K. R. M. Short, pp. 157–89. Knoxville: University of Tennessee Press, 1981.

Short, Ray LeRoy. "A Social Study of the Motion Picture." Master's thesis, State University of Iowa, 1916.

Short, William H. "The Effect of Motion Pictures on the Social Attitudes of High-School Children." *Journal of Educational Sociology* 6 (December 1932):220–26.

Shuttleworth, Frank K. "Measuring the Influence of Motion-Picture Attendance on Conduct and Attitudes." *Journal of Educational Sociology* 6 (December 1932):216–19.

Shuttleworth, Frank K., and Mark A. May. *The Social Conduct and Attitudes of Movie Fans.* New York: Macmillan, 1933.

Silverman, Stephen M. "Hollywood Cloning: Sequels, Prequels, Remakes, and Spin-Offs." *American Film,* July–August 1978, pp. 24–30.

Silverman, Syd. "Entertainment in the Satellite Era." *Variety,* Oct. 26, 1983, pp. 13, 99.

Silvey, Robert, and Judy Kenyon. "Why You Go to the Pictures." *Films and Filming* 11 (June 1965):4–5, 36.

Simon, Armando. "A Quantitative Nonreactive Study of Mass Behavior with Emphasis on the Cinema as Behavioral Catalyst." *Psychological Reports* 48 (June 1981):775–85.

Simon, Julian L. *Basic Research Methods in Social Science.* 2nd ed. New York: Random House, 1978.

Simonet, Thomas. *Regression Analysis of Prior Experiences of Key Production Personnel as Predictors of Revenues from High-Grossing Motion Pictures in American Release.* New York: Arno Press, 1980 (reprint of a Ph.D. dissertation, Temple University, 1977).

———. "Industry." *Film Comment,* January–February 1978, pp. 72–73.

———. "Performers' Marquee Values in Relation to Top-Grossing Films." Paper presented at the Society for Cinema Studies Conference, March 1978, Philadelphia.

———. "Market Research: Beyond the Fanny of the Cohn." *Film Comment,* January–February 1980, pp. 66–69.

———. "Conglomerates and Content: Remakes, Sequels, and Series in the New Hollywood." In *Current Research in Film: Audiences, Economics, and Law,* vol. 3, edited by Bruce A. Austin, pp. 154–62. Norwood, N.J.: Ablex, 1987.

———. Untitled and unpublished manuscript. Rider College, no date.

Simonet, Thomas, and Kenneth Harwood. "Popular Favorites and Critics' Darlings Among Film Directors in American Release, 1930–1971." Paper presented at the Society for Cinema Studies conference, March 1977, Evanston, Ill.

Sindlinger and Company. *An Analysis of the Motion Picture Industry 1946–1953, Volume 1.* Brigham Young University, Department of Archives and Manuscripts, National Association of Theater Owners file, Box 9, Folder 8.

Sklar, Robert. *Movie-Made America: A Cultural History of American Movies.* New York: Vintage Books, 1975.

Slater, Dan, and Teresa L. Thompson. "Attitudes of Parents Concerning Televised Warning Statements." *Journalism Quarterly* 61 (Winter 1984):853–59.

Slesinger, Donald. "The Film and Public Opinion." In *Print, Radio, and Film in a Democracy,* edited by Douglas Waples, pp. 79–98. Chicago: University of Chicago Press, 1942.

Smith, David M. "Explaining Everyday Life: Some Aspects of Children's Use of Mass Media for Information." *Gazette* 30 (no. 2, 1982):73–87.

Smythe, Dallas W.; John R. Gregory; Alvin Ostrin; Oliver P. Colvin; and William Moroney. "Portrait of a First-Run Audience." *Quarterly of Film, Radio and Television* 9 (Summer 1955):390–409.

Smythe, Dallas; Parker B. Lusk,; and Charles A. Lewis. "Portrait of an Art-Theater Audience." *Quarterly of Film, Radio and Television* 8 (Fall 1953):28–50.

Solomon, Stanley J. *Beyond Formula: American Film Genres.* New York: Harcourt Brace Jovanovich, 1976.

Somers, Dale A. "The Leisure Revolution: Recreation in the American City." *Journal of Popular Culture* 5 (Summer 1971):125–47.

Sontag, Susan. "Notes on 'Camp.'" In *Against Interpretation,* pp. 275–92. New York: Delta, 1966.

Sorokin, Pitirim A., and Clarence Q. Berger. *Time-Budgets of Human Behavior.* Cambridge, Mass.: Harvard University Press, 1939.

Spainhour, Con R. Letter to the editor. *Boxoffice,* December 1980, p. 4.

Spake, Amanda. "Dear Filmgoer . . ." *American Film,* November 1982, pp. 12, 16.

Spraos, John. *The Decline of the Cinema: An Economist's Report.* London: George Allen and Unwin, 1962.

Stabiner, Karen. "The Shape of Theaters to Come." *American Film,* September 1982, pp. 51–56.

Stagner, Ross. "Homeostasis, Discrepancy, Dissonance: A Theory of Motives and Motivation." *Motivation and Emotion* 1 (June 1977):103–38.

Stegman, Allan. "The Large-Screen Film: A Viable Entertainment Alternative to High-Definition Television." *Journal of Film and Video* 36 (Spring 1982):21–30, 72.

Steinberg, Charles S. "The Significance of Film Reviewers." In *The Movie Business,* edited by A. William Bluem and Jason E. Squire, pp. 237–49. New York: Hastings House, 1972.

Steiner, J. F. "Recreation and Leisure Time Activities." In *Recent Social Trends in the United States: Report of the President's Research Committee on Social Trends,* pp. 912–57. New York: McGraw-Hill, 1934.

Stephenson, William. *The Play Theory of Mass Communication.* Chicago: University of Chicago Press, 1967.

———. "Applications of Communication Theory: IV. Immediate Experience of Movies." *Operant Subjectivity* 1 (July 1978):96–116.

Sterling, Christopher H., and Timothy R. Haight. *The Mass Media: Aspen Institute Guide to Communication Industry Trends.* New York: Praeger, 1978.

Sterling, Christopher H., and John M. Kittross. *Stay Tuned: A Concise History of American Broadcasting.* Belmont, Calif.: Wadsworth, 1978.

"Still More Dire Predictions for Theatres." *Boxoffice,* May 1986, p. 62.

Strickland, Janet. "How Australian Film Censorship Works." *Cinema Papers,* January 1977, pp. 206–8, 280.

Stuart, Frederic. *The Effects of Television on the Motion Picture and Radio Industries.* New York: Arno Press, 1976 (reprint of a Ph.D. dissertation, Columbia University, 1960).

"Study Blames TV for Theatre Drop." *Broadcasting,* Feb. 3, 1958, p. 58.

Sturmthal, Adolf, and Alberta Curtis. "Program Analyzer Tests of Two Educational Films." In *Radio Research 1942–1943,* edited by Paul F. Lazarsfeld and Frank N. Stanton, pp. 485–506. New York: Essential Books, 1944.

Sullenger, T. Earl. "Modern Youth and the Movies." *School and Society* 32 (Oct. 4, 1930):459–61.

"Survey in Syracuse Shows Moviegoers Utilize Newspapers." *Variety,* July 31, 1985, pp. 7, 23.

Swanson, Charles E., and Robert L. Jones. "Television Owning and Its Correlates." *Journal of Applied Psychology* 35 (no. 5, 1951):352–57.

Swindell, Larry. "The Day the Silents Stopped." *American Film,* October 1977, pp. 24–31.

Sydenstricker, Edgar. "The Vitality of the American People." In *Recent Social Trends in the United States: Report of the President's Research Committee on Social Trends,* pp. 602–60. New York: McGraw-Hill, 1934.

Tannenbaum, Rob. "Soundtracks Thrived in Summer of '85." *Rolling Stone,* Nov. 21, 1985, pp. 15–17.

Taylor, Ryland A. "Televised Movies: Directors Win Audience." *Journal of Broadcasting* 20 (Fall 1976):495–500.

Thomas, Bob. *King Cohn: The Life and Times of Harry Cohn.* New York: G. P. Putnam's Sons, 1967.

Thomas, Sari. "Introduction." In *Film/Culture: Explorations of Cinema in Its Social Context,* edited by Sari Thomas, pp. 1–10. Metuchen, N.J.: Scarecrow Press, 1982.

Thompson, Warren S., and P. K. Whelpton. "The Population of the Nation." In *Recent Social Trends in the United States: Report of the President's Research Committee on Social Trends,* pp. 1–58. New York: McGraw-Hill, 1934.

Thorp, Margaret Farrand. *America at the Movies.* New Haven, Conn.: Yale University Press, 1939.

Thurstone, L. L. "Attitudes Can Be Measured." *American Journal of Sociology* 33 (January 1928):529–54.

———. "A Scale for Measuring Attitude Toward Movies." *Journal of Educational Research* 2 (September 1930):89–94.

Thurstone, L. L., and E. J. Chave. *The Measurement of Attitude.* Chicago: University of Chicago Press, 1929.

" 'Timing' Producer Has a Vex with 'X' Rating, Ad Censorship." *Variety,* Oct. 29, 1980, pp. 5, 42.

Tinsley, Howard E. A.; Thomas C. Barrett; and Richard A. Kass. "Leisure Activities and Need Satisfaction." *Journal of Leisure Research* 9 (fourth quarter, 1977):110–20.

Tinsley, Howard E. A., and Richard A. Kass. "Leisure Activities and Need Satisfaction: A Replication and Extension." *Journal of Leisure Research* 10 (third quarter, 1978):191–202.

Tocqueville, Alexis de. *Democracy in America.* New York: New American Library, 1956.

Toffler, Alvin. *The Culture Consumers.* New York: Vintage Books, 1964.

Tolman, Edward C. *Purposive Behavior in Animals and Men.* New York: Century, 1932.

Towriss, J. G. "A New Approach to the Use of Expectancy Value Models." *Journal of the Market Research Society* 26 (January 1984):63–75.

Traub, James. "Intrigues of the Story Trade: How Mega-Books Become Mini-Series." *Channels,* March–April 1985, pp. 22–26.

Traudt, Paul J.; James A. Anderson; and Timothy P. Meyer. "Phenomenology of Mass Communication: Unpacking the Media Experience." Paper presented at the Speech Communication Association conference, November 1985, Denver.

Trauth, Denise M., and John L. Huffman. "Obscenity and Cable Television: A Regulatory Approach." *Journalism Monographs,* no. 95 (March 1986).

"Trib-Star Checks Out Film Fans, and Where They Get Info (Not TV)." *Variety,* Dec. 15, 1976, p. 34.

Troland, Leonard Thompson. "Psychology of Natural Color Motion Pictures." *American Journal of Physiological Optics* 7 (1926):375–82.

Truffaut, Francois. "Une Certaine Tendance du Cinéma Française." *Cahiers du Cinéma,* January 1954.

Tudor, Andrew. "Film and the Measurement of Its Effects." *Screen* 10 (July–October 1969):148–59.

———. *Image and Influence: Studies in the Sociology of Film.* New York: St. Martin's, 1974.

Tunstall, Jeremy. *The Media Are American.* New York: Columbia University Press, 1977.

Tusher, Will. "Exhibs, Prods. Agree to Test a New Rating." *Variety,* Oct. 29, 1980, pp. 1, 31.

———. "Valenti Backs Bid to Revise Ratings." *Variety,* Feb. 1, 1984, p. 3.

———. "New PG-13 Rating Instituted by MPAA; Will Cover Some Pix That Would've Been R-Rated." *Variety,* July 4, 1984, pp. 3, 30.

———. "Majors Draw Up Strong Code on Drugs in Films." *Variety,* Jan. 22, 1986, pp. 1, 90.

———. "Col Survey Shows Vid Rentals Far Outdistancing Admissions; 'Staggering' VCR Growth Cited." *Variety,* May 21, 1986, pp. 3, 44.

"Twice as Many Drive-in Theaters?" *Business Week,* Jan. 1, 1949, pp. 44–45.

Twomey, John E. "Some Considerations on the Rise of the Art-Film Theater." *Quarterly of Film, Radio and Television* 10 (Spring 1956):239–47.

Ulloth, Dana R.; Peter Klinge; and Sandra Ellis. *Mass Media: Past, Present, Future.* St. Paul: West, 1983.

Unger, Lynette S., and Jerome B. Kernan. "On the Meaning of Leisure: An Investigation of Some Determinants of the Subjective Experience." *Journal of Consumer Research* 9 (March 1983):381–92.

United Media Enterprises. *Where Does the Time Go? The United Media Enterprises Report on Leisure in America.* New York: Newspaper Enterprise Association, 1983.

United States. Senate. *Motion Pictures and Juvenile Delinquency.* Report of the Committee on the Judiciary, Interim Report of the Subcommittee to Investigate Juvenile Delinquency. 84th Congress, 2nd Session, Report #2055. Washington, D.C.: U.S. Government Printing Office, 1956.

United States. Bureau of the Census. *Historical Statistics of the United States from Colonial Times to 1970.* Washington, D.C.: U.S. Government Printing Office, 1970.

United States. Bureau of the Census, Department of Commerce. *1970 Census of the Population,* vol. 1. Washington, D.C.: U.S. Government Printing Office, 1973.

United States. House of Representatives, Subcommittee on Special Small Business Problems. *Movie Ratings and the Independent Producer.* H.R. Rep. No. 966, 95th Cong., 2d Sess. Washington, D.C.: U.S. Government Printing Office, 1978.

United States. Senate Committee on the Judiciary, 97th Congress, 1st and 2nd Sessions. *Copyright Infringements (Audio and Video Recorders).* Washington, D.C.: U.S. Government Printing Office, 1982.

Utz, Walter Julius, Jr. "The Comparative Effect of Color and Black and White Film Clips upon Rated Perception of Reality." Ph.D. dissertation, University of Illinois, 1968.

"Valenti Brings in News Leak Experts." *Variety,* March 12, 1975, pp. 5, 24.

Valenti, Jack. "The Public Votes 'Yes' for the Rating System." Speech presented at the National Association of Theatre Owners Convention, Nov. 3, 1970, Bal Harbour, Fla. Brigham Young University, National Association of Theatre Owners Archives, Box 5, Folder 3.

———. "Remarks by Jack Valenti to the Annual Convention of the National Association of Theatre Owners," Oct. 26, 1977, Miami Beach.

———. "Who Really Knows Best? Film Fans or the Critics?" *Los Angeles Times,* Feb. 6, 1979, part IV.

————. "The Movie Rating System." Motion Picture Association of America, no date, mimeographed.

Van Leuven, Jim. "Expectancy Theory in Media and Message Selection." *Communication Research* 8 (October 1981):425–34.

Veblen, Thorstein. *The Theory of the Leisure Class: An Economic Study in the Evaluation of Institutions.* New York: Macmillan, 1899.

Vizzard, Jack. *See No Evil: Life Inside a Hollywood Censor.* New York: Simon and Schuster, 1970.

VonGunden, Kenneth. "The RH Factor." *Film Comment,* September–October 1979, pp. 54–56.

Vroom, Victor H. *Work and Motivation.* New York: John Wiley, 1964.

Wagner, Richard V. "The Study of Attitude Change: An Introduction." In *The Study of Attitude Change,* edited by R. V. Wagner and J. J. Sherwood, pp. 1–18. Belmont, Calif.: Brooks/Cole, 1969.

Walker, Alexander. *The Shattered Silents: How the Talkies Came to Stay.* New York: William Morrow, 1978.

Wall, W. D., and E. M. Smith. "The Film Choices of Adolescents." *British Journal of Educational Psychology* 19 (June 1949):121–36.

Wanderer, Jules J. "In Defense of Popular Taste: Film Ratings Among Professionals and Lay Audiences." *American Journal of Sociology* 76 (September 1970):262–72.

Ware, Norman J. *Labor in Modern Industrial Society.* Boston: D. C. Heath, 1935.

Warga, Wayne. "Major Film Exhibitor Won't Support New Rating System." *Los Angeles Times,* Nov. 11, 1968, part IV, pp. 1, 27.

Warner, Harry P. "Television and the Motion Picture Industry." *Hollywood Quarterly* 2 (1946):11–18.

Warner, W. Lloyd, and Paul S. Lunt. *The Social Life of a Modern Community.* New Haven, Conn.: Yale University Press, 1941.

Warshow, Robert. *The Immediate Experience: Movies, Comics, Theatre and Other Aspects of Popular Culture.* New York: Atheneum, 1970.

Wasko, Janet. *Movies and Money: Financing the American Film Industry.* Norwood, N.J.: Ablex, 1982.

————. "Hollywood, New Technology and International Banking: A Formula for Success." In *Current Research in Film: Audiences, Economics, and Law,* vol. 1, edited by Bruce A. Austin, pp. 101–10. Norwood, N.J.: Ablex, 1985.

Waterman, David. "Videocassettes, Videodiscs, and the Role of Theatrical Distribution." Paper presented at the Columbia University Research Program in Telecommunications and Information Policy conference, March 1984, New York City.

Waterman, David, and Arnold Glass. "Movie Concept Testing." Unpublished manuscript, Waterman, Glass & Associates, Los Angeles, November 1983.

Watzlawick, Paul. *How Real Is Real?* New York: Vintage Books, 1976.

Wax, Morton D. "When Do Exhibitors Get a Piece of the Royal Pie?" *Boxoffice,* March 1984, p. 54.

"WBBM in Live-Lens Survey; 75% of Kids Testing Chicago Theatres Admitted to 'R' Pics." *Variety,* May 9, 1979, p. 31.

Webb, Eugene J.; Donald T. Campbell; Richard D. Schwartz; and Lee Sechrest. *Unobtrusive Measures: Nonreactive Research in the Social Sciences.* Chicago: Rand McNally, 1966.

Webster, James G. "The Impact of Cable and Pay Cable Television on Local Audiences." *Journal of Broadcasting* 27 (Spring 1983):119–26.

Weigall, Arthur. "The Influence of the Kinematograph upon National Life." *Nineteenth Century* 89 (April 1921):661–72.

Weiner, Bernard. *Theories of Motivation: From Mechanism to Cognition.* Chicago: Markham, 1972.

Weir, L. H. *Recreation Survey of Buffalo.* Buffalo: Department of Parks and Public Buildings, 1925.

Weisgerber, Robert Arthur. "The Effect of Science Motivational Films on the Attitudes of Secondary School Pupils Toward the Field of Science." Ed.D. dissertation, Indiana University, 1960.

Wells, Carl D. "The Motion Picture Versus the Church." *Sociology and Social Research* 16 (1932):540–46.

Wenden, D. J. *The Birth of the Movies.* New York: E. P. Dutton, 1974.

"What and Who Influences Critics: Kael on Studio Execs." *Variety,* Dec. 17, 1980, p. 4.

"What Students Think of Movies." *Photo-Era* 62 (January 1929):49 and 62; (February 1929);102–3.

White, Lawrence J. "Antitrust and Video Markets: The Merger of Showtime and The Movie Channel as a Case Study." In *Video Media Competition: Regulation, Economics, and Technology,* edited by Eli M. Noam, pp. 338–63. New York: Columbia University Press, 1985.

Wicker, A. W. "Attitudes Versus Actions: The Relationship of Verbal and Overt Behavioral Responses to Attitude Objects." *Journal of Social Issues* 25 (1969):41–78.

Wickline, Lee Edwin. "The Effect of Motivational Films on the Attitudes and Understandings of High School Students Concerning Science and Scientists." Ed.D. dissertation, Pennsylvania State University, 1964.

Wiese, Mildred J., and Stewart G. Cole. "A Study of Children's Attitudes and the Influence of a Commercial Motion Picture." *Journal of Psychology* 21 (January 1946):151–71.

Williams, Dwight A., Jr. "Mass Media Preference Patterns: A Cross-Media Study." Paper presented at the International Communication Association conference, April 1971, Phoenix (available in ERIC ED 049 611).

Williams, Frederick; Amy Friedman Phillips; and Patricia Lum. "Gratifications Associated with New Communication Technologies." In *Media Gratifications Research: Current Perspectives,* edited by Karl Erik Rosengren, Lawrence A. Wenner, and Philip Palmgreen, pp. 241–52. Beverly Hills: Sage, 1985.

Williams, J. Harold. "Attitudes of College Students Toward Motion Pictures." *School and Society* 38 (Aug. 12, 1933):222–24.

Williams, Robert C. "Film Shots and Expressed Interest Levels." *Speech Monographs* 35 (June 1968):166–69.

Williams, Wenmouth, Jr. and Mitchell E. Shapiro. "A Study of the Effects In-Home Entertainment Alternatives Have on Film Attendance." In *Current Research in Film: Audiences, Economics, and Law,* vol. 1, edited by Bruce A. Austin, pp. 93–100. Norwood, N.J.: Ablex, 1985.

Wilner, Daniel M. "Attitude as a Determinant of Perception in the Mass Media of Communication: Reactions to the Motion Picture 'Home of the Brave.'" Ph.D. dissertation, University of California, Los Angeles, 1951.

Wilson, John. "Impresario of the Movie Teaser." *Los Angeles Times,* June 20, 1977, part IV, p. 10.

———. "A Campaign for 'Heroes': The Evolution of an Ad." *Los Angeles Times,* Oct. 16, 1977, Calendar section, pp. 40–41.

Wimmer, Roger D., and Joseph R. Dominick. *Mass Media Research: An Introduction.* Belmont, Calif.: Wadsworth, 1983.

Winge, John H. "The Critic's Success." *Sight and Sound,* Summer 1949, pp. 70–71.

Winick, Charles. "A Study of Consumers of Explicitly Sexual Materials: Some Functions Served by Adult Movies." In *Technical Reports of the U.S. Commission on Obscenity and Pornography,* vol. 4, pp. 245–62. Washington, D.C.: U.S. Government Printing Office, 1970.

Witt, Peter A., and Doyle W. Bishop. "Situational Antecedents to Leisure Behavior." *Journal of Leisure Research* 2 (Winter 1970):64–77.

Witty, Paul; Sol Garfield; and William Brink. "Interests of High-School Students in Motion Pictures and Radio." *Journal of Educational Psychology* 32 (March 1941):176–84.

Wolfe, Katherine M., and Marjorie Fiske. "The Children Talk About Comics." In *Communications Research, 1948–1949,* edited by Paul F. Lazarsfeld and Frank N. Stanton, pp. 3–50. New York: Harper, 1949.

Wolfenstein, Martha, and Nathan Leites. *Movies: A Psychological Study.* Glencoe, Ill.: Free Press, 1950.

Wolff, Harold. "Pre-Testing Movies." *Science Illustrated* 2 (February 1947):44–45, 115.

Wood, Peter. " 'Dressed to Kill'—How a Film Changes from 'X' to 'R.' " *New York Times,* July 20, 1980, sec. 2, pp. 13, 19.

Wozniacki, Janusz. "Kino i Teatr a Uczestnictwo w Kulturze." *Kultura i Spoleczenstwo* 21 (1977):163–73.

Wright, Charles R. "Functional Analysis and Mass Communication." *Public Opinion Quarterly* 24 (1960):602–20.

———. *Mass Communication: A Sociological Perspective.* 2nd ed. New York: Random House, 1975.

Wurtzel, Alan, and Stuart Surlin. "Viewer Attitudes Toward Television Advisory Warnings." *Journal of Broadcasting* 22 (Winter 1978):19–31.

Wyatt, Robert O., and David P. Badger. "How Reviews Affect Interest in and Evaluation of Films." *Journalism Quarterly* 61 (Winter 1984):874–78.

Yakir, Dan. "Bob Rehme: New Power in Hollywood." *Film Comment,* July–August 1981, pp. 74–76.

Yeager, Suzanne White. "G-PG-R-X: A Q-Study of the Movie Industry's Latest Attempt at Self-Regulation." Master's thesis, University of Missouri, 1971.

Young, Kimball. "Book Reviews" (of the Payne Fund series). *American Journal of Sociology,* September 1935, pp. 250–55.

Young, Paul T. *Motivation and Emotion: A Survey of the Determinants of Human and Animal Activity.* New York: John Wiley, 1961.

"Youth Barometer Tracks Patterns of Entertainment Habits, Spending." *Variety,* Feb. 13, 1985, pp. 2, 38.

Zacks, Richard. "Picture Windows." *Channels,* May 1986, pp. 40–41.

Zanna, Mark P.; James M. Olson; and Russell H. Fazio. "Attitude-Behavior Consistency:

An Individual Difference Perspective." *Journal of Personality and Social Psychology* 38 (March 1980):432–40.

Zeisel, Hans. "A Note on the Effect of a Motion Picture on Public Opinion." *American Sociological Review* 14 (August 1949):550–51.

Zeisel, Joseph S. "The Workweek in American Industry 1850–1956." In *Mass Leisure,* edited by Eric Larrabee and Rolf Meyersohn, pp. 145–53. Glencoe, Ill.: Free Press, 1958.

Zillmann, Dolf. "The Anatomy of Suspense." In *The Entertainment Functions of Television,* edited by Percy H. Tannenbaum. Hillsdale, N.J.: Lawrence Erlbaum, 1980.

Zimbardo, Philip, and Ebbe B. Ebbesen. *Influencing Attitudes and Changing Behavior.* Reading, Mass.: Addison-Wesley, 1969.

Zimmermann, Patricia R. "Entrepreneurs, Engineers, and Hobbyists: The Formation of a Definition of Amateur Film, 1897–1923." In *Current Research in Film: Audiences, Economics, and Law,* vol. 3, edited by Bruce A. Austin, pp. 163–88. Norwood, N.J.: Ablex, 1987.

Index

187